D1454214

FIRE IN THE THATCH

FIRE IN THE THATCH

The True Nature
of Religious Revival

EIFION EVANS

EVANGELICAL PRESS OF WALES

269.24
EVA

© Evangelical Press of Wales, 1996
First published, 1996
ISBN 1 85049 119 4

Cover photo by Dan Tennant

Published by the Evangelical Press of Wales
Bryntirion, Bridgend, Mid Glamorgan, CF31 4DX, Wales, UK
Printed in Wales by Bridgend Print Centre, Bridgend

CONTENTS

5

FOR
MEIRION AND SHARON

INTRODUCTION

For the traveller entering Wales from England the sight of mountains is never far away. They may not soar as high as the Alps, but their presence is always felt. Their names convey a sense of enchantment and mystery. Some, like the Berwyn, the two Black Mountains, the Beacons, Epynt, Prescelly, and Snowdonia, are mountain ranges, while others, like Cader Idris, Pen-y-fan, Plynlimon, and Tryfan are distinct, sometimes solitary peaks. It could be argued that their existence has influenced the character, culture, society and destiny of Wales.

In this respect the story of Christianity in Wales is similar to that of its geography. Since the Reformation that story has been characterised by mountainous religious activity, sometimes as a range of repeated revival movements, at other times remarkable peaks of localised spiritual awakenings. Like their physical counterparts, they show great diversity, and they too, in their features, have elevation, grandeur, and awesomeness. They impress and affect us profoundly. There is about them something beyond human ingenuity and effort, and they partake of an 'eternal' quality which marks them out as noteworthy landmarks for our earthly pilgrimage.

Nearly forty years have passed since I first became aware of this dimension to Christianity. It was a study of the truly apostolic ministry of Richard Baxter of Kidderminster in the 1640s and 1650s that first stimulated me. Here was extraordinary success attending ordinary means. Baxter's preaching and teaching were common enough ministerial activities, but the fruit of those labours could only have been the result of divine intervention. This prompted further investigation: the Reformation, the Great Awakening, the revivals in Wales, Scotland, Ulster, and the world over, since. And always the conclusion was the same: revivals are the sovereign activity of God. As God takes the initiative in man's salvation, giving eternal life to the spiritually dead, so in a sovereign and gracious manner He imparts life and fruitfulness to a decaying church. Certain consequences invariably follow: people are added to the church in great numbers, and the society in which they live is changed for the better.

Reading about revivals, however, must never be an end in itself. Our interest must never be merely academic or antiquarian. Knowing about the marvellous works of God in the past should produce in us a sense of worship, a thirst for closer acquaintance with the God of revivals, prayer that He would again visit His people in our day, and anticipation of further seasons of mercy.

For me, a fourfold impression lingers on. The first of these, the real sense of God's presence which is felt at a time of revival, is something I long for in my own life. However distant God may have seemed to be hitherto, even non-existent perhaps, in revival people become aware of God in a way that never happened before, and that remains with them ever afterwards. There is a nearness and immediacy about His coming among men at such times, which transcends the fleeting nature of a casual encounter. It is as if God takes us into His dwelling-place and the very atmosphere is saturated with Him: 'He brought me to the banqueting house, and his banner over me was love' (Song of Solomon 2:4). It is an atmosphere where trust, love, purity, truth, goodness, grace, and mercy in profound excellence satiate and mould the soul. For this knowledge and enjoyment of God we were created. To it we are restored by Christ's atonement and the Spirit's energies. Deprived of it, our souls are impoverished, inwardly we decay, and we become empty and shallow.

The second impression has to do with the display of God's power in revival. Whatever it is that mediates the sense of God's presence, and it is usually preaching, is characterised by an authority, a compulsiveness, an attraction, which is irresistible. It bears the stamp of authenticity and immediacy, of divine commission and warrant that carries with it a summons to appear before God, with a power that is vice-like in its grip, personal and direct in its application, and decisive in its outcome. The metaphors used of God's Word in the Bible which most closely convey the idea of power are 'hammer' and 'sword' (Jer.23:29; Eph.6:17; Heb.4:12), the one by its force, the other by its penetration. In this way, during revival seasons, the most profligate, resistant, and ignorant hearts are transformed. I long for this manifestation of God's might in my life, too, as I listen to sermons, read God's Word, sing hymns, seek His will, and do His pleasure. How cold, complacent, stubborn, wayward, and deaf towards God I become when left to myself! But the story of revivals holds before me the God who never changes, and hope is rekindled that He may yet visit my soul in power and glory. How else will I worship God with fervency and honesty, and live a godly and useful life?

The third impression leads, rightly, to the wider vision of the realisation of God's purpose for this world. Revivals have consistently been the most effective means of spreading Christ's kingdom. At such times, the numbers of those who come to faith in Christ always evoke surprise and praise. As a result of revival, Christian missions multiply in number, they extend their scope and show greater urgency. There is a renewed confidence in Christ's commission to take the gospel to every land, and a heightened expectancy that the darkest regions will yield to the Light of the nations. 'Let God arise, let his enemies be scattered' then becomes the watchword of the Church militant, and so the 'cords' of the gospel tent are lengthened, the 'stakes' are strengthened, the birth of a nation at once is awaited with eagerness (Ps.68:1; Isa.54:2, 66:8). How different has been the story of Wales for most of the twentieth century! The growth of Christ's kingdom has been slow, churches are abandoned, and the name of Christ is widely blasphemed. False religions lead many astray, self-gratifying pleasures and material possessions hold as much sway as the idols of silver and gold of former days, and the devil's activities have become more blatant and persuasive than ever. Revival history, in this situation, reminds me that God has not abandoned His plan. It is still the day of grace; we await only the day of His power to see again the realisation of His purpose in our midst (Ps.110:3). 'Oh that you would rend the heavens! That you would come down! That the mountain might shake at your presence' (Isa.64:1). It is neither too late, nor is it unrealistic or inappropriate, to make those words of Isaiah a prayer for our day.

Such a transition, from Isaiah's day to ours, from his desires to our prayers, highlights a fourth impression left by the study of revivals: the vindication of God's promise. So often in revival there has been the recognition, and the confirmation, that God's Word is truth. It has been proved to be true in the lives of individuals, for whole communities, in the destiny of empires and nations. The prophet Daniel's prayer (in chapter nine) is based on an understanding of God's promise through Jeremiah 'that he would accomplish seventy years in the desolations of Jerusalem', and what was 'written in the law of

Moses (vv.2,13). Peter's sermon on the Day of Pentecost affirmed that the events of that day were a fulfilment of God's promise through the prophet Joel (Acts 2:16). Another sermon of his summarised the entire Bible message when he spoke of 'the covenant which God made . . . saying to Abraham, "And in thy seed all the families of the earth shall be blessed"' (Acts 3:25). On this basis people have prayed for revival. I cannot escape the conviction that God's Word holds out the prospect of yet further blessings, under the terms of that tremendously glorious covenant.

God is a God of truth, and imparts to every covenant a binding quality which we, even in our human contacts and conversations, are to observe. Truth partakes of an absolute solemnity and sanctity, and that person or society which violates it reaps a disastrous and bitter harvest. But God never goes back on His promise, and revivals demonstrate this repeatedly. The fulfilment of His promise is a vindication of His character. The fact that I am dealing with the God who cannot lie, and who cannot change, gives my soul a firm foundation on which to build for eternity. It also provides me with the assurance that God's purposes of grace and glory for His people will infallibly be fulfilled.

These are some of the reasons why these chapters have been written.

Finally, a word about the title. Three centuries ago the Welsh Puritan preacher, Walter Cradock, felt that it was an age 'wherein God comes and fills his people with the glorious light of the Gospel'. He tells us why he felt that way: 'When God fills people's souls with the knowledge of Christ, who can keep it in? . . . I have observed and seen in the mountains of Wales the most glorious work that ever I saw . . . the gospel has run over the mountains between Breconshire and Monmouthshire, as the fire in the thatch'. (*The Works of . . . Walter Cradock*, Chester, 1800, pp.380-81). It is this last phrase which sums up admirably the sovereign work of the Holy Spirit in revival, a work which these chapters are intended to illustrate.

The reviving of God's work is like a powerful, irresistible, consuming blaze, carrying all before it, purifying, kindling, spreading, and transforming everything in its path. It was such a blaze which brought into being the Church at the time of Abraham, and gave it renewal after the Egyptian bondage in the days of Moses, and again amidst scenes of declension experienced by the prophets Elijah, Isaiah and Daniel. What more convincing and conclusive evidence could there be of this, than the emergence of the New Testament Church on the day of Pentecost, in 'tongues, as of fire'? (Gen. 15:17; Ex. 3:2; 1 Ki. 18:38; Isa. 6:6; Dan. 3:25; Acts 2:3). This collection of writings, therefore, is concerned with subsequent history, mainly but not exclusively in Wales, when God's Church was yet again being revived in the land. They were written not only to illustrate a theme, but also to activate faith and stimulate prayer.

SOURCES

Ten of the fifteen chapters in this book have appeared in print in English before. Permission to publish them in this form is gratefully acknowledged.

'What is Revival?' was first published in two issues of the American magazine, *The Wesleyan Advocate*, (Marion, Indiana), October 9 and October 23, 1978.

Revivals: Their Rise, Progress and Achievements, and 'John Davies, Tahiti' first appeared as publications of The Evangelical Library in London, the former in 1960, the latter in 1967.

'Preaching and Revival' first appeared as an article in *The Banner of Truth* magazine of December 1970.

'Early Methodist Apologetic' was published in the *Cylchgrawn Hanes* (Journal of the Historical Society of the Presbyterian Church of Wales), in 1979; 'The Bible and the Great Awakening' was first delivered in Welsh as The Historical Lecture at The General Assembly of the Presbyterian Church of Wales in 1988. amd subsequently published in Welsh in the *Cylchgrawn Hanes* of 1988/89. This is its first appearance in English.

'Adding to the Church—In the Teaching of the Welsh Calvinistic Methodists' was a paper given at The Westminster Conference in 1973, and privately printed with the other papers under the title *Adding to the Church* in 1974.

'David Jones of Llangan' first appeared as an article in *The Gospel Magazine* of April 1967.

'The Beddgelert Revival' was written for *Fellowship Magazine*, appearing in the July/August 1984 issue.

The chapters on 'Humphrey Jones' and 'Dafydd Morgan' were initially delivered as lectures. The first, under the auspices of the National Museum of Wales, in 1980, was published by the Museum in 1981; the second was given as the Annual Lecture of the Evangelical Library of Wales at Aberystwyth in 1983. They were jointly published under the title *Two Welsh Revivalists* in 1985.

Of the remaining chapters, 'Priorities in Revival' is based on 'George Whitefield and Wales' which appeared in The Evangelical Library *Bulletin* of Autumn 1970; and 'Why no Revival' was first delivered at a Bible Rally in Haverfordwest, Pembrokeshire, on 21 May 1992.

'Psalms and Sermons in the Streets', an account of Richard Baxter's Kidderminster ministry, and 'Spirituality Before The Great Awakening', an examination of the devotion of Griffith Jones, Llanddowror before 1735, are here offered in print for the first time.

1
WHAT IS REVIVAL?

In our Christian vocabulary, some words are overworked. They are burdened with meanings which they were never intended to carry. One such word is 'revival'. If we hold an evangelistic campaign with fervour and enthusiasm, with a prominent personality and profuse publicity, we sometimes talk glibly of 'having a revival'.

This is a travesty of language, and the only way to resolve the resulting confusion is to restore the true integrity of the word by restating its biblical usage.

Immediately, however, we are faced with a difficulty. The word 'revival' is not found in the Bible, only in its verbal form 'to revive'. Nevertheless, a biblical account of true revival is possible, inasmuch as revivals in the history of the Church have always shown a close affinity with specific ideas and events in both Old and New Testaments. Thus the word 'revival' can be defined in a biblical way by reference to these biblical principles and parallels.

But why should the Church today be so concerned about revival? There are several good reasons. Nothing exalts God's glory and demonstrates His sovereign power more than revival. The condition of the Church, the ineffectiveness both of our evangelism and the communication of our message, the all-pervasive poison of secularism, humanism and materialism, the blatant immorality and godlessness of the world, each of these considerations should compel prayer for the intervention of God the Holy Spirit.

The considered judgment of Thomas Charles, one of the founders of the Bible Society, and one who had wide experience of revival, was this: 'I am persuaded that unless we are favoured with frequent revivals, and a strong, powerful work of the Spirit of God, we shall, in a great degree, degenerate, and have only a name to live, religion will soon lose its vigour, the ministry will hardly retain its lustre and glory, and iniquity will, of consequence, abound.'

How can revival be defined? Revival is a sovereign, spontaneous, and saving activity of the Holy Spirit. It is widespread and powerful in its impact, effecting a universal sense of the presence of God, exalting Christ, invigorating and quickening the life of the Church, converting and transforming the world.

God initiates, sustains, and controls revival. Thus it is distinguished from evangelism, where the work of God is carried on by human agency. This is not to belittle evangelism, only to distinguish things that differ.

Revival is also a spontaneous activity of the Holy Spirit: unrehearsed, unsought, unexpected, and this distinguishes it from 'revivalism' and 'emotionalism'. This again is not to discount emotion, but to identify the source of true spiritual influence and power.

Jonathan Edwards recognized this: 'I am bold to assert that there never was any considerable change wrought in the mind or conversation [behaviour] of any person, by anything of a religious nature that ever he read, heard, or saw, that had not his affections [emotions] moved. Never was a natural man engaged earnestly to seek his salvation . . . nor was there ever a saint awakened out of a cold, lifeless frame, or recovered from a declining state in religion, and brought back from a lamentable departure from God, without having his heart affected.'

The saving and sanctifying effects of the Holy Spirit in revival are widespread, powerful, and general. God's presence becomes real, God's people are revitalized, there is unction, life, and authority in preaching, the ungodly are brought under strong conviction of sin, and the impact of the gospel is irresistible. In this way revival is distinguished from the ordinary work of the Church in ministering the Word of God.

Let it also be noted that revival takes place against the background of deadness and barrenness. Among God's people there appears widespread spiritual declension, in the work of the gospel there is neither lustre nor life, in the world there is a lack of awareness of God, of spiritual values and of eternal issues that is almost total. When there are neither inclination nor resources in men to change things, God steps in, the mountains melt at His presence, and the desert blossoms as a rose.

Listen to the Welsh hymn-writer, William Williams, speaking from experience, and describing the beginnings of a revival: 'One time, there were just a few of us, professing believers, gathered together, cold and unbelievably dead . . . we were about to offer a

final prayer, fully intending never again to meet thus in fellowship
. . . in such dire straits, on the brink of despair, with the door shut on
every hope of success, God Himself entered into our midst, and the
light of day from on high dawned upon us; for one of the brethren—
yes, the most timid of us all, the one who was strongest in his belief
that God would never visit us—while in prayer, was stirred in his
spirit and laid hold powerfully on heaven, as one who would never
let go.

'The fire took hold of others—all were awakened, the coldest and
the most heedless took hold and were warmed . . . This sound went
forth and was spread from parish to parish and from village to village . . . The tone of the whole district was changed . . . Today nothing counts but Christ, and He is all in all.'

That is revival.

Two words sum up the biblical teaching on revival: restoration
and effusion.

In the Old Testament, revival is portrayed as the restoration of
God's covenantal blessings. The Old Testament material can be conveniently grouped around three ideas: history, prayer, and prophecy.

The historical narratives of the Old Testament emphasize the re-
storing activity of God in covenantal grace after serious declension.
This was promised to the second-generation wilderness Israelites:
'But your little ones, which ye said should be a prey, them will I
bring in, and they shall know the land which ye have despised'
(Num. 14:31).

In the time of the judges, declension and restoration follow one
another in seemingly rapid succession, the one as a result of human
apostasy, the other at the instigation of divine mercy: 'And when the
Lord raised them up judges, then the Lord was with the judge, and
delivered them out of the hand of their enemies all the days of the
judge' (Judg. 2:18).

In the period of the kings the promise of covenant blessings motivated several seasons of restoration: under Asa, Hezekiah, and
Josiah (2 Chron. 15:12; 29:10; 34:31-32). The same covenantal
theme stimulated renewal in the time of Ezra and Nehemiah (Ezra
10:3; Neh. 9:32).

From such passages it is clear that the pathway to revival begins
with a sense of the broken covenant and of God's judgment upon
sin. This leads to a return to the terms of the covenant, and submission

to God's law. Finally there follows a desire for the blessings of the covenant and for God's gracious dealings with His people.

Turning to the prayers of the Old Testament, the importunity of Old Testament saints demonstrates the essential principles of revival. Most prominent among these is the intense longing for a manifestation of God's presence.

The closing chapters of Isaiah are a notable example. 'Look down from heaven . . . return for thy servants' sake . . . Oh, that thou wouldest rend the heavens, that thou wouldest come down . . . behold the Lord will come with fire . . . I will gather all nations and tongues; and they shall come, and see my glory' (63:15, 17; 64:1; 66:15, 18).

The same passionate pleas are found in the Psalms, the prosperity of God's people when He appears being contrasted with the calamity of His withdrawal. 'Wherefore hidest thou thy face and forgettest our affliction and our oppression? . . . Arise for our help, and redeem us for thy mercies' sake.' 'O God, how long shall the adversary reproach? shall the enemy blaspheme thy name for ever? Why withdrawest thou thy hand, even thy right hand? pluck it out of thy bosom.' 'Turn us again, O God, and cause thy face to shine; and we shall be saved.' 'Wilt thou not revive us again . . . show us thy mercy, O Lord, and grant us thy salvation . . . that glory may dwell in our land' (44:24,26; 74:10-11; 80:3; 85:6-7,9).

The outcome of such dramatic, divine intervention is a vindication of God's character and purpose, a realization of His salvation on an impressive scale in the history and experience of His people, and the spreading abroad of God's glorious kingdom.

In prophecy the same intensity of longing is expressed by pictures drawn from abundant temporal benefits. The blessings which they portray await fulfilment in Christ and by His Spirit; but use is made of the most vivid and superlative imagery to convey the transforming power of God.

'The desert shall rejoice, and blossom as the rose'; 'I will pour . . . floods upon the dry ground . . . thine offspring . . . shall spring up . . . as willows by the water courses'; 'that the mountains might flow down at thy presence'; 'shall a nation be born at once?'; 'their soul shall be as a watered garden'; 'there shall be showers of blessing'; 'this land that was desolate is become like the garden of Eden' (Isa. 35:1; 44:3-4; 64:1; 66:8; Jer. 31:12; Ezek. 34:26; 36:35).

Such passages speak of the gracious and extraordinary fulness of the gospel. They imply a divine source and the possibility of repeated seasons of spiritual restoration and expansion. Taken together they display the essence of true revival.

If the word 'restoration' epitomizes the Old Testament concept of revival, 'effusion' is its counterpart in the New. 'Effusion' stands for pouring out in abundant measure, and thus in the New Testament revival is looked upon as the effusion of God's covenantal Spirit.

The Gospels speak of the imminence of the great Gospel Day when this would be realized. At the outset, John the Baptist gave notice of this: 'He that cometh after me is mightier than I . . . he shall baptise you with the Holy Ghost, and with fire' (Matt. 3:11).

Our Lord refers to an outflowing of living water, speaking 'of the Spirit, which they that believe on him should receive: for the Holy Ghost was not yet given; because that Jesus was not yet glorified.' Furthermore, the Holy Spirit's great ministry was to glorify Christ, 'for he shall receive of mine, and shall show it unto you' (John 7:39; 16:14).

These things were yet in the future, and the disciples were to tarry in Jerusalem until they were endued with power from on high (Luke 24:49). The book of Acts gives repeated evidence of the promised effusion in the first 19 chapters, at Jerusalem, Samaria, Lydda, Joppa, Thessalonica, Corinth, and Ephesus.

The epistles were addressed, in many cases, to Christians who had experienced revival conditions. The Ephesians had been blessed 'with all spiritual blessings in heavenly places in Christ' (1:3); the Corinthians, according to the first epistle, were 'in everything enriched by God . . . even as the testimony of Christ was confirmed' in them (1:5-6); the gospel came to others, not 'in word only, but also in power, and the Holy Ghost, and in much assurance,' and their faith in God was already reaching out to others (I Thess. 1:5, 8).

'Effusion' also signifies abundance and copiousness. God's blessings in revival are such: widespread, powerful, lasting, generous. Note the numbers converted: Acts 2:41—3,000; Acts 4:4—5,000; Acts 5:14 and 6:1, 7—numbers multiplied. Christians in revival times met together 'with one accord', and enjoyed 'great power', 'great joy', and 'boldness of speech' (Acts 2:1; 4:24,31,33; 8:6,8; 9:29; 13:52).

To describe the spiritual ecstasy of revival experiences, even superlatives are inadequate: 'unsearchable riches', 'love passing knowledge', 'abounding grace', 'unspeakable and glorious joy', 'perfect and complete' (Eph. 1:18,19; 3:18-19; 2 Cor. 9:8; 1 Pet. 1:8; Col. 1:28; 2:2-3, 9-10; 4:12).

This does not mean that revivals are free from excesses—far from it! Satan sows tares among the wheat. There are, alas, counterfeit conversions and spurious experiences.

Nevertheless, the appearance of error and scandal does not invalidate revival, as John Wesley wrote of the Great Awakening in 1745: 'Do you delay fixing your judgment till you see a work of God without any stumbling block attending it? That never was yet, nor ever will, "it must needs be that offences will come." And scarce ever was there such a work of God before, with so few as have attended this.'

Jonathan Edwards, the great theologian of revival, adds his testimony in this way: 'The weakness of human nature has always appeared in times of great revival of religion, by a disposition to run to extremes, and get into confusion; and especially in these three things, enthusiasm, superstition, and intemperate zeal.'

From this survey of the biblical material, revival is seen to be initiated by the sovereign, saving, and surprising activity of the Holy Spirit. It is characterized by the twin themes of restoration and effusion, and has been repeatedly experienced in the history of the Church.

In the absense of revival, the responsibility of God's people is threefold. God's truth must be faithfully and perseveringly proclaimed; God's promises must be pleaded in humility and holiness; God's dealings in past revivals should be studied and His powerful intervention today diligently and patiently sought: 'If my people, which are called by my name, shall humble themselves, and pray, and seek my face, and turn from their wicked ways; then will I hear from heaven, and will forgive their sin, and will heal their land' (II Chron. 7:14).

Revival is not a substitute for evangelism, nor is it an excuse for complacency. It stems from a passion for God and for His glory in the extension of Christ's kingdom and fame.

> Teach me to love Thee as Thine angels love,
> One holy passion filling all my frame —

> The baptism of the heaven-descended Dove,
> My heart an altar, and Thy love the flame.

Its advent is near when holy men lift up their hearts to God with fervency and urgency for His gracious visitation. 'Sow to yourselves in righteousness, reap in mercy; break up your fallow ground: for it is time to seek the Lord, till he come and rain righteousness upon you' (Hosea 10:12).

2
REVIVALS:
Their Rise, Progress and Achievements

The history of revivals is the history of God's gracious dealings with men. It is that which Jonathan Edwards styled 'the history of redemption', and as such it is the only true history, that is, the only study of the past which is properly 'in perspective', for therein is delineated the unfolding and outworking of God's sovereign purpose. To regard it as a mere intellectual exercise therefore betrays a gross underestimate of the meaning, implications, and consequences of revival. The subject is full, not only of interest, but also of instruction, and he who seriously undertakes the study of revivals should not expect to proceed far without becoming intimately involved in and passionately concerned for the issues that arise. There can be no neutrality or sterility here, for this study challenges faith, stimulates prayer, and motivates praise.

It may be necessary in the minds of some to make an apology, or at any rate to give a reason, for proposing the subject at the present time. Evangelical forces are seemingly becoming more concentrated and more prominent, and the need for an effusion of the Holy Spirit in revival, in the opinion of some, is far from desperate or urgent. While more and more attention is being given to men and methods, the significance and importance of the person and work of the Holy Spirit is being gradually diminished. But an enquiry of this kind, perhaps more than any other, demonstrates conclusively the deity, holiness, and sovereignty of the third person of the Trinity. In such a study His gracious manner of working, in glorifying Christ, in decrying sin and exalting righteousness, and in conforming men to the divine image, is forcefully and convincingly brought into focus.

Furthermore, the study of revivals has often been used of the Holy Spirit to promote an interest in, and a desire for, another 'season of refreshing from the presence of the Lord'. Thus Jonathan Edwards, in urging the publication of a periodical containing accounts of the progress of the 1740 revival in America, states: 'It has been found by experience, that the tidings of remarkable effects of the power and grace of God in any place, tend greatly to awaken and engage the minds of persons in other places.'

Now a word as to procedure and purpose. It will be found that in the main, reference is made to revivals of the eighteenth century. This is an historical enquiry rather than a theological treatise. Its purpose parallels the several parts of its title, being an attempt to demonstrate that the Spirit's work is sovereign in instigating, irresistible in advancing, and sanctifying in establishing, the glory of God in revival.

1. Darkness Before Dawn

Before proceeding to consider the sovereign work of the Spirit in the rise of revivals, it is necessary to list some elements in the prevalent situation previously obtaining, and to indicate their relevance in the light of subsequent events. At the risk of over-simplification it can be maintained that the revivals of the sixteenth and eighteenth centuries came to an apostate, declining, expiring Church, while those of the seventeenth and nineteenth centuries took place against the background of a dormant, listless, and unconcerned Church. The former situation witnessed the emergence of particular leading doctrines and outstanding figures, while the latter situation was radically altered by invigorated prayer together with a return to the apostolic preaching of the whole counsel of God.

A general apostasy

The apostasy of the Church at the beginning of the eighteenth century is evident from many considerations. In America the Church allowed an unconverted ministry as valid and harmless, and allowed an unconverted membership to its sacramental occasions without examination or enquiry. This had grave repercussions, in that the necessity for regeneration and a 'saving closure with Christ' were seldom insisted upon, and the vast majority of Church members were strangers to the covenant of grace. Arminianism was making inroads into some of the congregations, and its man-centred system was becoming more and more attractive to the natural mind. There were however many exceptions, the congregation at Northampton in 1734 being the most notable, as Edwards himself wrote: 'About this time began the great noise, in this part of the country, about Arminianism, which seemed to appear with a very threatening aspect upon the interest of religion here. The friends of vital piety trembled for fear of the issue; but it seemed, contrary to their fear, strongly to be overruled for the promoting of religion. Many who looked on themselves as in a Christless condition, seemed to be awakened by it, with fear that God was about to withdraw from the land, and that we should be given up to heterodoxy and corrupt principles; and that then their opportunity for obtaining salvation would be past.'

Much of the contemporary theological thought in England and Wales was the product of a philosophical Arminianism, that is, of Arminian principles developed philosophically so as to elevate the reason or will of man. The resultant systems of Deism, Rationalism and Moralism had crippled the Church, reducing its effectiveness and bringing about a drastic degeneration in its spiritual life. The leaders of the Evangelical Awakening were neither slow nor compromising in their denunciations of these systems.

Such was the theological background of the eighteenth century revival, and it is necessary to list some of the other elements in the religious situation in the period immediately preceding the great revivals of 1735.

Widespread spiritual darkness

That religion was at a low ebb was the universal complaint of the revivalists as they came to an experience of the gospel and became acquainted with the condition of the Church. While God had not left Himself without witness in any land, it grieved the evangelical leaders to find that those around them who professed religious beliefs, ministers and members alike, were in spiritual darkness and deadness.

The situation at New Londonderry, Pennsylvania, previous to 1740 is depicted by the minister of the parish, and can be regarded as general and typical throughout America.

'The most part seemed to rest contented, and to satisfy their consciences just with a dead formality in religion. A very lamentable ignorance of the main essentials of true practical religion, and the doctrines next related thereto, very generally prevailed. The nature and necessity of the new birth was but little known or thought of. The necessity of a conviction of sin and misery, by the Holy Spirit opening and applying the law to the conscience, in order to a saving closure with Christ, was hardly known at all to most. It was thought that if there was any need of a heart-distressing sight of the soul's danger, and fear of divine wrath, it was only needful for the grosser sort of sinners. There was scarcely any suspicion at all of any danger of depending upon self-righteousness, and not upon the righteousness of Christ alone for salvation.'

Jonathan Edwards' analysis of the situation at Northampton in 1734 has more particular reference to the state of the youth: 'The greater part seemed to be at that time very insensible of the things of religion, and engaged in other cares and pursuits . . . Licentiousness for some years greatly prevailed among the youth of the town; they were many of them very much addicted to night-walking, and frequenting the tavern, and lewd practices, wherein some, by their example, exceedingly corrupted others. It was their manner very frequently to get together, in conventions of both sexes for mirth and jollity, which they called frolics; and they would often spend the greater part of the night in them, without regard to any order in the families they belonged to.'

Meanwhile, in England as early as May 26, 1739, George Whitefield was able to report considerable progress in the revival in the London area, and also that he had found 'some thousands of secret ones living who have not bowed the knee to Baal.' On the other hand, he had not been in Oxford long as a student before he was 'solicited to join in their excess of riot with several who lay in the same room'; and that those who desired to live godly in Christ Jesus must suffer persecution—witness the members of the 'Holy Club' who received the holy eucharist only after going through 'a ridiculing crowd'. Whitefield's first sermon was characterized by his plain speaking, and it is significant that two of the practices he denounced were the not-so-innocent entertainments of professing Christians, and the commonly accepted belief in baptismal regeneration.

During the early years of the revival the evangelistic activity of the Welsh revivalists had been confined to the south. Howel Harris visited parts of North Wales in 1740, and he had cause to mourn over the darkness, superstition, and immorality which characterized the land. 'This country is all ruined for want of experimental preaching of Christ powerfully; no Gospel light but in a few places . . .

went to Trefeglwys church to hear—Morris, he preached on 'in keeping of them there is good reward', the sum of it was, do this, be good and live . . . had a desire to expose him . . . O Lord I can't help mourning over the darkness of the country of North Wales! North Wales! Thy guides are blind, the magistrates are persecutors, and the instruments for Thee are all weak . . . dreadful things do I hear of all the ministers in these parts.' When he surveyed the situation in North Wales in February 1741, he could list one dissenting minister in Caernarvonshire 'full of the love of God', one minister in Merioneth, 'a very godly man', two such in Montgomeryshire, and the remaining portion of the country is tragically summed up thus: 'I don't find there is any religion in Anglesey or Flintshire, but near papists; some little dawning in Denbighshire.'

That these accounts were not the exaggerated opinions of biased men appears from several facts. The leaders of the revival felt constrained from Scripture premises to raise aloud their protests against the doctrines and practices of the times. They saw clearly that multitudes were being deluded by error and false teaching even within the Church, and they were grieved at the evils, immorality, and vice which abounded in the land on all sides. For their uncompromising stand with regard to these matters and because they sought to lead the nation, the clergy, and the Church back to New Testament principles and practices, they were often excluded from the churches by their enemies, persecuted by mobs, and attacked in the pamphlets and printed works of the time.[1] Nevertheless, God caused them to triumph and many were added to the Church, having been 'born again of God'. These converts soon formed themselves into religious societies for prayer and fellowship.[2] There could be only one explanation for these phenomena: God had visited the land in a tremendous outpouring of His Spirit and of power, making that to blossom as the rose which had been formerly a desolate wilderness.

2. The Dawn of Revivals

The 17th and 19th centuries

The seventeenth century was a period of expansion and consolidation for the gospel, when the full implications of the sixteenth century Reformation were being worked out theologically and practically. Much the same was true of the nineteenth century, the churches reaping tremendous benefits from the Evangelical Awakening of the previous century. The condition of the Church varied greatly from time to time and from place to place, but there was no widespread, deep-rooted apostasy in the fullest sense of the word. Rather, the Church experienced times of decline and inactivity interspersed with revival periods of vigorous energy and spiritual prosperity. These revivals were mainly localized, and the human instruments used of the Spirit were generally famous for their work at that place. Here are some obvious examples: David Dickson and the Stewarton revival of 1625; John Livingstone and the Kirk O'Shotts revival in 1630; Richard Baxter's ministry at Kidderminster especially between 1647 and 1660;[3] William C. Burns and Robert Murray M'Cheyne and the Dundee revival of 1839; and David Morgan, whose name is inseparable from Ysbyty Ystwyth and 1859, even though he was used in a far wider sphere than the mountainous region of north Cardiganshire.

The revivals of these two 'odd-number' centuries—generally speaking, of course—show distinct characteristics. The Spirit blessed a faithful, zealous ministry in the context of a few godly families, or perhaps a particular sermon at a sacramental occasion. At other times, the godly who had fallen into a deep slumber and become oblivious of their own state and indifferent to that of others, were awakened to pray more frequently and more fervently. It is significant, for example, that in the 1859 revival in Wales, the message which burned in the hearts of Humphrey Jones and David Morgan,[4] the two leading revivalists, was that of Amos 6:1, 'Woe to them that are at ease in Zion'. It is also significant that Humphrey Jones, upon his arrival at his home in Cardiganshire in 1858, having given an account of the revival in America from whence he had come, constrained the church to hold prayer meetings every night. Most of the church members had seen or experienced previous revivals—there had been at least fifteen major awakenings in Wales during the previous ten decades—and in setting themselves to pray, their desire was that God would again visit them by His Spirit in a similar fashion. When the churches had been thus led to pray, the preaching of the Word became more powerful, and the substantial truths of the gospel, presented plainly and earnestly, and applied closely and personally, were signally used to the recovery of vast multitudes of men.

The amazing 1730s

One of the most compelling and convincing facts which go to demonstrate the sovereignty of the Holy Spirit in instigating revivals is the simultaneous manner of manifesting His work in various places and in various persons. The seventeen-thirties must surely be reckoned the most amazing decade in modern history for, during those years God graciously visited America, England, Scotland and Wales in powerful revivals. At first these events were apparently unrelated and localized, but within the scope of only a few years they were fused into one mighty awakening, when whole countries and vast tracts of land were submerged in a surge of divine power and momentous spiritual upheaval. It was to Howel Harris a perpetual call to wonder and praise that God had worked thus: '16 March, 1747 . . . when God visited me and sent me first to speak to people near twelve years ago, I did not know there was a believer living; nor did I as much dream there was a reformation to go on, or that I was to be a preacher; till about two years I heard of a clergyman, one Mr Rowland, and then a young clergyman here in London that preached four times a day—Mr Whitefield; and now see how the little cloud has spread over the land, so that God only knows where it will end.'

Jonathan Edwards had been converted in the period 1720-22, and had been ordained in 1727, becoming assistant minister to his grandfather over the congregation at Northampton. Evidences of a divine visitation in revival were found in the congregation towards the end of 1733, and during the following year the Holy Spirit's operation was as glorious as it was manifest, so that by the summer of 1735 'the town seemed to be full of the presence of God'. In the sovereign purpose of God, similar stirrings were felt in the north of Scotland during the same period. John Balfour was appointed minister of the parish of Nigg, Ross and Cromarty, in 1730. 'From that date, Balfour of Nigg became the acknowledged leader of the northern evangelical revivals. In his own parish, from 1730 to 1739, there was a gradual quickening, 'with stops and intermissions', in the spiritual life of the people. In 1739, we notice the unmistakable beginning of a spiritual movement which powerfully affected not only Nigg, but many parishes in Ross and Sutherland, and which is traceable throughout the rest of the century, and well into the next.'

The work of the Holy Spirit in conversion was brought to fruition in George Whitefield, Howel Harris, and Daniel Rowland in 1735, in John and Charles Wesley in 1738. Each of these events, as well as being perpetual monuments to the saving grace of God, are also witnesses to the sovereign purpose and plan of God in revival, for from those incidents stems the powerful spate of blessing which revolutionized the spiritual life of the Church in the eighteenth century.

Shortly afterwards, in 1742, William McCullough of Cambuslang and James Robe of Kilsyth were being used of God, having preached consistently and repeatedly in their churches for an appreciable time on several aspects of the Spirit's work in regeneration. By 1747 there were similar revivals on the continent, and Howel Harris could record in his diary for 14th January of that year the irrepressible progress of the gospel: 'Heard refreshing news today of a great revival in France in Montauban by two ministers that preached a month there, and were saved by God from being taken up, and went away. They came through from Geneva. Great was the power of God, and there were gathered 30,000, they came thirty leagues (or ninety miles) to hear.'

The revival spread to Ireland in 1745 when 'an English soldier in Dublin formed a small society of pious people, and began to preach to them'. This society was visited by various Methodist preachers during 1746, and by John Wesley in 1747, so that during Wesley's visit two years later, the preaching of the Word was attended with unusual unction and power, and his voice 'could not be heard for the voice of those who cried for mercy, or praised the God of their salvation'.

A minister in Holland, reported astonishing revival scenes experienced at Nieuwkirk, near Amersfoort, towards the end of 1749, being apparently the climax of a gradual, progressive work of the Spirit. 'The Spirit of the Lord began to work in an astonishing manner (during a sermon on Psalm 72:16 preached on 9th November, 1749); all that had passed before seemed to have been a preparation for greater and more glorious things . . . the trouble of conscience and emotion of affections was general. There was a great lamentation; rivers of tears gushed out, and several fell trembling and astonished to the earth unable to stand by reason of the agony and agitation of their spirits, arising from the sudden, strong impression made upon them of the dreadful state and crying necessity of their souls ... The following Thursday he (the minister) preached upon Acts 16:16,30,31; where many were brought to a more distinct view of their true state and condition. From that day the work increased beyond description; there is no painting of it to the life; it was a perfect commentary on the second chapter of Acts.'

The sovereignty of the Holy Spirit

The Holy Spirit alone could reproduce so exactly in the eighteenth century manifestations such as were seen on the day of Pentecost. What other explanation could be offered for these similar, simultaneous, widespread and powerful blessings, than that the sovereign God was pouring out His Spirit upon all flesh as He purposed and pleased? That which had been found impossible with man was accomplished gloriously, effectively and triumphantly by the Holy Spirit. Human philosophy and morality, pagan superstition, and a corrupt pretence at worship had driven men further from God and had filled the land with darkness, immorality, and hypocrisy. From this hopeless chaos there seemed no deliverance until God intervened in sovereign grace and divine pity, 'bringing a clean thing out of an unclean' far beyond human capability, device or intention.

Further illustration of the Spirit's sovereignty in the work of revival is provided by the manner of their beginning. Many factors were involved, sometimes singly and separately, at other times unitedly or as a combination of several such. The Spirit used remarkable providences, sacramental occasions, revival reports, fast days and prayer meetings, as He willed, but supremely it was the preaching of the Word which He especially countenanced and blessed, often together with one or more of the occurrences noted. Jonathan Edwards, the Tennents, George Whitefield, John Wesley, Daniel Rowland and others like them were called and equipped primarily to preach, and it was in the capacity of preacher that each was most signally blessed and most widely used.

The preaching of a minister in his own parish was often the means honoured by God in a time of revival, as is seen for instance, at New Londonderry in the spring of 1740. The minister, Samuel Blair, wrote his account of the awakening in August 1744: 'Religion lay as it were dying, and ready to expire its last breath of life in this part of the visible church. I had some view and sense of the deplorable condition of the land in general; and accordingly the scope of my preaching through that first winter after I came here (1739), was mainly calculated for persons in a natural, unregenerate state. I endeavoured, as the Lord enabled me, to open up and prove from His Word, the truths which I judged most necessary for such as were in that state to know and believe in order to their conviction and conversion. I endeavoured to deal searchingly and solemnly with them; and through the concurring blessing of God, I had knowledge of four or five brought under deep convictions that winter . . . The number of the awakened increased very fast. Frequently under sermons there were some newly convicted, and brought into deep distress of soul about their perishing estate. Several would be overcome and fainting; others deeply sobbing, hardly able to contain; and a solemn concern appearing in the countenance of many others. And sometimes the soul-exercises of some (though comparatively but very few) would so far affect their bodies as to occasion some strange unusual bodily motions . . . The general carriage and behaviour of people was soon very visibly altered. Those awakened were much given to reading in the Holy Scriptures and other good books. Excellent books that had lain by much neglected, were then much perused, and lent from one to another; and it was a peculiar satisfaction to people to find how exactly the doctrines they heard daily preached, harmonized with the doctrines contained and taught by great and godly men in other parts and former times.'

3. The Progress of Revivals

The Preaching of the Word

Revivals thus display great variety in the manner of their beginnings, but preaching seems to be prominent in each case. God's dealing—sometimes drastic—with the parish or local minister often brought about a radical change in the success of the gospel at that place, as the above instances show, and these instances could be multiplied.

The famous Gilbert Tennent was distressed with the want of success of his ministry after being at New Brunswick for about six months. Here are his subsequent experiences:

'It pleased God to afflict me about that time with sickness, by

which I had affecting views of eternity. I was then exceedingly
grieved that I had done so little for God, and was very desirous to
live one half year more, if it was His will, that I might stand upon
the stage of the world, as it were, and plead more faithfully for His
cause, and take more earnest pains for the conversion of souls. One
thing among others pressed me sore; viz. that I had spent much time
in conversing about trifles, which might have been spent in examin-
ing people's states towards God, and perusading them to turn to
Him. After I was raised up to health, I examined many about the
grounds of their hope of salvation, which I found in most to be nothing but as the sand. With such I was enabled to deal faithfully and
earnestly, warning them of their danger, and urging them to seek
converting grace. By this method, many were awakened out of their
security; and of those, divers were to all appearances effectually
converted, and some that I spoke plainly to were prejudiced. I did
then preach much upon original sin, repentance, the nature and
necessity of conversion, in a close examinatory and distinguishing
way; labouring in the meantime to sound the trumpet of God's judg-
ments, and alarm the secure by the terrors of the Lord, as well as to
affect them with other topics of persuasion; which method was
sealed by the Holy Spirit in the conviction and conversion of a considerable number of persons.'

Many such ministers were stirred up by the Holy Ghost at much
the same time, to greater earnestness and faithfulness in their particular duties, and their quickened labours were made effectual to their
congregations.

Time and time again in Scotland between 1600 and 1800 God
was graciously pleased to pour out a plentiful effusion of the Holy
Spirit on sacramental occasions. People would flock to these from a
wide area, and the many ministers who attended not only helped at
the tables but also preached several times. According to one writer,
during this period, 'the sacramental assembly and the parochial fellowship meeting were the supreme evangelising agencies; and to
one or other of them we can trace all or most of the awakenings and
revivals which have quickened the spiritual life of the people.'

Fast days or days set apart for prayer sometimes witnessed the
first open manifestations of a divine visitation in revival, as was the
case at Wrentham, Massachusetts, in February 1741, when the minister preached on Zechariah 12:10, 'And I will pour upon the house

of David, and upon the inhabitants of Jerusalem, the spirit of grace and of supplications . . . ' 'There appeared,' according to the account, 'especially in the afternoon, a very uncommon attentiveness unto the word, a wonderful tenderness upon the assembly; the tokens of a very serious concern were visible on many faces.' The effects spread to neighbouring congregations, the convictions becoming more intense and the conversions more frequent. In August of the same year, Halifax, in the county of Plymouth, witnessed the beginning of great things on a similar occasion.

Itinerant preaching

The itinerant ministries of George Whitefield, John Wesley, the Tennents, Howel Harris, and Jonathan Edwards, must also be mentioned as being, under the good blessing of God, instrumental in a large measure to commence awakenings in various parts. Their journals and accounts are full of descriptions of their journeys and the unparalleled success they met with in preaching the gospel. There were not a few who objected to their itinerant labours for various reasons, with the result that they often met opposition from ministers, in that the parish church would be refused to them, and from magistrates who sought to bring them under legal restrictions. The usefulness of their preaching tours, however, can hardly be over-estimated, and they contributed in no small measure, under the blessing of God, to the progress as well as to the rise of revivals.

Itinerant preaching accomplished at least two purposes in the progress of the eighteenth century revival. Firstly, it was a means of continued expansion and propagation by preaching; and secondly, it was the means of consolidation and instruction of the converts in the religious societies by exhortation.

The leaders of the revival began itinerating for a variety of reasons. While on a visit to Bristol, George Whitefield was called upon during a service to address the congregation, and he instantly complied with the request. More invitations followed, and each he regarded as a divine call to preach the gospel. Furthermore, the remarkable success which followed his ministry, first in Bristol, and later in London, could only be interpreted in Whitefield's mind as being a clear indication of its validity, expediency and usefulness in the divine purpose. This work commenced early in 1737 in Bristol, and by September, in London, Whitefield could record that 'for near three months successively, there was no end of the people flocking to hear the Word of God'.

To Howel Harris likewise the urge to itinerate came from within, an irresistible consequence of the nature of his spiritual experience of God's free and sovereign grace. Soon after his conversion on Whit-Sunday 1735 he set up family worship in his own home, and visited the neighbouring farms and houses. Upon his return home after an abortive attempt to settle at Oxford to study, he busied himself with 'going about' amongst the nearby parishes spreading the message which 'did so burn' in his soul, giving him no rest 'day or night, without doing something' for his God and Saviour. His own account is particularly striking. 'After my return, I was occupied in going from house to house until I had visited nearly the whole of the parish in which I was born, together with some of the neighbouring ones. The people began now to assemble in vast numbers, so that the houses in which I addressed them were too small for the congregations. The Word was attended with such power, that many cried out on the spot for the pardon of their sins.' That account refers to 1736; by 1742 his zeal and fervour had by no means diminished, as this extract from his diary for 4th September of that year will show: 'I was often led to cry: We are about soul's work! Eternity work and God's work. There is no jesting with God.'

Daniel Rowland's usefulness was by no means confined to his ministry at Llangeitho. It is true of him, as it was to be of Thomas Charles of Bala later, that his chief contribution to the rise and progress of the revival was his amazing labours at that preaching centre. From Llangeitho to Bala there radiated forth to the rest of the Principality such an influence for good that hitherto has never been surpassed. Daniel Rowland, however, had commenced preaching outside his own parish by August 1737, as Howel Harris heard him at Devynock, Breconshire, on the 13th of that month. By August the following year he had been to at least two parishes in Carmarthenshire, and by 1740 Daniel Rowland had visited North Wales at least once.

John Wesley, being refused access to many pulpits in London, began his itineraries in 1738, and fifty years later he could write in retrospect, 'God has been pleased to bless the itinerant plan . . . it must not be altered . . . I hope it will remain till our Lord comes to reign upon earth.'

The visit of Jonathan Edwards to Enfield was the beginning of a revival which spread over a wide area. On that occasion, 8th July, 1741, he preached on 'sinners in the hands of an angry God', basing his remarks on Deuteronomy 32:35, '. . . their foot shall slide in due time . . .' 'Before the sermon was ended, the assembly appeared deeply impressed and bowed down with an awful conviction of their sin and danger. There was such a breathing of distress and weeping that the preacher was obliged to speak to the people and desire silence, that he might be heard. This was the beginning of the same great and prevailing concern in that place, with which the colony in general was visited.'

No effort against such itinerant ministries was successful, and God prospered the work under the hands of the ministers so mightily that it grew beyond all imaginable proportions. When God wills success, no man can impose failure.

Field preaching

Field preaching was in effect only the inevitable consequence of itinerant preaching. Whereas it was found by the leaders of the revival to be necessary because of closed churches, they came to regard it as nothing short of the providential ordering of God. In fact, the revival which their enemies desired to quench and end, prospered and progressed all the more because of it. Furthermore, it would have been impossible to accommodate the tens of thousands which flocked to hear the Word of God had not Whitefield and the others taken to preaching in the open air.

The 'ice' was broken on 17th February, 1739, when Whitefield preached to some 200 colliers at Kingswood, and his joyful comments were these: 'I believe I never was more acceptable to my Master than when I was standing to teach those hearers in the open fields. Some may censure me; but if I thus pleased men, I should not be the servant of Christ.' A few months later he noted in his *Journal* what must have been, to him, ample justification for that memorable decision to preach in the open air: 'Thousands at the great day will have reason to bless God for field-preaching.' By May of 1748 the desirability and usefulness of field preaching had so impressed itself upon Howel Harris's mind that he was concerned lest anything should arise to deny the revivalists this means of publishing the gospel tidings. 'If we'll be obliged to license ourselves and houses, it will cramp the work and stop field-preaching.'

Religious societies

Another important factor in the progress of the revival was the setting up of the religious societies, or, as Whitefield described them in 1742 to the Bishop of Bangor, 'little fellowship meetings, where some well-meaning people meet together, simply to tell what God has done for their souls.' The first society was formed in Breconshire by Howel Harris as early as 1736, and by 1739 about thirty of them had been organized and regulated in South Wales, 'in imitation of the Societies which Dr (Josiah) Woodward had given an account of.'

These religious societies were set up by the revivalists in an attempt to ensure the spiritual growth and well-being of their converts. Their meetings were times of prayer, fellowship, and Bible study, and very often would include the singing of a hymn or psalm, followed by the leader's exposition of a passage of Scripture, or catechism, together with an opportunity for discussion, and the sharing of spiritual experiences and difficulties. Inasmuch therefore that by these means the young converts were nurtured in spiritual things, their contribution to the progress and eventual achievement of the revival was an important one. Very often they supplied a deficiency which the parish clergy were either unable or unwilling to supply.

Religious literature

The religious literature produced by the Evangelical Awakening added further fuel to the fires of the revival. Between 1740 and 1745 accounts of the success of the gospel in various parts appeared in a weekly periodical bearing the title successively of *The Christian's Amusement, The Weekly History, An Account of the Progress of the Gospel,* and *The Christian History.* The Scottish counterparts of those London publications were *The Glasgow Weekly History,* and James Robe's *Monthly History.* A similar periodical appeared in Boston in America, under the title *The Christian History.*

Extracts from these were read in the societies on 'letter days', and in many instances quickened interest in the revival's progress, and stimulated prayer for the revival's continued success. They consisted chiefly of letters sent by the leading revivalists or portions of their journals. The publication of the latter, by Whitefield and John Wesley in particular, together with the publication of their sermons, had the same effects, as did also the appearance in print of the hymns of Charles Wesley and William Williams. One Welsh revival, that of 1762, received tremendous impetus from the appearance in print of a collection of William Williams' hymns, and gave rise to outbursts of praise and rejoicing which were hardly equalled anywhere during the whole of the eighteenth century. The Welsh catechisms of Griffith Jones, Llanddowror, proved eminently profitable to the religious societies and in the 'charity schools'. The latter could be regarded as the religious nurseries of the revival in Wales, and their work was carried on by Thomas Charles of Bala in the Sunday schools.

Doctrinal emphasis

Such were some of the leading factors in the progress of the eighteenth century revival and it remains only to outline some of the emergent characteristics as the work progressed. The leading figures rose to prominence at an early stage, and it was not long before their doctrinal emphasis also became apparent. Thomas Prince of Boston defined the broad principles of the revival in his statement concerning the work in his own parish: 'Nor, in all the preaching of the instruments of this work in town, did I ever hear any teach to follow impulses or any religious impressions but of the Word of God upon our minds, affections, wills, and consciences; and which, agreeable to the Holy Scriptures, the most famous Reformers and Puritan ministers, both in England, Scotland and New-England, have in their writings taught us. As to the doctrinal principles of those who continue in our congregations, and have been the subjects of the late revival, they are the same as they have been instructed in all along, from the Westminster Assembly's Shorter Catechism.'

A similar statement is given by the minister of Golspie (Sutherland) which was blessed with an outpouring of the Holy Spirit in November 1743: 'The terrors of the Lord denounced in His Word against the wilful transgressors of his holy laws, and the impenitent unbelieving despisers of his gospel grace; the impossibility of salvation

on the score of self-righteousness; the absolute necessity of the effi-
cacious influences of the grace and Spirit of God, in order to a vital
union with Christ by faith, for righteousness and salvation; that all
the blessings of the new covenant, freely given by the Father to the
elect, and purchased for them by the sufferings and death of Christ
the Son, are effectually applied to them by the Holy Ghost—these
were the doctrines insisted on to the people of this congregation.'

Emphasis on regeneration

If, however, one doctrine received more prominence than any other
during the eighteenth century awakening, it was that of regeneration.
It was as characteristic of that movement of the Spirit, as justification by faith was of the Reformation of the sixteenth century. It
seems to have been the doctrine above any other, which was honoured of the Holy Spirit during the whole period of eighteenth century revivals. From 1734, when 'a ray of divine light . . . darted in'
upon the soul of George Whitefield, when he knew that he had to be
'a new creature', until the Moulin revival of 1798, this particular
doctrine was kept to the fore. Thus Whitefield refers to the subject at
least forty-six times in his Journals in the decade 1734-44, while,
during the same period, justification by faith is mentioned about
eight times. It is not without significance that his first publication as
early as August 1737 was a sermon on 'The Nature and Necessity of
our New Birth in Jesus Christ, in order to Salvation'. The fact that it
passed through at least three editions before the end of the same
year, having 'sold well to persons of all denominations and dispersed very much at home and abroad', lends added weight to the
contention.

The fact that preaching on regeneration was so universally
blessed of the Holy Spirit secures for it further recognition as a
salient doctrine in the revival. The minister of Hopewell and
Amwell in New Jersey preached for six months on the subjects of
conviction and conversion before the Holy Spirit's powerful influence descended upon his congregations in May 1739. The same
truths were insisted upon to the congregation at New Londonderry
before their 'seasons of refreshing' in 1740. Multitudes were affected under the preaching of Whitefield on the subject at Boston in
1740. William McCulloch had been over ten years at Cambuslang

before he decided to preach on those subjects 'which tend most directly to explain the nature, and prove the necessity of regeneration.' This he did for about a year before February, 1742, when the truths he had been preaching and insisting upon became a reality in the experiences of vast numbers of his congregation. The same was true at Kilsyth under James Robe's ministry in 1740, and at Llangeitho, under Daniel Rowland's ministry, in 1781.

These facts must surely indicate that even as the Holy Spirit in His sovereign choice used certain human instruments, so also He signally honoured certain doctrines, not exclusively, but more especially. The choice is necessarily His and bears no robot-like imitation. The impulse must come from Him, even as the power accompanying the Word must be ascribed to Him.

Physical manifestations

The severity and intensity of the convictions during revivals deserve a comment. These were not constant but fluctuated from place to place. There were amazing conversions in people of all ages. The revival manifestations or phenomena, such as physical prostrations, crying out, fainting, and so on, were witnessed in many places both in Europe and America. They were objected to by some and counterfeited by others. Jonathan Edwards' *Treatise on the Religious Affections* was an attempt to answer the objections and to correct the abuses attendant upon such phenomena. Perhaps the most amazing account of such incidents is given by Jonathan Edwards himself in alluding to the revival experiences at Northampton in 1741: 'The months of August and September were the most remarkable of any this year, for appearances of conviction and conversion of sinners, and great revivings, quickenings, and comforts of professors, and for extraordinary external effects of these things. It was a very frequent thing to see a house full of outcries, faintings, convulsions, and such like, both with distress, and also with admiration and joy. It was not the manner here to hold meetings all night, as in some places, nor was it common to continue them till very late in the night: but it was pretty often, so that there were some that were so affected, and their bodies so overcome, that they could not go home, but were obliged to stay all night at the house where they were.'

Whitefield obviously experienced some difficulty at first in accepting these phenomena as being truly the work of God and not of the devil, for John Wesley had occasion to reprimand him of thus censuring the sovereignty and power of the Holy Spirit. Wesley notes in his Journal for 7th July, 1739: 'I had an opportunity to talk with him of those outward signs which had so often accompanied the inward work of God. I found his objections were chiefly grounded on gross misrepresentations of matter of fact. But the next day he had an opportunity of informing himself better: for no sooner had he begun (in the application of his sermon) to invite all sinners to believe in Christ, than four persons sunk down close to him, almost in the same moment. One of them lay without either sense or motion; a second trembled exceedingly; the third had strong convulsions all over his body, but made no noise, unless by groans; the fourth, equally convulsed, called upon God, with strong cries and tears. From this time, I trust, we shall all suffer God to carry on His work in the way that pleaseth Him.'

Such evidences of the work of the Spirit which resulted in conversion and sanctification, then, demonstrate the intensity of the revival, and the irresistible power of the Spirit in bringing the truth to the mind with reality and force. The vast majority of occurrences of this nature could only be attributed to the divine authorship.

That is not to say that there were no spurious conversions or false manifestations; but they appear to have been detected sooner or later and exposed, as is seen from the following report relating to New Londonderry: 'They endeavoured just to get themselves affected by sermons, and if they could come to weeping, or get their passions so raised as to incline them to vent themselves by cries, now they hoped they were got under convictions, and were in a very hopeful way; and afterwards, they would speak of their being in trouble, and aim at complaining of themselves, but seemed as if they knew not well how to do it, nor what to say against themselves. And thus, much in such a way as this, some appeared to be pleasing themselves just with an imaginary conversion of their own making.'

Unworthy and detrimental incidents of this nature, were, however, comparatively few, and lost significance in the great weight of testimony concerning the more valid and genuine experiences of innumerable others.

Some of the factors involved in the progress of revivals have been outlined, and together they serve to emphasise the omnipotence of

God in His gracious dealings with men. Revivals, therefore, in their rise and progress are supremely the work of the Holy Spirit. Their effects and achievements are glorious; being the Lord's doing, they are marvellous in the eyes of all who see them.

4. The Fruits of Revivals

What, then, were the achievements? The revivals of the eighteenth century brought about the overthrow of the prevailing philosophical systems which pretended to a theological character. That philosophy which is the product of the natural mind and of worldly wisdom is quite incompatible with 'the simplicity which is in Christ', and it was from this latter position that the evangelical leaders of the eighteenth century sought to lead the Church. They offered no apology for doing so, they merely yielded to an inward compulsion to preach the gospel of Christ in simple scriptural terms. They therefore held forth the free offer of salvation by grace, preaching plainly, closely and personally the substantial truths of the New Testament with zeal, earnestness and fervour, being constrained by the love of Christ to do so. 'Two things exceeding needful in ministers,' says Jonathan Edwards, 'as they would do any great matters to advance the kingdom of Christ, are zeal and resolution.' He continues: 'Zeal and courage will do much in persons of but an ordinary capacity; but especially would they do great things, if joined with great abilities. If some great men who have appeared in our nation, had been as eminent in divinity as they were in philosophy, and had engaged in the Christian cause with as much zeal and fervour as some others have done, and with a proportional blessing of heaven, they would have conquered all Christendom, and turned the world upside down.'

Deism, Socinianism and Unitarianism were swept aside as the revival spread, and many of those churches which had been under their shadow were restored into full gospel light and liberty. A faithful ministry returned to the land which ensured the safety and prosperity of the churches for many years.

Spiritual experiences

Not the least of the blessings which ensued from the revival were the elevated spiritual experiences of the members of Christ's

Church, and the sense of the divine love which pervaded the churches. By 1736 Jonathan Edwards was able to list some of the achievements of the 1734 revival at Northampton in this way: 'Persons after their conversion often speak of religious things as seeming new to them; that preaching is a new thing; that it seems to them they never heard preaching before; that the Bible is a new book; they find there are new chapters, new psalms, new histories, because they see them in a new light . . . Some who before were very rough in their temper and manners, seemed to be remarkably softened and sweetened. And some have had their souls exceedingly filled, and overwhelmed with light, love, and comfort, long since the work of God ceased to be so remarkably carried on in a general way . . . There is still a great deal of religious conversation continued in the town, amongst young and old; a religious disposition appears to be still maintained amongst our people, by their holding frequent private religious meetings . . . we still remain a reformed people, and God has evidently made us a new people.'

Sanctifying effects

This visible reformation in morality and society of which Jonathan Edwards speaks was not confined to his congregation, but appeared universally wherever the Holy Spirit had been poured out in revival. They can best be defined as sanctifying effects, the Holy Spirit working to the glory of God in churches and communities through the changed lives of their members. In answer to several queries from the Presbytery of Aberdeen regarding the revival of 1839 at Dundee, Robert Murray M'Cheyne could write in 1841: 'The Sabbath is now observed with greater reverence than it used to be; and there seems to be far more of a solemn awe upon the minds of men than formerly. The private meetings for prayer have spread a sweet influence over the place. There is far more solemnity in the house of God; and it is a different thing to the people now from what it once was. Any minister of spiritual feeling can discern that there are many praying people in the congregation. When I first came here, I found it impossible to establish Sabbath schools while, very lately, there were instituted with ease nineteen such schools, that are well taught and well attended.'

These effects and achievements were typical of those attained irrespective of country or time or instrument. The Holy Spirit was at work, glorifying Christ in the salvation of sinners, bringing men into subjection, by His powerful operations, to the truth as it is in Jesus, and establishing that righteousness in a nation which alone exalts it.

Whole communities transformed

In the experience of the Church the eighteenth century was one continuous flow of revivals, which the Holy Spirit moulded from its infinite variety of situations, circumstances, impossibilities, instruments and conditions, into one great healing stream. The leading revivalists were 'men of like passions as we are', subject to errors, sin and temptations, but the Holy Spirit used them in spite of their limitations and failings. As they preached, the Holy Spirit accompanied the Word with power and it became the 'savour of life' to many. The deadness and barrenness which had prevailed in the Church, and the indifference and immorality which had abounded in the world, could not withstand the surge of spiritual life which flowed through mere men, but issued from a divine source. Whole communities were affected and transformed, great churches were reformed and invigorated, vast countries took on a new aspect. From this movement of God's Spirit new missionary enterprises were born, philanthropic institutions blossomed forth, and ecclesiastical foundations were consolidated. The repercussions of the movement not only traversed continents, but also periods and ages, giving cause for generations to come to praise God, and securing for them a priceless heritage.

Our greatest need

Alas! that it is necessary to bemoan in these days the scarcity of such divine visitations as were so frequent in the eighteenth century! Is it not to the grief of Christians today that so few know 'the years of the right hand of the most High', that few have witnessed and experienced those blessed effusions of the Holy Spirit which so radically altered the condition of God's Church and the appearance of human society? How poverty-stricken must be the condition of Christ's Church today, when so many years have passed without a revival! Oh! may the Holy Spirit grant to His people in these days a

realization of their state, and be led by the Spirit of adoption to cry
to their heavenly Father: 'O God, how long shall the adversary
reproach? Shall the enemy blaspheme thy name for ever? Why
withdrawest thou thy hand, even thy right hand? Pluck it out of thy
bosom' (Psalm 74:10,11). 'Awake, awake, put on strength, O arm
of the Lord; awake, as in the ancient days, in the generations of old'
(Isa. 51:9).

REFERENCES

1. See chapter 8, 'Early Methodist Apologetic'.
2. See chapter 7, 'Adding to the Church'.
3. See chapter 3, 'Psalms and Sermons in the Streets'.
4. See chapter 13, 'Humphrey Jones', and chapter 14, 'Dafydd Morgan'.

3
PSALMS AND SERMONS IN THE STREETS
Richard Baxter's Kidderminster Ministry

The seventeenth century was a time of great revolutionary changes for both Church and State. Early in the century, under King James I, the Authorized Version of the Bible was published. This remained for three centuries highly esteemed both for the integrity of its translation and the quality of its style. The disturbances of the Civil War gave prominence to Oliver Cromwell, and brought Charles I to his execution. Religious intolerance became acute in the sixties, and died down only in the closing decades of the century.

In the midst of this turbulent period, which determined so much of the national character and liberties in both Church and State, Richard Baxter cuts a remarkable figure indeed. His life (1615-1691) spans almost the entire century. The early skirmishes between the Puritans (those who laboured for a more Protestant, Reformed, Church of England), and the High Churchman, William Laud, took place in the days of Baxter's youth. He greatly admired the major and lasting contribution to Christian theology made by the Westminster Assembly of Divines in the forties. He himself was caught up in the painful struggles for ecclesiastical freedom which followed the 1662 Act of Uniformity.

It was as a Christian minister, labouring in the midst of profound and far-reaching civil, theological, pastoral, and ecclesiastical events, that Richard Baxter excelled. J. C. Ryle, Anglican bishop of the last century, made this assessment of him: 'Take Baxter for all together, and there are few English ministers of the Gospel whose names deserve to stand higher than his. Some have excelled him in some gifts, and some in others. But it is seldom that so many gifts are to be found united in one man as they are in Baxter. Eminent personal holiness, amazing power as a preacher, unrivalled pastoral skill, indefatigable diligence as a writer, meekness and patience under undeserved persecution, all meet together in the character of

43

this one man.' One who has studied Baxter in some depth, Dr J. I. Packer, echoes Ryle's sentiments, calling Baxter 'the most outstanding pastor, evangelist and writer on practical devotional themes that Puritanism produced.'

Chief among his labours was his ministry at Kidderminster from 1647 to 1661. Here God blessed his labours in an eminent degree. This period of diligent gospel sowing and plentiful gospel harvesting provides us with significant pointers to a right method of pursuing similar goals in our own day.

First, however, a word about the man himself, and about God's dealings to prepare him for the task. Baxter was born at a village called Eaton Constantine, near Wrekin Hill outside Shrewsbury, in November 1615. His father, although a freeholder, was often beset by gambling debts. Spiritual help was hard to find: ignorance, immorality, neglect, and decay were widespread. Sundays were hardly restful or peaceful:

though we had no better teachers, it pleased God to instruct and change my father by the bare reading of the Scriptures in private, without either preaching, or godly company, or any other books but the Bible . . . In the village where I lived the Reader read the Common-Prayer briefly, and the rest of the day even till dark night almost, except eating-time, was spent in dancing under a Maypole and a great tree, not far from my father's door, where all the town did meet together . . . so that we could not read the Scripture in our family without the great disturbance of the Taber and Pipe and noise in the street.

These comments were made by Baxter in his later years, but while in his mid-teens the stirrings of spiritual change were beginning in his own heart, partly on account of the change he had witnessed in his father. Another influence upon him was the reading of good books:

A poor day-labourer in the town . . . had an old book which he lent my father, which was called Bunny's *Resolution* . . . In the reading of this book (when I was about fifteen years of age), it pleased God to awaken my soul, and show me the folly of sinning, and the misery of the wicked, and the inexpressible weight of things eternal, and the necessity of resolving on a holy life . . . And about that time it pleased God that a poor pedlar came to the door that had ballads and some good books. And my father bought of him Dr (Richard) Sibbes' *Bruised Reed* . . . which opened more of the love of God to me, and gave me a livelier apprehension of the mystery of redemption, and how much I was beholden (indebted) to Jesus Christ.

Baxter applied himself to reading more good books, both while he was at home, and during short stays at Ludlow and London. The doctrinal and devotional works of Puritan authors such as William Perkins and Richard Sibbes were devoured with both spiritual and intellectual appetite. His friendship with godly ministers in the Shrewsbury area, and some severe illnesses (smallpox among them), influenced his outlook on life and brought a growing conviction of God's call to the ministry. The 'fervent prayers and savoury conference and holy lives' of the former impressed upon him a sense of the great majesty of God and the need for 'a painful [painstaking] ministry, and for discipline.' His experiences 'in the school of affliction' he regarded as a 'great mercy . . . to keep my sluggish soul awake in the constant expectation of my change [death].' In retrospect he was to say, 'Weakness and pain helped me to study how to die, that set me on studying how to live.' By the end of 1638 Baxter had been encouraged to become a clergyman in the Church of England, and had been ordained as deacon by the Bishop of Worcester.

Three short periods of ministry now followed, before his five years' chaplaincy in Cromwell's army. At Dudley he found an eager response, confirming his confidence in preaching as God's chief means of sinners' conversion:

In this town of Dudley I lived in much comfort, among a poor, teachable people, lately famous for drunkenness, but commonly more ready to hear God's Word with submission and reformation, than most places where I have come; so that having set up a monthly Lecture [preaching service], the Church was usually as much crowded within and at the windows, as ever I saw any London congregations.

It was at Dudley, too, that ecclesiastical issues increasingly disturbed his conscience. 'Godly, honest people,' he says, 'lent me manuscripts and books which I never saw before'. While he fought off the seemingly censorious implications of these views, he was impressed by the gracious lives of those who suffered because they held them.

These misgivings intensified at Bridgnorth, his next sphere of labour. Here the people had been privileged with a sound, biblical ministry, but Baxter found unexpected obstacles to fruitfulness:

The people proved a very ignorant, dead-hearted people (the town consisting too much of inns and Ale-houses, and having no general trade to employ
the inhabitants in, which is the undoing of great towns); so that though,
through the great mercy of God, my first labours were not without success,
to the conversion of some ignorant, careless sinners unto God . . . yet were
they not so successful as they proved afterwards in other places. Though I
was in the fervour of my affections, and never anywhere preached with
more vehement desires of their conversion, yet with the generality, an
applause of the preacher was most of the success of the sermon which I
could hear of; and their beer-drinking and ill company and dead-heartedness
quickly drowned all.

For an all-round Gospel ministry, Baxter was coming to see that both
hard work and close, disciplined, personal dealing were necessary.

An eighteen-month initial period at Kidderminster followed. The
town was a busy, industrial community of some 4,000 inhabitants.
Baxter was drawn there 'because . . . an ignorant, rude and revelling
people . . . had need of preaching, and yet had among them a small
company of converts, who were humble, godly, and of good conversation . . . but above all, because they had hardly ever had any lively,
serious preaching among them'. During these months Baxter was
struggling. Ill-health was a continuing problem, but he was supported by the prayers of believing friends, 'who were importunate with
God on my behalf', and on more than one occasion he found himself
'suddenly relieved upon their prayers'. Doubts tormented him, too,
about 'the certain truth of the Sacred Scriptures; and also the life to
come, and immortality of the soul.' But they were triumphantly
resolved, and much of his best-selling book, *The Saints' Everlasting
Rest* is a sustained affirmation of these truths. 'I was fain to dig to
the very foundations . . . that so my faith might indeed be my own.
And at last I found that nothing is so firmly believed, as that which
hath been sometime doubted of.'

Perhaps his greatest struggle, however, had to do with the nature of a
gospel ministry, its character, priorities, and aims. When he was to return
to Kidderminster in five years' time, he would have opportunity to work
out his deepening convictions. Meanwhile, a work of grace among the
young people evidenced itself:

My first and greatest success was upon the youth. And . . . when God had
touched the hearts of young men and girls with a love of goodness and

delightful obedience to the truth, the parents and grandfathers who had grown old in an ignorant worldly state, did, many of them, fall into liking and love of piety, induced by their children, whom they perceived to be made of it much wiser and better, and more dutiful to them.

For his part, Baxter, 'took special notice of every one that was humbled, reformed or converted', and looked upon them as 'jewels'.

At this time Baxter held two Sunday services, the sermon in each lasting for at least an hour. Some found his preaching offensive: he was forthright in his denunciation of sin, and relentless in his determination to establish a disciplined congregation. His work at Kidderminster was, however, interrupted by the Civil War. When he left the town to join the Army, he was not alone. He could say that he had 'many score of my neighbours with me in the wars'. Later, at Coventry he tells us, 'the religious part of my neighbours at Kidderminster that would fain have lived quietly at home, were forced . . . to be gone: and to Coventry they came.'

For Baxter the war and army life presented, as well as the harrowing exiences, opportunities for doing good. He vigorously opposed the 'sectaries', those partly religious, partly political groups, whose emphases were apocalyptic in tone, who were extremist in doctrine, and often unbridled in practice. Baxter's debates with them taught him much about human nature, and demanded even greater familiarity with Scripture. Even their defeat, however, did not bring about a truly Reformation settlement, the victors in the war jostling for supremacy and influence. Baxter eventually returned to Kidderminster, a somewhat disillusioned, but wiser man:

O what sweet idolizing thoughts of our future state had we in the time of the wars! What full content did I promise my soul! when I should enjoy peace, and see the Gospel set up in power and plenty, and all the Ordinances in purity, and true discipline exercised in the churches, and ignorance cured, and all persecution ceased . . . And now, where is the rest that I promised my soul? even that is the greatest grief from which I expected most contentment.

It was lessons such as these which added urgency and fervency to his preaching. In this world there is no perfection or paradise. It takes faithful gospel preaching to convince people of eternal realities, and that we have here no continuing city.

The Cromwellian settlement did, however, bring one great benefit: freedom to preach. The Parliamentary Committee for Plundered Ministers had suspended the Kidderminster parish incumbent on account of his unfitness for service. This left open the appointment of a successor, and in 1647, 265 Kidderminster parishioners signed an invitation to Baxter to be their minister, with a promise to give him 'all due encouragement and assistance'.

Of the 1800 people 'at age to be communicants', most refused any religious commitment beyond listening to Baxter preaching. Drunkenness was common in the town, 'the sin of which we were in most danger', says Baxter. Two minority groups differed widely in their religious affiliation. There were the sceptics and the ignorant on the one hand, and 'the religious sort' on the other. The latter, by their 'holy, humble, blameless lives, zeal and diligence' gave Baxter much support and encouragement. He was to witness a remarkable increase in their number: 'When I first entered on my labours I took special notice of everyone that was humbled, reformed or converted; but when I had laboured long, it pleased God that the converts were so many, that I could not afford time for such particular observations . . . families and considerable numbers at once . . . came in and grew up I scarce knew how.'

The means of this dramatic transformation was, quite simply, Baxter's diligent ministerial labours. His great objective, he tells us, was to preach 'Christ crucified to myself and the country people'. This he did, not only from the pulpit, but also in close personal dealings during his pastoral visits.

The thing which I daily opened to them, and with greatest importunity laboured to imprint upon their minds, was the great fundamental principles of Christianity . . . even a right knowledge, and belief of, and subjection and love to, God the Father, the Son, and the Holy Ghost, and love to all men, and concord with the church and one another. I did so daily inculcate the knowledge of God our Creator, Redeemer and Sanctifier, and love and obedience to God, and unity with the Church, and love to men, and hope of life eternal, that these were in the matter of their daily consideration and conversation, and indeed their religion.

He shared this prior objective with neighbouring ministers:

We must labour, in a special manner, for the conversion of the unconverted. The work of conversion is the first and great thing we must drive at; after this we must labour with all our might. Alas! the misery of the unconverted is so great, that it calleth loudest to us for compassion . . . It is so sad a case to see men in a state of damnation, wherein, if they should die, they are lost forever, that methinks we should not be able to let them alone, either in public or private, whatever other work we may have to do. I confess, I am frequently forced to neglect that which should tend to the further increase of knowledge in the godly, because of the lamentable necessity of the unconverted. Who is able to talk of controversies, how excellent soever, while he seeth a company of ignorant, carnal, miserable sinners before his eyes, who must be changed or damned? . . . Whatever you pass over, forget not poor souls that are under the condemnation and curse of the law, and who may look every hour for the infernal execution, if a speedy change do not prevent it. O call after the impenitent, and ply this great work of converting souls, whatever else you leave undone.

That Baxter gave himself to this urgent task at Kidderminster is clear from some of his earliest—and most fervent—published works. These were first preached as sermons, and then printed for a wider public. This is how he introduced his *Treatise of Conversion*, which appeared in 1657 as 'the substance of some plain sermons on the subject': 'I believe God, and therefore I know that you must, every soul of you, be converted or condemned to everlasting punishment. And knowing this, I have told it you over and over again.' *A Call to the Unconverted*, another book on the same theme published in 1658, met with astonishing success, over 20,000 being sold in just over a year. Also in 1658 he issued *Directions and Persuasions to a Sound Conversion*. Two other works in similar strain appeared in 1662: *Now or Never*, and *A Saint or a Brute*, written, like these others, with white-hot intensity, and conveying both urgency and earnestness.

If that was the message, what of Baxter's manner? Liveliness and plainness best describe his preaching, and he deliberately, rigorously, diligently applied himself to both. In his *Divine Appointment of the Lord's Day* he urges ministers to 'preach with such life and awakening seriousness; preach with such grateful holy eloquence, and with such easy method, and with such variety of wholesome matter, that the people may never be weary of you.' And in *The Reformed Pastor*, the classic manual of ministerial labour which he published in 1656, he pursued the theme with deep conviction:

Preach to yourselves the sermons which you study before you preach them to others . . . when I let my heart get cold, my preaching is cold . . . when I have grown cold in preaching, the hearers have grown cold too . . . How few ministers do preach with all their might, or speak about everlasting joys and everlasting torments in such a manner as may make men believe that they are in good earnest! Alas! we speak so drowsily or gently, that sleepy sinners cannot hear. The blow falls so lightly that hard-hearted sinners cannot feel . . . In the name of God, brethren, labour to awaken your own hearts, before you go to the pulpit, that you may be fit to awaken the hearts of sinners . . . Oh, speak not one cold or careless word about so great a business as heaven or hell.

Two of Baxter's contemporaries bear witness to the way in which Baxter realised in himself these ideals. Edmund Calamy said that ' he talked in the pulpit with great freedom about another world, like one that had been there, and was come as a sort of an express from thence to make a report concerning it.' Matthew Sylvester, although he knew Baxter only in old age, confirmed this: 'when he spoke of weighty soul concerns, you might find his very spirit drenched therein.' Baxter's serious illnesses had brought him to the edge of eternity. Thereafter, he tells us:

> I preached, as never sure to preach again
> And as a dying man to dying men.

For Baxter, seriousness and liveliness were twin, indispensible qualifications for a gospel ministry.

Baxter was no less concerned about plainness in preaching, and was keenly aware that many of his flock were ordinary weavers. 'All our teaching must be as plain and evident as we can make it. For this does most suit a teacher's end. He that would be understood must speak to the capacity of his hearers, and make it his business to be understood. Truth loves the light, and is most beautiful when most naked.' Again, he urges, 'God bids us be as plain as we can, for the informing of the ignorant, and as convincing and serious as we are able, for the melting and changing of unchanged hearts.' It was essential, therefore, for ministers to study their flock as well as their books:

Too many are strangers to the people whom they teach, and know not the weakness of the common people, and therefore neither justly resolve their doubts, not answer their objections, nor indeed speak that language which the people understand. They have been bred from their childhood in the Universities among scholars, and have little conversed with plough-men and poor people and ignorant persons, who have quite other conceptions and expressions than scholars have. Their accurate styles and well-couched words and elegant phrases, are most of them like an unknown tongue, to the greatest numbers of their hearers.

In Baxter's opinion the most blameworthy, inexcusable failure of any minister was the failure to be diligent. Laziness, self-indulgence, carelessness, negligence, all these were to be vigorously resisted.

What skill doth every part of our work require!—and of how much moment is every part! To preach a sermon, I think, is not the hardest part; and yet what skill is necessary to make the truth plain; to convince the hearers, to let irresistible light in to their consciences, and to keep it there, and drive all home; to screw the truth into their minds, and work Christ into their affections; to meet every objection, and clearly to resolve it; to drive sinners to a stand, and make them see that there is no hope, but that they must unavoidably either be converted or condemned—and to do all this, as regards language and manner, as beseems our work, and yet as is most suitable to the capacities of our hearers. This, and a great deal more that should be done in every sermon, must surely require a great deal of holy skill. So great a God, whose message we deliver, should be honoured by our delivery of it . . . O brethren! do you not shrink and tremble under the sense of all this work? Will a common measure of holy skill and ability, of prudence and other qualifications, serve for such a task as this? . . . Do not reason and conscience tell you, that if you dare venture on so high a work as this, you should spare no pains to be qualified for the performance of it? It is not now and then an idle snatch or taste of studies that will serve to make an able and sound divine . . . O therefore, brethren, lose no time! Study, and pray, and confer, and practise; for in these four ways your abilities must be increased.

Above all, Baxter claimed, 'we must study how to convince and get within men', a task that demanded not only sustained diligence, but also true spirituality.

Such spirituality had a divine, not a human source. It was right for God's messengers to use all diligence, but God's message reached men's hearts only by the power of the Holy Spirit. Head knowledge must become heart knowledge. 'A man is not so prone to live according to the truth he knows, except it do deeply affect him, so neither doth his soul enjoy its sweetness, except speculation do pass to affection. The understanding is not the whole soul, and therefore cannot do the whole work . . . Knowledge is not the end of knowing: but it is as eating is to the body, where health, and strength and service is the end.' The believer is to grow 'downwards in a clearer insight into the foundation of the Christian faith.' How vital, then to seek for, and depend on, the powerful influences of the Holy Spirit in the work of the gospel:

All this work must be done spiritually, as by men possessed of the Holy Ghost. There is in some men's preaching a spiritual strain, which spiritual hearers can discern and relish; whereas, in other men's, this sacred tincture is so wanting, that, even when they speak of spiritual things, the manner is such as if they were common matters . . . Our whole work must be carried on under a deep sense of our own insufficiency, and of our dependence on Christ. We must go for light, and life, and strength to him who sends us on the work.

It was in this way of close, sustained self-examination that Baxter exercised his ministry in Kidderminster. If his gospel opportunity as a minister was great, his responsibility in that capacity was solemn.

Baxter faced the challenge with a firm belief in the efficacy of prayer. First, however, he must prove its power in his own life.

In my labours at Kidderminster, after my return [from the Army] I did all under languishing weakness, being seldom free from pain . . . Many a time have I been brought very low, and received the sentence of death in myself, when my poor, honest, praying neighbours have met, and upon their fasting and earnest prayers I have been recovered. Once when I had continued weak three weeks, and was unable to go abroad, the very day that they prayed for me, being Good Friday, I recovered, and was able to preach and administer the sacrament the next Lord's Day, and was better after it.

His passionate belief in the God who answers prayer found poignant application when it came to the sickness of a young woman who was later to become his wife. 'A special prayer meeting was held, with fasting . . . in which compassion made us all extraordinary fervent, and God heard us and speedily delivered her.' It is no wonder that his advice to ministers includes some strong exhortations about prayer:

Above all, be much in secret prayer and meditation. Thence you must fetch the heavenly fire that must kindle your sacrifices . . . Prayer must carry on our work as well as preaching; he preacheth not heartily to his people, that prayeth not earnestly for them. If we prevail not with God to give them faith and repentance, we shall never prevail with them to believe and repent.

Baxter's days were always full, and often troublesome, but prayer, in public and in private, he always looked on as so much fuel with which to maintain the fire of his devotion. 'Pray with that heavenly life and fervour as may wrap up the souls of those that join with you, and try then whether they will be weary; praise God with that joyful alacrity which is fitting for one that is ready to pass into glory, and try whether this will not cure the people's weariness.'

One-third of Baxter's *Reformed Pastor* is taken up with 'The duty of personal catechizing and instructing the flock'. By this he meant a pastoral interview with each family in the parish at least once every year. For Baxter that meant some 800 families, each closely examined as to their spiritual state, in systematic order, taking some seven or so on each of two afternoons a week. He was aware that some would object on grounds of the work-load being too heavy. His answer to the objection was ready:

The labour in which we are engaged is not likely to impair your health. It is true, it must be serious; but that will but excite and revive our spirits, and not so much spend them . . . What have we our time and strength for, but to lay them out for God? What is a candle made for, but to burn? Burned and wasted we must be; and is it not fitter it should be in lighting men to heaven, and in working for God, than in living for the flesh?

How then did Baxter set about the task of transforming the spiritual condition of Kidderminster?

Before the wars, I preached twice each Lord's day; but after the war, but once, and once every Thursday, beside occasional sermons. Every Thursday evening, my neighbours who were most desirous, and had opportunity, met at my house, and there one of them repeated the sermon . . . And last of all I caused sometimes one, and sometimes another to pray (to exercise them); and sometimes I prayed with them myself: which (beside singing a Psalm) was all they did. And once a week also some of the younger sort, who were not fit to pray in so great an assembly, met among a few more privately, where they spent three hours in prayer together. Every Saturday night, they met at some of their houses, to repeat the sermon of the former Lord's Day, and to pray, and prepare themselves for the following day.

The 'private meetings' provided an opportunity to safeguard the 'seed' sown by preaching. They also provided Baxter with 'feedback' as to the people's response to his sermons,

a marvellous help to the propagating of godliness among them: for thereby truths that slipped away were recalled, and the seriousness of the people's mind renewed, and good desires cherished; and hereby their knowledge was much increased; and here the younger sort learned to pray, by frequently hearing others. And here I had opportunity to know their case, for if any were touched and awakened in public, I should presently see him drop in to our private meetings; and I was usually present with them, answering their doubts, and silencing objections, and moderating them all.

So much for public ministry, and dealing with those who showed some concern for their souls.

Baxter also found that unconverted people often became aware of their godless state when dealt with on an individual basis. 'Some ignorant persons, who have been so long unprofitable hearers, have got more knowledge and remorse in half an hour's close discourse, than they did from ten years' public preaching. I know that preaching the Gospel publicly is the most excellent means, because we speak to so many at once. But it is usually far more effective to preach privately to a particular sinner.' Consequently, Baxter's public ministry to his congregation was complemented by systematic, homely, penetrating application of the truth in private conference. Two afternoons each week were taken in this way by Baxter and his assistant, the schoolmaster, Thomas Baldwin:

First they recited the catechism to us (a family only being present at a time, and no stranger admitted); after that I first helped them to understand it, and next enquired modestly into the state of their souls, and lastly, endeavoured to set all home to the convincing, awakening and resolving of their hearts according to their several conditions; bestowing about an hour (and the labour of a sermon) with every family. And though the first time they came with fear and backwardness, after that they longed for their turn to come again. Few families went from me without some tears, or seemingly serious promises for a godly life.

This was Baxter's distinctive emphasis and contribution while at Kidderminster. The success he met with encouraged him to recommend the same effective practice to others. Many neighbouring ministers followed his example, and the 'Worcestershire Association' of ministers was known for its diligent ministerial labours on the Baxter pattern.

Rightly does Bishop J. C. Ryle say of Baxter, that he was 'one of the most successful pastors of a parish and congregation that ever lived'. In all Baxter spent fourteen years at Kidderminster, and he was the first to acknowledge God's mercy in crowning his labours with success:

The congregation was usually full [the building could accommodate about a 1,000 people], so that we were fain to build five galleries after my coming thither . . . Our private meetings, also, were full. On the Lord's Day there was no disorder to be seen in the streets, but you might hear a hundred families singing Psalms and repeating sermons as you passed through the streets. In a word, when I came thither first, there was about one family in a street that worshipped God and called on his name, and when I came away there were some streets where there was not past one family in the side of the street that did not so; and that did not, by professing serious godliness, give us hopes of their sincerity . . . Some of the poor men did competently understand the Body of Divinity, and were able to judge in difficult controversies. Some of them were so able in prayer, that very few ministers did match them in order and fulness and apt expressions and holy oratory, with fervency . . . The professors of serious godliness were generally of very humble minds and carriage; of meek and quiet behaviour unto others; and of blamelessness and innocency in the conversations . . . And the zeal and knowledge of this poor people provoked many in other parts of the land.

Such were the effects of a faithful ministry, effects which left their mark on the town for a long time. Another famous preacher, also greatly owned of God in the conversion of many, George Whitefield, visited Kidderminster a full century later. 'I was greatly refreshed', he says, 'to find what a sweet savour of good remained to this day, from Mr Baxter's doctrine, works, and discipline.'

Several matters stand out as significant in considering the great work wrought by God through Baxter at Kidderminster. Baxter had an implicit confidence in his message, both in its source, the Bible, and its power, as being God's chief agency in conversion. He was just as insistent on the exercise of pastoral discipline, not in the sense of a legalistic 'lording it over God's heritage', but in the sense of supervised, personal assessment of spiritual experience. With discernment and compassion, he led people into closer dealings with God, and therefore into spiritual maturity. The gospel preacher in Baxter was also shepherd, teacher, brother, and friend. Furthermore, in all these capacities he was a labourer, diligent, unsparing of himself, always at full stretch. In his manner there was fervency, directness, and total commitment. One, who heard Baxter preaching in his old age, spoke of 'a strange fire and pathos' in the sermon.

Within two years of Baxter's departure from Kidderminster came The Act of Uniformity. All clergymen were required to confine their ministrations to forms and words set out in the Prayer Book of the

Church of England. Along with some 2,000 others, Baxter's conscience would not submit to that limiting, and in some parts, biblically unwarranted sanction. On this account he was often imprisoned, deprived of his books, and persecuted. Baxter had been, even in Kidderminster, a prolific writer: from 1662 to his death in 1691 some ninety or so books issued from his pen.

Baxter's Kidderminster ministry, however, remains an abiding testimony to the effectiveness of an all-round ministry of the Word of God. Towards the end of his life he wrote, 'My Lord, I have nothing to do in this world, but to seek and to serve Thee; I have nothing to do with a heart and its affections, but to breathe after Thee; I have nothing to do with my tongue and pen, but to speak to Thee, and for Thee, and to publish Thy glory, and Thy will.' Baxter's Kidderminster ministry makes it clear that a gospel ministry demands such single-mindedness. It also holds out the hope that, as then, so again in God's mercy, such devotion may be a means of reviving God's work.

SELECT BIBLIOGRAPHY

Reliquiae Baxterianae, 1696. Baxter's massive and detailed Autobiography and commentary on the events of his times, published posthumously by the editor, Matthew Sylvester. Subsequent abridged and edited editions are listed in Keeble, below.

N. H. Keeble, *Richard Baxter, Puritan Man of Letters*, Oxford, 1982. An excellent 'Baxter Bibliography' is given at the end. Keeble has also written, 'Richard Baxter's Preaching Ministry: its History and Texts', in the *Journal of Ecclesiastical History*, vol.35, No.4 (October 1984), pp.539-59.

Geoffrey F. Nuttall, *Richard Baxter*, London, 1965.

J. I. Packer, *Among God's Giants, the Puritant Vision of the Christian Life*, Eastbourne, 1991. A superb study of Puritan theology: comprehensive, reliable, and stimulating. The same applies to Packer's various pieces on Baxter: 'Introduction' to *The Reformed Pastor*, Edinburgh, 1974; 'Introducing' *A Christian Directory*, Ligonier, Pa., 1990; 'A Man for All Ministries', in *Reformation & Revival*, vol.i, No.1, Winter 1992, pp.53-74.

J. C. Ryle, *Light from Old Times*, Fourth Edition, London, 1903, pp.303-42.

4
SPIRITUALITY BEFORE
THE GREAT AWAKENING
The personal devotion of Griffith Jones, Llanddowror

The revival of religion in the eighteenth century which came to be known as 'The Great Awakening' was the result of several powerful and widespread movements of God's Holy Spirit. Markers of their beginning and cessation can rarely be precisely set. The year 1735 is usually taken as the starting point in Wales, with the conversion of Howel Harris and Daniel Rowland. Some time was to pass, however, before the success which attended their labours could justifiably be acknowledged as a season of refreshing from the presence of God.

Our concern is with people and events before this date, and in particular with the Christian conviction and devotion (which together made up the piety or spirituality) of one man, Griffith Jones.[1] He was born in 1683, and lived to his seventy-eighth year. After spending some time as a shepherd, he came to faith in Christ and was constrained to become a clergyman. His education at Carmarthen grammar school was followed by ordination in 1708, eventually being appointed Rector of Llanddowror in Carmarthenshire in 1716, where he remained until his death. Even before this date his fame as a preacher attracted both success (large crowds attended his ministry everywhere), and opposition (from prejudiced colleagues). From 1713, when he became a corresponding member of the Society for Promoting Christian Knowledge [SPCK], he also showed great zeal as a Christian educator. This aspect of his work involved the publication of Welsh editions of the Bible, distributing Christian books, and organising schools where people of all ages could learn to read.

Extensive diaries of Griffith Jones are not available to us, and so we lack a sustained, personal account of God's dealings with his soul. What we have are letters, sermons, and published works, all, to a greater or lesser extent, public. And in all of them he is teaching, expounding, applying the Scriptures. Only occasionally do we have glimpses of his own joys and sorrows. Nevertheless, his ideals and priorities come through with forcefulness and clarity. From these it is immediately apparent that his godliness is biblical in its source, Reformed in its allegiance, and Anglican in its devotion. Even though the Evangelical Revival was still in the future, he displays a depth and warmth in the fervency of his spirit, combined with a profound commitment to evangelistic effort, that was later so characteristic of that Revival. Christian experience in revival is not another kind of experience; it is experience heightened, enlivened, invigorated by more powerful manifestations of God's Spirit. But it is for this reason that Jones is sometimes referred to as 'the Morning Star of the Revival'. If Jones could enjoy and exhibit such lively spirituality in his day, why not us, in ours?

It is true that conditions in Jones's day were similar to ours. Here are some of his typical comments on the state of religion then:

That excellent text, Isa.59:19, 'When the enemy comes in like a flood, the spirit of the Lord shall lift up a standard against him', contains in it a most comfortable promissory prophecy . . . If we consider how numerous and shameless . . . how common and impudent the despisers and opposers of serious piety are in our days, what shall we think but that the enemy is coming in like a water-flood, and threatens to overflow our land with a worse deluge than that which drowned the world in the days of Noah. And though . . . it may be suffered to proceed to a greater extremity than we have yet seen, yet in God's due time, I trust he will seasonably and surprisingly lift up a standard against the enemies and persecutors of Jesus Christ . . . Reason and human means only will not serve to stop the tide of iniquity, which now flows so fast upon us. No standard will suffice to oppose it but that of the Holy Spirit's lifting up; which should remind us always to have recourse to the Spirit of God for direction, assistance, and success in every thing we attempt.[2]

Personal godliness and public witness were to be nurtured in the face of great discouragements. In Jones's day, most people remained in ignorance of the gospel, and superstition, immorality, and misery held sway in their lives. Others denied the need for divine relevation or supernatural grace, trusting in the power of reason and outward morality as sufficient religion for this world and the next. Few acknowledged the need for personal salvation from sin through Jesus Christ, and daily conformity to God's will in the light of Scripture and by the power of the Holy Spirit.

For these reasons, then, a study of Jones's spirituality should be both salutary and encouraging. What was it that sustained the believer's spiritual life in those days? How did they manage the conflict with unbelief, sin, and Satan's opposition? When there was no apparent evidence of a reviving of the work of God, what gave them hope, and courage to persevere? What convictions gave meaning to everyday life and duties, and where did believers find strength to glorify God therein?

Both Puritan and Anglican thinking influenced Griffith Jones. The method and thoroughness of his treatment of his subjects betray close familiarity with Puritan practice. His views of the Christian life, his emphasis on knowledge, his use of Scripture, and its close, practical application, reflect Puritan convictions.[3] Jones was a minister in the Anglican communion, and the SPCK worked closely with its bishops, clergy and laity, providing educational and publishing resources. Hence it is not surprising that Jones owned allegiance to The Book of Common Prayer with its distinctive devotional culture, and widely used the Anglican religious classics produced by the SPCK.[4]

During the early decades of the eighteenth century, believers outside the Anglican Church were also facing bravely this period of spiritual declension and barrenness. One of them, the Dissenting minister Philip Doddridge, spoke of 'a secret strength' among them. Another, the Kidderminster merchant Joseph Williams, recorded some remarkable experiences in his diary at various times between 1717 and 1725:

Under the sermons I have heard today, being our sacrament day, Christ's love to souls was the subject of discourse. Never did I experience such a flame of divine love as was kindled in me. The word came to me with life and power. I have this day been made again to experience what it is to enjoy communion with, and communications of love from, a kind and gracious God. Oh! the sweet rays of love, wherewith he was pleased to shine in and upon my soul.

Yet another, Timothy Thomas, whose short ministry of three years at Pershore, Worcestershire, ended with his death at 1720 at the age of twenty-two, had similarly lively occasions:

Such a night had I of God's dealings with my heart, and my heart taking hold of him, and wrestling with him, as I do not remember before, as far as I can look back! . . . When I have seen the forgiveness of God, and this plenteous redemption . . . my heart would no longer hold . . . 'Oh! the love, the grace!' I could not but cry out, and repeat it often in a flood of tears . . . He communes with me often, and my soul holds communion with him . . . in prayer I meet with him, and in meditation I hold him fast, and cannot let him go.[5]

Such evidence of a vigorous spirituality, however scanty, in the midst of widespread religious indifference and impotence, deserves acknowledgement and examination. In Wales, its most illustrious representative, Griffith Jones, was to be found in the Anglican Church. His spirituality found its centre as well as its sufficiency in God Himself:

It is the end of religion to have God for our portion, who is the Author, fountain, life and substance of all happiness, and the all-sufficient, yea, the only and sufficient support and felicity of our souls. It is God and his Christ, with the Holy Spirit, that is our all in all, the everlasting and overflowing fountain of bliss. It is from this fund of all-sufficiency that we must be supplied with all we want—all grace and mercy, all peace and pardon, all help and wisdom, all our righteousness, sanctification and redemption.[6]

Just as God's regenerating power breathes life to the soul 'dead in trespasses and sins', so His renewing power supplies and satisfies that soul, however arid the desert around it.

Early in his ministerial career, Jones had to seek God's guidance. An eminent layman, Sir John Philipps of Picton Castle, Pembrokeshire[7], regarded him as 'a very worthy Clergyman', 'one of the most sincerest Christians I ever had the happiness to converse with'. In October 1712, he communicated to the SPCK that Jones had 'lately discovered an inclination' to go to India as a missionary.[8] With this in mind, the Society sent him a Portuguese Grammar and Dictionary.

Discerning God's will in the matter caused him a great deal of heart-searching. At first he seemed inclined to accept the Society's invitation: he learned some Spanish, and arranged that the Society should send part of his financial allowance to his mother. Sir John could report of her, 'she is very tender of him and yet willingly resigns him up to the hand of Providence.' At about the same time, the Society informed Sir John that it would 'be impossible for Mr Jones to go by the next ship', and the issue was delayed.[9] Wise counsel came in the form of a letter from A. W. Boehm, who translated into English the account of A. H. Francke's schools and orphanage at Halle, Germany (*Pietas Hallensis*, a title which gave Jones the idea for Welsh Piety as a title for the reports of his own work). Boehm's advice is worth quoting at some length:

The concern you are under at present about a sure and certain knowledge of the will of God is a concern common to all those that have begun to study the very first and initial lesson of the Christian religion. I mean the great duty of self-resignation to the Divine will. If we follow the Lord in whatever we undertake we have then the promise that He will guide us with His eye, and, if we run before Him, we must needs fall into many dangers and untrodden byways and lose ourselves at last in the devices of our own heart . . . Now, to manage so momentous a matter with the greater hope of success, the Lord promised us the Spirit of power, of love and of sound mind. Power makes us bold, love makes us willing, and the soundness of mind makes us prudent in the administration of the mystery of the Gospel . . . As it is God alone who must prepare us, so it is God alone who, by a Divine impression, must convince us. I say by a Divine impression. Human persuasions, can at the best beget but human conviction . . . But when I speak of a Divine conviction, I do not undervalue all my mutual conference with friends and other such helps as may be fetched from souls acquainted with the ways of Providence . . . but the application of the work is still, and only, in the hands of God, by whom the external light given by a friend is impressed both upon the will and understanding with a divine assurance, and thereby our evidence rendered far and effectual on all sides. Faith itself, you know, is of that nature, that it never rests in general promises, but must have every promise of the Gospel in particular appropriated to itself by a higher Being than man is.[10]

Jones took over a year to come to a final decision: 'as to the invitation of going to the Indies as a missionary, he thinks himself obliged to decline it, upon the prospect he had of doing more service in his native country than he can propose to do abroad.'[11] But this was only after going up to London for an interview, during which visit he preached before Queen Anne.[12] Jones was later to speak of God's will as being unfolded to us in two ways: the revealed will of His Word, to which we must always yield obedience, and the secret will of His Providence, to which we must always yield submission.[13]

Once the decision was taken to remain in Wales, Jones seems to have given himself unreservedly to prayer and preaching. At the time he was a curate at Laugharne in Carmarthenshire, a place better known today for Dylan Thomas's literary labours from 1949. In 1713 Jones's preaching attracted people from a wide area, and his congregations grew to several hundreds. William Williams, in his elegy to Jones, refers to him as 'stuffing the churches to capacity, transforming graveyards into churches.'[14] Jones's constant aim in preaching is best described in a letter of his written some twenty years later:

I need not tell you that those always are the best sermons which bring one's heart nearer to God, which render Christ dearer to us, by representing our need of him, our misery without him, and our privileges by him, and which convince us of the necessity of holiness, and of the Spirit's influence to that end, exciting and assisting us to mortify the dearest sin, and to vanquish the strongest temptation, and weaning us from earthly enticements, teaching us to live in communion with God, and to bear up comfortably under all the disquietudes of this life, and fitting us for a comfortable passage through the pangs of death.[15]

His sermons were written with careful exegesis of the text, a thorough exposition of its teaching, and a practical application, a method bearing closer resemblance to Puritan, rather than Anglican, practice.[16]

An early published Summary of Jones's life and character gives a detailed description of his preaching. It mentions his 'reverence and holy fear' as he entered the pulpit, 'his mind . . . full fraught with the idea of his subject', and 'as he advanced, his subject fired him more and more.' The account continues:

In refuting, remonstrating, and reproving, he assumed the tone of conviction, and majestic authority; but when he came to the Application, he gave way to a still superior burst of religious vehemence, which, like the impetus of an irresistible torrent, mightily carried all before it. Great was the power of the divine Spirit that accompanied the word. The prayerless cried for mercy; and the ignorant were made wise unto salvation. He warmly invited the poor to become spiritually rich; the indigent and guilty to accept of pardon. He enforced the necessity of doing good works, and at the same time displayed the madness and impiety of trusting in them. CHRIST WAS ALL to him; and it was his greatest delight to publish and exalt the unsearchable riches of his Redeemer.

According to one of the SPCK's correspondents, Edward Dalton, Jones combined 'uncommon industry', 'eminency in Scriptural and Christian knowledge' on the one hand, with 'fluency of speech' and 'plain and familiar dialect' on the other.[17] His was a spirituality that reached out to others in their plight because of sin, and used every gift that God had given him to that end.

Between 1714 and 1716 Jones had to answer charges levelled against him by his fellow-clergymen. Sir John Philipps reported to the SPCK:

That Mr Jones of Laugharne has lately undergone a sort of trial before the Bishop of St. David's at Carmarthen, where several of the clergy appeared against him, whose principal accusation was his neglecting his own cure and intruding himself into the churches of other ministers without their leave, the contrary whereof was manifestly proved; namely, that he never preached in any other place without being invited, either by the incumbent, curate, or some of the best inhabitants of the Parish. That he had indeed preached twice or thrice without the wall of the church, the reason of which was because the church was not large enough to contain the hearers, which sometimes amounted to 3 or 4,000 people.[18]

Jones's explanation to the bishop is full and forthright, and his determination to persevere is equally candid: 'None can cultivate a wilderness without being sometimes scratched by the thorns and briars; we can't . . . think that we are rightly sowing God's pearls unless some dogs turn again and rend us.'[19] A year later, his zeal was unabated, as Sir John reported to his wife: 'I should be pleased to hear Mr Jones were more careful of his health, but he seems to have a spring of thirst in him for the salvation of souls, that will make that advice impracticable, at least till some further weakness convinces him that this cannot be so effectually carried on without the other.'[20]

Ill-health and suffering for Christ seem to go hand in hand in Jones's experience. From a very early age he was plagued with asthma. In 1731 he reported to the SPCK that it was 'a very sickly time near his neighbourhood where many die and many more are sick of a nervous kind of fever.' From time to time he availed himself of the medicinal waters at Bath.[21] Scribbled beside a sermon on Psalm 86:12-13, preached on 27 February 1737, are the words, 'Mr Jones's first sermon after his recovery from the pleuritic fever [pleurisy]'.[22] He carried on in spite of such adversities: 'Though I went from home with a cold, and returned with a hoarseness, yet I have been carried through the duties of the day with some strength and cheerfulness. My Sundays are always my best days with regard to the health of my soul and my body too. I wish I was employed in the same manner every day, and that all my days were holy-days.'[23] A conviction that the ways of God's providence are intended for our good kept that resolution firm: 'It is necessary there should be some alloy attending the most favourable circumstances here, in order to unite our affections more closely to Him alone, in whom we shall be sure to find relief under all our disappointments from other quarters.' The gaze of the believing soul must be on the God who controls our circumstances, rather than on the circumstances themselves:

It is well that the mixing of our cup belongs to God; if we had ourselves the tempering of it, we should soon destroy ourselves by taking out all the bitter ingredients; and by so making it more pleasant, we should render it very unwholesome. We should have the thorn in the flesh removed from us; and if our petition were granted, it would ruin, or at least endanger, our souls . . . Oh! for a more improved degree of faith. According to our measure of it will be our strength in the day of trial. This is the grace that crowns our head in the day of battle . . . For certainly that which causes us to sink in times of trouble, is rather from within, from our unsubdued and clamorous thoughts, than from the troubles themselves. But by committing the whole affair to our dear Lord, the soul is quickly brought to rest.[24]

Nor was the comfort that Jones derived from his beliefs merely theoretical or selfish. When in 1733 he had been made aware of the plight of some 25,000 Protestants from Salzburg, exiled on account of their faith, he collected nearly £70 for their relief. And his convalescence at Bath was not a time of idleness. Lady Cox, the wife of the Gloucester Member of Parliament, 'derived much profit from the preaching and heart-searching conversation of the apostolic Griffith Jones.'[25]

Underlying all of Griffith Jones labours and sufferings was a strong conviction regarding the integrity and authority of the Scriptures. As the Summary of his life related, 'He earnestly inculcated the WHOLE truth of the Gospel in his ministrations . . . He had a most reverential esteem for the divine word, and was well-versed in the holy Scriptures . . . The oracles of heaven were his study, his delight, and his counsellors.' Unlike the mystics, his spirituality was nourished by familiarity with, and meditation on, the Word of God. This it was which set forth the only Mediator between God and man, Christ Jesus, and apart from Him access to God, and saving knowledge of Him, is impossible. For Jones, then, Scripture was the norm, the point of reference, the framework, from which, and within which, the whole of life was to be brought into harmony with God's mind and will. 'In the holy Scriptures are the most important and needful subjects for all to know, and they should be most inculcated and conferred about, as the necessity, advantage, and evidence of our union with Christ Jesus; from which foundation of all comforts flow our covenant relation to God, forgiveness of sin, justification, everlasting peace, adoption, access before the throne in prayer, and eternal life, and every thing that pertains unto it . . . The Holy Bible . . . has the Holy Ghost for its Author, infallible truth for its subject-matter, and eternal life for its end.'[26]

Those words were written in 1737, before the Great Awakening's powerful influences had been felt. Nearly ten years later, with revival manifestations widespread, and large numbers professing conversion, there was a danger that the regulatory function of Scripture was being neglected or even despised. Jones therefore reminded one of the Revival's leaders, Howel Harris, of the Scripture's importance: 'He urged much', says Harris, 'and how the work may be marred, and how all should be stirred up to read, or else they may come to follow their experiences, and not the Word.'[27]

With such convictions, Jones wrote catechisms, expositions of the Apostles Creed, the Lord's Prayer, the Ten Commandments, and the Sacraments, and other books. From 1731 he set up schools 'for all comers to learn to read and be supplied with books, and taught gratis'. Such was their success that by 1761 some 3,500 schools had been set up in Wales, with over 158,000 scholars, and their fame had spread as far as Russia.[28] His was a spirituality based upon the premise that truth must first enter the mind, if it is to affect the soul in its relationship with God. Only then will men's lives be changed from self-seeking to neighbourliness, and a genuine concern for the eternal welfare of others. Furthermore, of all the enemies to godliness, ignorance was chief, as it was also the means of hindering men's saving acquaintance with Christ. But reading was a means, not an end. Jones taught people to read Bibles and works of divinity and devotion with this end in view: the salvation of their souls. His *Letter Regarding the Duty of Catechising Children and the Unlearned* may not have appeared in print until 1749, but its precepts had been implemented throughout his ministry.

'Nor', adds the author of the Summary of his life, 'was his devotion confined to the pulpit . . . He thought it his incumbent duty . . . to build an altar unto the Lord, in his family . . . His constant method, morning and evening, was to call his domestics together, and his neighbours were welcome to come and join with him. This stated worship consisted of introductory prayer; expounding a chapter; singing [Psalms]; and then a conclusion of the whole by additional prayer and thanksgiving.' All this gives the clear impression that for Jones growth in godliness, the nurture of a genuine spirituality, was only possible in the context of disciplined learning, a schooling of the soul for communion with God, and for life in the world. It was the spirituality of the later Methodists, too, summed up in George Whitefield's definition of Methodism: 'It is no more nor less than "Faith working by Love. A holy method of living and dying, to the glory of God."'[29]

Mention of love is a reminder that Jones viewed the two sacraments as occasions to renew faith and love. They are the seals of the Covenant of Grace, whereby we are assured of our saving interest in Jesus Christ. In this area Jones's doctrinal position reflects the classical Puritan emphasis on the Covenant. At the same time, the implications of covenantal privileges and responsibilities are unashamedly woven into Anglican sacramental usage. The sacraments are a means of grace, confirming our position in Christ, but also constraining our devotion to His Person and to His purpose in the world. 'If the dying love of our Redeemer does not influence us to live to Him, to what purpose was the holy Supper appointed to be solemnized in remembrance of Him?', he asks in one letter.

A fuller answer to this rhetorical question is given in another:

The Lord's Supper was ordained to be a solemn commemoration of our Lord's death and passion, and to keep up a lively and affectionate remembrance of it in our minds until His coming again . . . to be a solemn renewing of the holy Covenant . . . as a lively and solemn means, whereby the Spirit of Christ may stir up . . . our repentance, faith, love, desire, hope, joy, thankfulness and new obedience . . . to be a public and solemn profession of our faith, love, obedience and gratitude to the blessed Trinity . . . to be a solemn sign, badge and confirmation of our brotherly love and union in Christ, and readiness to communicate to each other.[30]

Jones rejects the Roman Catholic teaching that the bread and wine become in reality the body and blood of Christ, and instead affirms that believers' reception of Christ is three-fold:

in a Sacramental sense, receiving the visible signs for the right ends, as they signify and seal to them invisible realities . . . in a Covenantal sense, as they receive Christ . . . in all His offices, under a solemn and sure obligation to believe faithfully and submissively in Him, and to cleave to Him for ever . . . in a Spiritual sense . . . to nourish them by faith to eternal life.[31]

God's Word, the visible signs, and faith: these together constituted a right use of the Sacraments. In this way the believing soul receives inner, spiritual nourishment for the demands of a hostile environment in which his temporal body resides.

The believer's life in this world is a life of faith. Living among things which are seen, he looks to the things which are unseen, and he does so by faith. 'The sum of the Christian duty is to live, not under the directions of sense, but, in all concerns of the present and future world, to live by faith, and to continue under the power and conduct, and comfort of it all our days.' Thus Jones's understanding of faith provides another key to his spirituality. By faith he means not just assent to 'the Christian faith', a vague kind of imbibing beliefs and values from Church or tradition. Nor is it a general, loose idea of derivation from, influence by, and obligation to some undefinable force or spirit outside ourselves. Quite the contrary:

FAITH . . . is not only an undoubted belief of all that God has revealed in the holy Scriptures, but likewise an entire dependence upon the grace and mercy which God has promised us through Christ, in our sincere use of the means He has appointed . . . True faith in Christ is an active and vital principle, and worketh effectually in the soul, to lead men to endeavour after a real conformity to the Spirit and life and doctrine of the blessed Redeemer . . . Divine love must sway their delights, desires and affections, for faith worketh by love. They must cleans themselves from all pollutions of flesh and spirit; for faith purifieth the heart . . . Faith will work an admirable change for the better in every part of man; for if any be brought by it into Christ Jesus, he is a new creature, old things are done away, and behold all things are become new.[32]

'An active and vital principle, and worketh . . . ': this divinely-planted gift is within the believer, a constant generator of heavenly-mindedness, goodness, and humility in a world that is earth-bound, evil, and arrogant in its self-assertiveness. It has no life of its own, but draws upon the life of God Himself, ministered to the soul by the Holy Spirit, and sought earnestly by prayer and waiting on God.

'It is the Holy Spirit of God who must dispose and fit us for every duty. It is He that draws the soul near to God, and teaches us how to converse with Him.' This strong affirmation about prayer comes in one of nine lengthy letters on the subject by Jones. They are separate from his exposition of the Lord's Prayer, which forms Part Four of his *Directions to a Saving Knowledge of the Principles and Duties of Religion,* published in 1746. There are, he tells us, 'three prerequisites of prayer . . . a due consideration of God's marvellous perfections . . . a knowedge and consideration of the holy Scriptures . . . ', and 'a knowledge and consideration of ourselves.' His main concern was not with the structure, or mechanics of prayer, but with the more dynamic, inner experience of desire and dependence.

How greatly the Spirit of prayer differs, either from the best form, or from the brightest gifts of prayer, for these are but the outside of the duty; it is the spirit that gives it life, vigour and efficacy, and that renders it acceptable to God, and of real advantage to us . . . Perfection is not the necessary term of our acceptance; but where there is sincerity in the heart, and faith applying to Christ's mediation, our gracious God will overlook many defects and weaknesses in our performance.

This is why, in an earlier letter, he expresses a longing 'to be favoured with the gracious breathings of the good Spirit, to move our affections towards the things of God.' He adds, 'If our duties and prayers do not through Christ prevail for the stirring up of these kindly gales, our profession will come to a shipwreck, or we shall hardly be able to set out for, much less to arrive at, the desired haven.'[33] True godliness could only be nurtured by a conscious dependence on the assistance of God's Spirit.

Griffith Jones was fully aware, too, that Christian experience was subject to change and fluctuation. Writing in 1734, he refers to that greater freedom and intensity of prayer which on occasions surprises the believer:

Indeed there is a considerable difference between believers and themselves at different times and seasons, according to the presence or absence of our Divine Helper . . . some pious persons, at some special seasons, are carried up into a very high degree of divine rapture in their praying, singing, meditation, communion, or some other branch of devotion. Their thoughts, desires and affections are all set on fire. What they say, hear, and every thing at that time, is full of sweet savour. Their paths are full of fatness, their fingers drop with sweet smelling myrrh upon the handles of the lock; the flesh is, as it were, swallowed up of the spirit, and mortality swallowed up of life; heaven seems to be poured down upon them. And now the lame runs, the feeble is made strong. They are carried through all duties and difficulties with great ease and pleasure, their wheels run glibly on. Surely they are anointed with the precious oil of the Spirit; they are surely overshadowed with the power of the Most High. Oh! one such day in the courts of the Lord is better than a thousand. A bright sunshine day it is. Oh, lovely day! But as long as we are in the body, it will come to an evening. Yet another day, after some hours of night, will follow. The sun will set, but then in order to rise again . . . Christians must be cautioned not to wonder or be surprised, if they find not the same measure and assistance from the Spirit of God in prayer at all times.[34]

And, in a sermon on the Song of Solomon 3:1-4, preached at Llanddowror on 27 June 1731, Jones drew out the following doctrines:

1. The godly sometimes lose Christ, as if they had never possessed Him, or, Even the best saints feel the absence of Christ at times, Ps.13:1. The Lord sometimes withdraws from His people, to prove their love, and to intensify their longing for Him more than for all else in the world. At other times it is by way of reproof, for their neglect of staying close to Him in the past. 2. The godly man's soul delights in Christ, whatever his condition in the world, Ps.73:25. 3. Those who love Christ earnestly seek for Him when they realise that He has withdrawn from them, Ps.42:1-2. 4. Such as seek Him without success are under grievous affliction on that account, Ps.30:7 . . . when Christ, the Sun of Righteousness, is hidden from them it is as the horror of a dark night to their souls.[35]

Truly, the Christian life is a warfare, in which battles are sometimes lost, but at all times the conflict must go on. 'We must a little while combat with oppositions from without and with corruptions from within . . . so that we have need to take unto us the whole armour of God; and after all, our spiritual victories must be sought for at the hands of God.'[36] After expounding to his correspondent, Bridget Bevan, the sevenfold nature of the Christian armour mentioned in Ephesians 6, he concludes:

We are here it is true in the field of battle, and we have many enemies to fight with; but then remember the Prince and Captain of our salvation, whose banner of love we fight under, and forget not the prize we fight for. Let us put on his armour, and he will perfect his strength in our weakness, that we shall not fail to manage it.[37]

Griffith Jones often expressed a deep concern on many occasions for his own spiritual state, and for that of religion generally. Here is a typical example:

I wish I had more of the unction of this Holy Spirit to carry me through the work of my day, and to assist me to live in a closer communion with God. It has sometimes refreshed my soul to consider that among all the precious promises in the holy scriptures, there is not one more full, and worded in stronger terms of assurance, than that of the heavenly Father giving the Holy Spirit to them that ask him, Luke 11:13. And this should put us upon asking in faith, which can never fail to succeed.

In March 1735 he laments that 'our neglect about religion, especially in the spiritual part of it, has caused our sins to increase to a vast height; and it is evident that we ripen very fast for some terrible judgment, which we must expect to feel soon, if God in infinite mercy prevents it not by sending a double portion of a reforming spirit among us.' That concern issued in prayer and renewed efforts in preaching and teaching. He felt the same burden in August: 'I am more and more convinced that the joint and resolute endeavours of several clergymen would have a good effect, by the blessing of God, towards reforming a wicked world. But I fear we shall yet grow worse, and come to smart for it, before we begin to grow better.' He continued:

Never was the world fuller of hindrances to the good work of stirring ourselves up to lay hold on God; and yet this work was never more necessary; since we have reason to fear that God is now about leaving our land and departing from us. It is now, if ever, we should stir ourselves up to lay hold on him, as the prophet says, and by earnest resolution, fixed thoughts, and flaming affections, solicit his return and stay with us. All that is within us must be summoned up and awakened to this employment, and all is little enough.

In May 1736 he was convinced that 'atheism, infidelity and other various fatal errors' were coming like a deluge upon the land, so that all Christians should 'prepare speedily for suffering times and fiery trials.'[38]. A mere two weeks later Jones received a visit from Howel Harris, seeking advice about evangelism and ordination. This visit to Llanddowror at the end of May 1736 was the first of over thirty occasions for consultation on the work of the gospel. With Daniel Rowland, too, coming to him for ministerial guidance at about the same time, Jones must have felt that his prayers for the reviving of God's work in the land were about to be answered.

The godly concern for the salvation of others which characterised Jones's spirituality was thus not without hope. On occasions, too, his spirit was sustained and refreshed by joy and delight in God. A very long letter, dated 14 September 1736, bears this out:

Although the Holy Spirit, the free dispenser of his own gifts, according to the good pleasure of his will, does sometimes in this life cast into the soul the comfortable gleams of his refreshing consolations immediately, when and how he pleaseth; yet ordinarily he causeth this sensible and gracious cheerfulness to revive the hearts of his people at certain times and under certain circumstances. For instance:- 1. When sinners, visited with the day of God's power, are thoroughly made a willing people to become espoused to Jesus Christ. There is commonly then a wedding feast of joy in the soul. The affections are raised, the passions are melted, the heart is filled with zeal and gladness, although it be perhaps with tears, like a sun that shines through a shower of rain . . . 2. It is a more promising evidence that all is right, when men are intent, serious, humble, and constant in divine worship. They are sometimes brought to a nearer and warmer closure with God, and feel more than a common degree of communion with him. They taste the sensible sweetness of the Lord's gracious presence, and the joy of his Divine Spirit within them . . . 3. Sometimes more than common cheerfulness of heart is felt upon doing some great or difficult service for the honour of God and the benefit of men . . . 4. The Most High does usually favour men with high degrees of inward joy and comfort, upon great instance of self-denial, when they forsake and willingly part with what is dear to them for his sake . . . 5. When any of Christ's disciples willingly bear the cross and endure any great sufferings for his sake . . . they are generally favoured then with more sensible joy and comfortable communion with God than is common at other times. Their hopes are revived, and the love of God is shed abroad in their hearts, so that they are made to rejoice in their tribulation, to sing in chains and prisons . . . 6. When we resolutely and with steady faithfulness resist and overcome the violent and repeated assaults of strong temptations, and keep ourselves pure from their contagion; then also usually follows a greater flow than common of inward consolation . . . 7. When we fix and settle ourselves in the bosom of divine love . . . Our dear Lord received every beloved disciple into his bosom, and why should not we embrace the beloved Saviour in our bosom? . . . A high degree of joy is vouchsafed, when we receive a believing view of Christ, after many doubtful combats with despair and fear. This is always accompanied with reviving joy and gladness . . . When we have much afflicted ourselves and deeply humbled ourselves before God for our sins, then he is wont graciously to turn towards us, and smile upon us . . . When under some pressing distress and uncommon exigency, we pour forth our souls with bitter cries to God in prayers, and procure an answer of peace. Exodus 14:13 . . . When serious, humble, and heavenly-minded Christians sweetly commune and converse

together about the great things of their salvation, the spiritual presence of
their dear Lord, according to his promise, is wont sometimes in a peculiar
manner to be with them . . . Great joy is given when we zealously lay out
ourselves in our best endeavours for the good of others; more especially for
the good and welfare of other men's souls.[40]

Few men so zealously laid themselves out for others as Jones did.
The dawn of the most significant and far-reaching revival of religion
in Wales was about to break when he wrote those words. After the
night of tears, burden and conflicts, there was to be a glorious morning of joy.

By the nature of his spirituality and the vigour of his labours he
demonstrates convincingly that the expectation of such momentous
events, which can only be initiated and sustained by God, do not
paralyse devotion or action. Such spirituality, firmly anchored in the
Scriptures, nourished by prayer, and finding practical expression in
compassionate, evangelistic activity, is the most profound antidote
to lethargy and discouragement in trying times. Listen to Griffith
Jones's own testimony: 'Have we not sometimes found the un-
deniable evidence of God's gracious presence with us, softening,
moulding and renewing the inward man into higher degrees of zeal
and love? And have we not found, not only by the melting frame of
spirit and inward testimony, which we have had, but also by the
answer of prayers and fulfilling of our desires, which followed afterwards, that God has often most graciously accepted our prayers and
praises?'[41] As it was for him, so shall it be for us too.

REFERENCES

1. In addition to the entry for Griffith Jones in *The Dictionary of Welsh Biography
    down to 1940*, London, 1959, the following short studies have also appeared:
    David Boorman, 'The Morning Star of the Methodist Revival', an article in *The
    Evangelical Magazine of Wales*, vol.21, No.4 (Aug–Sep,1982), pp.9–11; Gwyn
    Davies, *Griffith Jones, Llanddowror, Athro Cenedl*, Bridgend, 1984; Geraint H.
    Jenkins, *Hen Filwr dros Grist: Griffith Jones, Llanddowror*, 1983; and an article,
    'Yr Hen Filwr ymdrechgar', by R. Tudur Jones in *Cristion*, Tach-Rhag, 1983,
    pp.4-5. For Rowland and Harris, see Richard Bennett, *Howell Harris and the
    Dawn of Revival*, Bridgend, 1987; Eifion Evans, *Daniel Rowland and the Great
    Evangelical Awakening in Wales*, Edinburgh, 1985; *Howel Harris, Evangelist*,
    Cardiff, 1974; Geoffrey F. Nuttall, *Howel Harris 1714-1773, The Last
    Enthusiast*, Cardiff, 1965.

2. Edward Morgan, *Letters of the Rev Griffith Jones*, London, 1832, pp.20,21-2. Henceforth shortened to L, followed by the page number(s).

3. For Puritan spirituality see J. I. Packer, *Among God's Giants*, Eastbourne, 1991, especially Chapter 12, 'The Spirituality of John Owen'; and Richard C. Lovelace, 'Puritan Spirituality:The Search for a Rightly Reformed Church', in *Christian Spirituality, Post-Reformation and Modern*, ed. Louis Dupré and Don E. Saliers, New York, 1991, pp.294-323.

4. For Anglican spirituality see Gordon S. Wakefield, 'Anglican Spirituality' in Louis Dupré and Don E. Saliers, *op.cit.*, pp.257-93; for the contribution of the SPCK to Wales in this period, see M. G. Jones, *The Charity School Movement*, Cambridge, 1938; Mary Clement, ed. *Correspondence and Minutes of the SPCK Relating to Wales 1699-1740*, Cardiff, 1952; and Geraint H. Jenkins, *Literature, Religion and Society in Wales, 1660-1730*, Cardiff, 1978.

5. Quoted in Geoffrey F. Nuttall, 'Methodism and the Older Dissent: Some Perspectives', in the United Reformed Church Historical Society *Journal*, vol.ii (1981), pp.261, 263. Dr Nuttall is quoting from *Calendar of the Correspondence of Philip Doddridge*, ed. G. F. Nuttall, 1979, Letter 663; *Joseph Williams, Enlarged series of Extracts from the Diary, Meditations and Letters*, ed. Benjamin Hanbury, 1815, pp.34-5; and [Timothy Thomas], *The Hidden Life of a Christian exemplified in the diary, meditations, and letters of a young minister* . . . ed. Thomas Gibbons, [1752], pp.129-130, 122, 168-9.

6. L 56.

7. For Sir John Philipps, see *The Dictionary of Welsh Biography down to 1940*, London, 1959.

8. Mary Clement, ed. *Correspondence and Minutes of the SPCK Relating to Wales 1699-1740*, Cardiff, 1952, p.52 abst 3322; p.53 abst 3383; p.55 abst 3460. Henceforth shortened to C with page number and abstract number, if relevant.

9. C p.54 abst 3404; p.207 abst 2830.

10. C pp.330,331,332,333.

11. C p.62 abst 3803.

12.   C p.62, n.164.

13. *Hyfforddiad i Wybodaeth Iachusol o Egwyddorion a Dyledswyddau Crefydd* . . . Y Bedwaredd Ran, 1746, pp.30-31.

14. N. Cynhafal Jones, *Gweithiau Williams Pant-y-celyn*, cyf.1, p.439.

15. L 22.

16. Several volumes of these exist in manuscript, at The National Library of Wales, Aberystwyth, and at Cardiff. Two volumes of sermons were translated and published by the Rev. John Owen, and an incomplete list of texts and occasions appears in *Cylchgrawn Cymdeithas Hanes y Methodistiaid Calfinaidd*, cyf.ix 53-37, in an article on Jones and the Methodists. Henceforth shortened to CCH followed by volume and page number.

17. CCH xxix.3.

18. C pp.71-2 abst 4163.

19. National Library of Wales, Ottley Papers No 100.

20. C pp.336-7.

21. C p.163 abst 11,373; p.176 abst 14,006.

22. National Library of Wales, Calvinistic Methodist Archives MS 8326, p.568.

23. L 79

24. L 75,77-78.
25. C p.235 abst 15643; p.307, 5 May 1733; and see p.167, n.332 [A. C. H. Seymour], *The Life and Times of Selina Countess of Huntingdon*, vol.i, 1844, p.53,n.
26. L 216, 217.
27. CCH xxv.20.
28. C p.163, abst 11,373 and n.332: M. G. Jones, *The Charity School Movement*, pp.297-314. For a list of Jones's published works see M. H. Jones, 'Bibliography of the Works of Griffith Jones' in *Transactions of the Carmarthenshire Antiquarian Society*, vol.xvi.
29. John Gillies, *Memoirs of the Late Reverend George Whitefield* . . . , London, 1811, p.224; A more recent two-volume biography of Whitefield, by Arnold A. Dallimore, was published at London, 1970, and Edinburgh, 1980. In 1743, Jones's published *Crynodeb y Salmau Canu* [Selection of Metrical Psalms]. It was intended for family as well as for public worship, p.iv, and a second edition was called for in 1774.
30. L 58,59.
31 *Hyfforddiad i Wybodaeth Iachusol* . . . Y Bummed Ran, 1746, p.62.
32. L 220, 230, 240-41.
33. L 332, 285-358, 285, 286, 333, 99.
34. L 335, 341.
35. National Library of Wales, Calvinistic Methodist Archives MS 8326 vol.II, p.712,f.
36. L 100.
37. L 4-11: For Bridget Bevan, see *The Dictionary of Welsh Biography down to 1940*.
38. L 27, 317, 86-7, 135-6.
39. CCH xxix.10.
40. L 168-73.
41. L 158-9.

5
PREACHING AND REVIVAL

Preaching and revival are both biblical concepts. The activity of preaching and the phenomenon of revival are found in both Old and New Testaments, even though there is a preponderance of evidence for preaching over that for revival. In the Old Testament there are great prophetic pictures, comparisons and descriptions of revival. Coming to New Testament times, there are a number of occasions when revival is very much in evidence even though the word itself is not mentioned. From these sources, however, it is possible to trace the permanent principles of God's activity in revival, and the relation it bears to the instrumentality of preaching.

Preaching is consistently represented in Scripture as the activity of one sent by God for the purpose of setting forth to men a God-given message for a God-given purpose. Christ's prophetic office is depicted in these terms by Isaiah and confirmed by Christ Himself in the synagogue at Nazareth. These three elements, a sense of divine commission, the good news of God's free favour, and the divine purpose of salvation for sinners are always present in true preaching. Together, they form a divine ordinance of abiding validity and relevance. They also fuse into a balanced whole, and the absence or distortion of any one of those vital elements seriously hampers the realization of the biblical ideal.

While preaching is a human responsibility, revival is a divine activity. Both have in common the fulfilment of the divine purpose in man's salvation, but revival depends on God's initiative rather than man's. Revival, then, is God manifesting Himself in a sovereign, spontaneous, powerful and general manner, bringing about the quickening of spiritual life in His people and the conversion of the ungodly.

This activity originates with God and takes place in His sovereign, providential ordering when and where He pleases. It invariably exalts the person and work of Christ, especially the redemption which He accomplished, and sanctification is intensified. For these reasons, revival can be said to be an extraordinary season of activity on the part of the blessed Trinity.

In the Bible there are prayers for such reviving periods, as in Psalm 80 and the later chapters of Isaiah; prophetic pictures of them, as in Isaiah 35 and Joel 2; and narratives relating their progress as in 2 Chronicles 34 to 35 and Acts 2 to 12. The outcome is always one of rapturous joy and spiritual pleasure: Psalm 85:6, 'Wilt thou not revive us again, that thy people may rejoice in thee?'

Today's diminishing interest in preaching and revival is due to many factors. With regard to preaching, there is no longer a general acceptance of its abiding validity and relevance. The churches are turning to newer methods for the solution of their missionary problems. So much of present-day preaching lacks that authority which is derived from a conviction of the divine source of its apostolic nature, message and purpose. Few look upon it any longer as a divine institution and force. As a discipline it is thought of more in terms of human ingenuity and effort, bringing about the adoption of that very principle which Paul explicitly disowned in his own evangelistic strategy, 1 Corinthians 2:1-5.

The category of revival no longer appears on the horizon of ecclesiastical policy. Whereas the spiritual leaders of only a few generations ago would have thought, prayed, and worked in terms of revival, this is no longer the case. Today there is a proliferation of human substitutes by way of methods meant to attract. There is less consciousness of dependence on the divine initiative, and far less longing than ever for a supernatural intervention on the part of God the Holy Spirit to resolve the predicament of the Church.

The close relationship between preaching and revival is never questioned in Scripture. On the contrary, it is so axiomatic that it is asserted rather than expounded, 1 Thessalonians 1:5, 'For our gospel came not unto you in word only, but also in power, and in the Holy Ghost, and in much assurance.' Josiah's reform stemmed from the finding of the law in the temple, and the preaching of it which followed. In the book of Acts, apostolic labours are founded upon the presentation of the cross and resurrection, related to Old Testament prophecy and applied to the hearers in a close, personal, and saving manner. Historically, those revivals have been purest and most permanently beneficial which have given to preaching the same Scriptural priority and predominance. During the nineteenth century the blighting influence of rationalism and humanism took its toll of the Church's preaching, so that in the Welsh revival of 1904, for example, there was a serious neglect of that ordinance, and the fruit of that work of God was but partly consolidated.

In order to see the intimate relationship between preaching and revival it will be necessary to examine the characteristics, content, and effect of preaching in those seasons of refreshing from the time of the Reformation to the present day.

There are certain prerequisites in the preacher himself which God demands whether He gives revival or not. Richard Baxter, who had experienced revival under his own ministry at Kidderminster during the 1650s, in his *Reformed Pastor* puts some searching questions on this very issue: 'Can it be expected that God will bless that man's labours who worketh not for God, but for himself? Now, this is the case of every unsanctified man. None but the upright do make God their chief end, and do all or anything heartily for His honour: they make the ministry but a trade to live by . . . do you think it is a likely thing that he will fight against Satan with all his might that is a servant of Satan himself? . . . A traitorous commander, that shooteth nothing against the enemy but powder, may cause his guns to make as great a sound as some that are laden with bullets; but he doth no hurt to the enemy by it. So one of these men may speak loud and mouth it with an affected fervency, but he seldom doth any great execution against sin and Satan . . . Is that man likely to do much good, or fit to be a minister of Christ, that will speak for Him an hour, and by his life will preach against Him all the week beside? . . . If you stand at the door of the kingdom of grace, to light others in, and will not go in yourselves, when you are burnt to the snuff you will go out with a stink, and shall knock in vain at the gates of glory that would not enter at the door of grace.' Another of Baxter's cryptic sayings was this, 'It is a fearful case to be an unsanctified professor, but much more to be an unsanctified preacher.'

God dealt with such a man before He gave revival to his parish when the minister of Moulin, Perthshire, was converted in 1796, ten years after he had settled in it, during which time he had 'felt nothing of the power of religion' in his life. Here is his story: 'The writings of pious men, which were put into my hands by one or another Christian friend were made the means of bringing me acquainted with the truths of the gospel . . . From that time, I began to teach and to preach Jesus Christ with some degree of knowledge and confidence. From August 1797 to January 1798 I preached a course of sermons on the fundamental doctrines of Christianity. The novelty of the matter, and some change in the manner of the preaching, excited attention. People began to think more, and sometimes to talk together, of religious subjects, and of sermons they heard.'

This was only the beginning of the work, for the minister, together with two others newly converted like himself began to meet for prayer in a smoky cottage where an old, godly, infirm woman lived. The sacrament of the Lord's Supper the following summer was an occasion of blessing and many were brought under conviction. This had followed a course of sermons on the 'nature of the Ordinance, and the character of those who, under the denomination of disciples, were commanded to keep it.' 'More general awakening', attended the preaching of 'a course of practical sermons on regeneration' between March 1799 and July 1800. During that period, seldom 'a week passed in which we do not see or hear of one, two, or three persons, brought under deep concern about their souls, accompanied with strong convictions of sin, and earnest enquiry after a Saviour.'

A manifestation of God's presence and power to the minister's soul prove to be the source of his power in the pulpit. General revival and personal revival can never be divorced in the experience of the preacher. Revival preaching is impossible without revival experience.

Such an experience came to Howel Harris of Wales before he entered on his revivalist activities in 1735. 'June 18th, 1735. Being in secret prayer I felt suddenly my heart melting within me like wax before the fire, with love to God my Saviour. I felt not only love and peace, but also a longing to be dissolved and to be with Christ; and there was a cry in my inmost soul, with which I was totally unacquainted before, it was this—"Abba, Father; Abba, Father". I could not help calling God my Father: I knew that I was His child, and that He loved me; my soul being filled and satiated, crying, "It is enough—I am satisfied; give me strength, and I will follow Thee through fire and water". I could now say that I was happy indeed. There was in me "a well of water, springing up into everlasting life", yea, the love of God was shed abroad in my heart by the Holy Ghost.'

It was this very experience of God which motivated his future labours in England and Wales. Five years later he was with John Cennick at Swindon, ablaze with the same heavenly flame in their souls, a fire which no degree of persecution could quench. Cennick recorded the incident in this way:

'We found a large company assembled in the grove, with whom I sang and prayed, but was hindered from preaching by a great mob, who made a noise, and played in the midst of the people and then with guns fired over our heads, holding the muzzles of their pieces so near our faces that we were both black as tinkers with the powder.

'We were not frightened, but opened our breasts and told them we were ready to lay down our lives for our doctrine, and had nothing against it if their guns were levelled at our hearts. Then they got dust out of the highway and covered us all over, and then played an engine, which they filled out of the stinking ditches, till we were just like men in the pillory.

'But as they played on Brother Harris, I spoke to the congregation, and when they turned the engine on me, he preached, and thus they continued until they had spoiled the engine, and they threw whole buckets of water over us.'

For such men there could only be one overriding, dominating constraint: the love of Christ. George Whitefield—perhaps the greatest preacher of the eighteenth-century Awakening in England—makes this abundantly clear in a sermon on John 7:37-39, 'The Indwelling of the Spirit, the common privilege of all believers':

When Joseph was called out of the prison-house to Pharoah's court, we are told that he stayed some time to prepare himself; but do you come with all your prison-clothes about you; come poor, and miserable, and blind, and naked, as you are, and God the Father shall receive you with open arms, as was the returning prodigal. He shall cover your nakedness with the best robe of His dear son's righteousness, shall seal you with the signet of His Spirit, and feed you with the fatted calf, even with the comforts of the Holy Ghost. O! let me not go back to my Master and say, "Lord, they will not believe my report". Harden no longer your hearts, but open them wide, and let the King of glory enter in; believe me, I am willing to go to prison or death for you; but I am not willing to go to heaven without you. The love of Jesus Christ constrains me to lift up my voice like a trumpet; my heart is now full: out of the abundance of the love which I have for your precious and immortal souls, my mouth now speaks; and I could now not only continue my discourse until midnight, but I could speak until I could speak no more.

This earnestness and lively expression of love for the souls of men was a God-given grace. It characterized not only the preaching of Whitefield, but also that of many other useful men. Baxter's outstanding success at Kidderminster was due to a divinely-planted longing for the conversion of his people.

Long have I travailed in birth till Christ be formed in you. For this I have studied, and prayed, and preached . . . I believe God, and therefore I know that you must, every soul of you, be converted or condemned to everlasting punishment; and, knowing this, I have told it to you over and over again. I have shown you the proof and reasons of it, and the certain misery of an unconverted state; I have earnestly besought you and begged of you to return, and if I had tears at command I should have mixed all these exhortations with my tears . . . the God that sent me to you knows that my soul is grieved for your blindness, and stubbornness, and wickedness, and misery, more than for all the losses and crosses in the world; and that my heart's desire and prayer for you to God is, that you may yet be converted and saved.

A further characteristic of preaching in revivals is plainness of speech. Baxter's strategy was 'to preach, not only to a popular auditory, but to the most ignorant, sottish part of that auditory.' He had learnt from experience that preaching with the polish and finish of scintillating words and impeccable grammar may be pleasing to the ear but is not necessarily conducive to convince the soul of sin. Mere oratory without plainness and directness breathes death to any congregation, as Baxter had found: 'When I read such a book as Bishop Andrewes' Sermons, or heard such kind of preaching, I felt no life in it. I thought they did but play with holy things . . . But it was the plain and pressing downright preacher, that only seemed to me to be in good sadness, and to make somewhat of it, and to speak with life and light and weight.'

In another passage he pursues the same theme: The commonness and the greatness of men's necessity commanded me to do anything that I could for their relief, and to bring forth some water to cast upon this fire, though I had not at hand a silver vessel to carry it in, nor thought it the most fit. The plainest words are the most profitable oratory in the weightiest matters. Fineness is for ornament, and delicacy with delight, but they answer not necessity . . . We are not to stand upon compliment when we run to quench a common fire, nor to call men out to it by an eloquent speech. If we see a man fall into fire or water, we stand not upon mannerliness in plucking him out, but lay hands upon him as we can without delay.

Fervency and eloquence, so effective in the preaching of reviving times, are special qualities. They are not put on in the sense in which an advocate uses fervency to plead his case, or an actor practises eloquence to enchant his audience. In preaching they must issue from the preacher's sense and practice of God's presence.

A preacher thus rightly related to God feels with unavoidable compulsion the duty to direct his hearers solely to God's Word. There can be no attempt to substitute human, synthetic ideas for truths revealed in Holy Scripture. So we read of Calvin's sermons, 'Calvin's preaching is an echoing-board of the Scriptures. His mind is steeped in the Bible, and allusions are as plentiful and as elusive as gnats on a summer evening.' In all true revivals the preaching of God's servants has substantially followed Calvin's example. The truths of divine revelation are those which the Holy Spirit has consistently honoured in revival.

These preachers of the past were not induced to take the by-paths of obscure points of theology, or prophecy, where they could air their speculative theories; they kept rather to the basic doctrines of Scripture, cast in the framework of the Westminster Confession of Faith and its Catechisms. The sum of all their preaching was Christ; the fulness of it, the whole counsel of God. These doctrines were not preached without the closest application being made to the sinner's condition. Whitefield is always careful, as were the Puritans before him, to 'press home' with life and vigour, with fervency and urgency, with earnestness and entreaty, the invitation or warning, the commands or promises of Scripture. Here is the closing part of his sermon on 1 Corinthians 1:30, 'But of him are ye in Christ Jesus, who of God is made unto us wisdom, righteousness, santification and redemption', which he refers to as 'the believer's golden chain of privileges':

Whatever you may pretend, if you speak truth, you must confess, that conscience breaks in upon you in your more sober intervals whether you will or not, and even constrains you to believe that hell is no painted fire. And why then will you not come to Christ? He alone can procure your everlasting redemption. Haste, haste away to Him, poor beguiled sinners. You lack wisdom; ask it of Christ. Who knows but He may give it you? He is able: for He is the wisdom of the Father; He is that wisdom which was from everlasting. You have no righteousness; away therefore to Christ: He is the end of the law for righteousness to every one that believeth; you are unholy, flee to the Lord Jesus: He is full of grace and truth; and of His fulness all may receive, that believe in Him. You are afraid to die; let this drive you to Christ: He has the keys of death and hell; in Him is plenteous redemption; He alone can open the door which leads to everlasting life . . . why, why will you die? Why will you not come unto Him that you may have life?

The effect of such preaching during revival seasons was nothing less than extraordinary. The impact of the message, under the power of the Holy Spirit, transformed entire congregations; the face of society was changed, the standard of morality was raised, the spread of Christ's kingdom was urgently desired, and the name of Christ was held in the highest esteem.

Some of the effects were more powerful and startling than others, and often varied from one place to another. Under Daniel Rowland's ministry in Wales, these were very remarkable indeed, and continued, with greater or lesser intensity, for over fifty years! One contemporary description of the scenes witnessed under his preaching was given by Howel Harris in 1743 in a letter to Whitefield.

I was last Sunday at the Ordinance with brother Rowland, where I saw, felt, and heard such things as I can't send on paper any idea of. The power that continues with him is uncommon. Such crying out and heartbreaking groans, silent weeping and holy joy and shouts of rejoicing I never saw. Their 'Amens' and crying 'Glory in the highest' would enflame your soul. It is very common when he preaches for scores to fall down by the power of the Word, pierced and wounded or overcome by the love of God and the sights of the beauty and excellency of Jesus, and lie on the ground, nature being overcome by the sights and enjoyments given to their heaven-born souls that it can't bear, the spirit almost bursting the house of clay to go to its native home. Some lie there for hours, some praising and admiring Jesus, free grace, distinguishing grace; others wanting words to utter. You might read the language of a heart running over with love and solid rest in God. Others meeting when the word is over to sing and you might feel God among them there like a flame; others falling down one after another for a long time together, praying and interceding, and you might see and feel it is the prayer of faith, and that they are worshipping a God that they know, and love, and delight in, and that now there is no veil between. Others lie wounded under a sense of their piercing Jesus, so that they can hardly bear it; others mourning and wailing for the Comforter, and such love and simplicity that a spiritual eye must see and acknowledge that God is there. This is but a very faint idea of it, but what words can express spiritual things?

God has always honoured the preaching of His Word. Those who preached God's truth with simplicity in the power of the Holy Spirit have been widely used to the glory of Christ. There is talk sometimes of the 'problem of communication', implying that modern man cannot understand the 'old' truths of regeneration and justification. Whitefield's preaching at Bristol, nevertheless, got through to the Kingswood miners in spite of their ignorance and superstition. 'The first discovery of their being affected was to see the white gutters made by the tears which fell plentifully down their black cheeks, as they came out of their coal pits. Hundreds and hundreds of them were soon brought under deep convictions, which, as the event proved, happily ended in a sound and thorough conversion.'

Whitefield always preserved biblical imagery and preached biblical truth. It was the energy of the Holy Spirit which made those truths powerfully effective in the minds and hearts of men and women.

Today we need a fresh conviction of the abiding validity and relevance of preaching as a divine institution, and also a plentiful effusion of the Holy Spirit. We need nothing less than the holy 'boldness' which the disciples received at Pentecost. We need to pray again their prayer: 'Grant unto thy servants that with all boldness they may speak thy word, by stretching forth thine hand to heal, and that signs and wonders may be done by the name of thy holy child Jesus.'

6
PRIORITIES IN REVIVAL
George Whitefield and the Revival in Wales

George Whitefield, 'the Great Evangelist of the eighteenth century revival', lived from 1714 to 1770. Born in Gloucester and converted while at University in Oxford, a great part of his ministry was spent in America, where he died. He visited Wales on some twenty occasions between 1739 and 1768.

There are several very good reasons for a study of George Whitefield's Welsh connections. Chief among them is his affinity with Welsh Calvinistic Methodism. At a formative stage in its emergence in Wales from 1739 onwards Whitefield gave guidance and inspiration. He did so by his preaching and counsel, so that its distinctive elements of evangelistic zeal and experimental godliness remained a powerful influence in the land well into the next century.

During the four years between his conversion in 1735 and his first visit to Wales, Whitefield had applied himself to the pursuit of godliness, and his preaching had met with considerable success. Within him there was an insatiable thirst for closer communion with God, and he soon established habits of daily Scripture reading and prayer:

I began to read the Holy Scriptures upon my knees, laying aside all other books, and praying over, if possible, every line and word. This proved meat indeed, and drink indeed, to my soul. I daily received fresh life, light, and power from above. Sometimes as I was walking, my soul would make such sallies as though it would go out of the body. At other times, I would be so overpowered with a sense of God's Infinite Majesty, that I would be constrained to throw myself on the ground, and offer my soul as a blank in His hands, to write on it what He pleased.[1]

Others urged him to seek ordination, but this he strenuously resisted, until the Holy Spirit's constraints compelled him to yield:

I never prayed against any corruption I had in my life, so much as I did against going into holy orders, so soon as my friends were for having me to go . . . I prayed a thousand times, till the sweat has dropped from my face like rain, that God, of his infinite mercy, would not let me enter the church before he called me to, and thrust me forth in, his work . . . these words came into my mind, 'My sheep hear my voice, and none shall pluck them out of my hand'. O may the words be blessed to you . . . as they were to me when they came warm upon my heart; then, and not till then, I said, Lord, I will go, send me when Thou wilt.[2]

Diligence and fervency characterised his ministry. Here are his own sentiments:

Expounded twice or thrice every night this week. The Holy Ghost so power-fully worked upon my hearers, pricking their hearts, and melting them into such floods of tears, that a spiritual man said, 'he never saw the like before'. God is with me of a truth. Adored be His unmerited goodness; I find His grace quickening me more and more every day. My understanding is more enlightened, my affections more inflamed, and my heart full of love towards God and man. (6 Jan 1739) True faith in Jesus Christ will not suffer us to be idle. No, it is an active, lively, restless principle; it fills the heart, so that it cannot be easy, till it is doing something for Jesus Christ. (8 Feb 1739) I am now weary. I am not idle through grace; but when I go to bed I weep, and am ashamed I can do so little for God. (16 Sep 1742)[3]

This was the man whose reputation preceded him as he prepared to visit Wales for the first time in March 1739.

George Whitefield's first important contact with Wales was by way of the pious philanthropist, Sir John Philipps of Picton Castle, Pembrokeshire. Two favours in particular made Whitefield deeply conscious of his debt to this eminent Welshman. Firstly, for part of his time at Oxford, Whitefield received financial support from him; and secondly, by virtue of Sir John's interest in the Society for Promoting Christian Knowledge, Whitefield was chosen a corres-ponding member. The allowance of £30 a year was conditional on Whitefield's superintendence of the affairs of the Methodists at Oxford. Membership of the SPCK had the advantage of giving Whitefield 'an opportunity of procuring books at a cheap and easy rate for the poor people'. Whitefield had every reason to regard Sir John as 'a great and good man', 'a blessed instrument of supplying our wants, and of encouraging us in our weak endeavours to pro-mote the Gospel'.[4]

Griffith Jones of Llanddowror is the next link between George Whitefield and Wales. While a curate at Laugharne, Carmarthen-shire, he had been instrumental in an awakening of considerable local impact as early as 1714.[5] He had suffered censure from the ecclesiastical authorities on account of his itinerant preaching, undertaken with the permission, if not the approval, of the parish incumbent. By 1738 he had firmly pioneered a system of adult religious education in South Wales. The ties between Sir John and Griffith Jones were both spiritual and natural. Sir John shared Griffith Jones's evangelical convictions and fully supported his reforming activities, and Jones's wife was Sir John's sister.[6]

Whitefield had evidently heard of Griffith Jones before 1738. On returning through Ireland from his first visit to America, he was moved with compassion for the people. 'I can think of no likelier means to convert them from their erroneous principles, than to get the Bible translated into their own native language, to have it put in their houses, and charity schools erected for their children, as Mr Jones has done in Wales.' The two men met for the first time at Bath on 22 February 1739. Whitefield recorded in his Journal, 'I was much comforted by meeting with several who love our Lord Jesus Christ in sincerity. More especially, I was edified by the pious conversation of the Rev Mr Griffith Jones, whom I have desired to see of a long season. His words came with power, and the account he gave me of the many obstructions he had met with in his ministry convinced me that I was but a young soldier just entering the field.'[7] Two weeks later, Whitefield was in Wales, meeting, not as one might expect, Griffith Jones, but Howel Harris.

Harris had been converted at the age of twenty-one in 1735, the same year as Whitefield. Despite extraordinary zeal for the conversion of souls, and a sound, growing knowledge of the Christian faith, he had been twice refused ordination, in July 1736 and February 1739. He had heard of Whitefield in a letter from Bristol in February 1738, and in November of that year his reading of Whitefield's Journal moved him deeply to 'vast sympathy of soul with him' and 'to the most ardent desires'. Whitefield's first letter to him dated 20 December 1738 expressed delight at his labours and requested news of God's dealings with him. In his reply some three weeks later, Harris reported 'a sweet prospect' in his own native Breconshire, as well as 'a great revival in Cardiganshire through Mr D[aniel] Rowland . . . who has been much owned and blessed in Carmarthenshire also.' The 'field preaching' already undertaken by Harris confirmed in Whitefield the conviction that this was another instrument of doing good at a time 'when there was no end of the people flocking to hear the Word of God.' Whitefield already knew of two clergymen who had ventured to break with tradition in this way: Griffith Jones preaching in cemeteries when churches were full, and Richard Morgan at Kingswood, Bristol, to coal miners who never attended a church.[8]

Harris was undoubtedly Whitefield's closest ally in the early years of the Revival. Their meeting in Cardiff on Whitefield's first visit was as memorable as it was historic. At the sight of Harris, Whitefield was 'much refreshed', and his 'heart was knit closely to him'. Whitefield 'wanted to catch some of his fire, and gave him the right hand of fellowship'. Harris, for his part, was struck by White-field's greeting, 'Do you know that your sins are forgiven?' 'The question rather surprised me', Harris confessed, 'having never heard it asked before.' Of the private conversation after Whitefield's ser-mon on John 3:3 Harris reported, 'I had my soul filled with heaven'. Whitefield would have told Harris about the crowds attending his ministry in London and Bristol, about the conversion of the Wes-leys, and about his first visit to America.[9]

From Harris, Whitefield had a full account of the Revival's pro-gress in Wales. He heard of Griffith Jones's fifty charity schools, Harris's thirty fellowship meetings, and of Rowland's extraordinary preaching and success: 'People make nothing of coming twenty miles to hear a sermon'. There were other gospel ministers too, Edmund Jones a Nonconformist minister near Pontypool, the Angli-can Thomas Jones of Cwm-iou near Abergavenny, among them. All in all, Whitefield wrote in his Journal, 'a most comfortable prospect of the spreading of the Gospel in Wales'. There were other matters too, which they agreed on: 'such measures as seemed most con-ducive to promote the common interest of our Lord'; the best way of supplying an urgent need for Welsh Bibles; and the doctrine of election.[10] To Harris's surprise and delight, Whitefield supplied him 'with a horse and money for Bristol', and asked him 'to go to London'.

Such accounts of gospel success must have stirred within them a realisation that God was reviving His work in their hands, as well as through others. A copy of Jonathan Edwards's *Narrative of Sur-prising Conversions* had been in Harris's hands for over a year. He had already commented to Rowland, 'Sure the time here now is like New England', a significant observation.[11] What Whitefield and

Harris were witnessing could only be explained in terms of divine initiative and activity. The spiritual vigour, authority and power which attended their labours, could not have been produced by human agency. The Holy Spirit alone could reproduce apostolic preaching and pentecost-like conditions.

Three areas of mutual concern emerge from Whitefield's first meeting with Harris. They reflect emerging priorities in the work to which they were both committed, and which appeared to them in such 'comfortable prospect'. Their first concern was to exploit the opportunities for preaching the gospel which were presented to them, in the providence of God. Ever since their conversion they had both felt burdened for the spiritual welfare of others. Both divine revelation and personal experience constrained them to regard sinners as in great danger and to make Jesus Christ known to them as the only way to God and salvation. Harris could have been speaking for Whitefield as well when he wrote:

An universal deluge of swearing, lying, reviling, drunkenness, fighting, and gaming had over-spread the country, like a mighty torrent . . . Seeing thus, rich and poor going as it were hand in hand in the broad way to ruin, my soul was stirred up within me . . . ministers were . . . not in earnest, and did not appear to have any sense of their own danger, nor any sense of the love of Christ . . . This view of their darkness, deadness, and indifference, made me out of the abundance of my heart, speak to some of those with whom I was acquainted . . . I could not help making it my business to speak to all I came near, of their danger . . . death and judgment were my principal subjects of conversation . . . I began to set up family worship in my mother's house; and on Sunday morning some of the neighbours would come to hear me reading the Lessons and Psalms, etc.[12]

Preaching therefore had priority and prominence in their labours from the outset, and its importance grew as the leaders saw it as the means of sanctification as well as conversion. During their time together the decision was made to translate Whitefield's sermon on 'The New Birth' for publication in Welsh, and it duly appeared before the end of the year.[13] Furthermore, Whitefield's future visits would be preaching tours, as well as times of fellowship and counsel. The progress of the Revival was unthinkable without preaching.

A second area of priority had to do with the beliefs they shared in common. The preaching of Whitefield, Rowland and Harris was nothing if not doctrinal. Joint evangelism and fellowship would only prosper if there was agreement in the truth which governed their lives and burned in their hearts. It was Whitefield's sermon on 'Regeneration or New Birth' 'which under God began the awakening at London, Bristol, Gloucester, and Gloucestershire'. He had found that 'the Word, through the mighty power of God, was sharper than a two-edged sword. The doctrine of the New Birth and Justification by Faith in Jesus Christ . . . made its way like lightning into the hearers' consciences.'[14] At Cardiff, Whitefield had preached on John 3:3, 'Except a man be born again, he cannot see the kingdom of God', and here, too, he had questioned Harris about his assurance of forgiveness. On their journey together to Bristol, Harris 'found we agreed about election, which united us the more', while at Bristol in the next few days, he heard Whitefield preaching several times on 'free grace'.[15]

Whitefield, Rowland and Harris were Anglicans, and their adherence to the Thirty-Nine Articles was wholehearted. Their understanding of those Articles grew as time went on, but even in 1739 it provided a common bond, believing them in a distinctly Calvinist sense. 'Our principles agree', Whitefield was to say in a letter to Harris in November, 'as face answers to face in water'.[16] Their ordered, experimental emphasis in the area of Christian experience constituted their Methodism. It was their conviction about the sovereignty and freeness of God's grace which described that Methodism as Calvinistic. It established, through Whitefield in England, through Rowland and Harris in Wales, a distinct spiritual culture and ethos, which they would have claimed reflected that of the New Testament.

'We took an account of the several Societies', says Whitefield of the first evening he spent with Harris. Here was a third priority. With great numbers coming to faith in Christ, devising appropriate means by which to monitor their integrity, safeguard their experience, and promote their growth and knowledge was a matter of the greatest urgency. Whitefield had realised this at an early stage, and three editions of a sermon on 'The Nature and Necessity of Society in general, and Religious Society in Particular', had appeared before the end of 1737.[17] Both Rowland and Harris had set up 'fellowship meetings' for the same purpose, and were providing guidelines for their usefulness.[18] In his *Letter . . . to the Religious Societies* which appeared in 1740, Whitefield urged the young converts: 'Form yourselves into little companies of four or five each, and meet once a week to tell each other what is in your hearts; that you may then also pray for, and comfort each other, as need shall require . . . I know not a better means in the world to keep hypocrisy out from amongst you. Pharisees and unbelievers will pray, read, and sing Psalms; but none, save an Israelite indeed, will endure to have his heart searched out.' They were to return to the subject often: Whitefield's *Letter . . . to the Religious Societies* was translated into Welsh; Rowland and Harris published in Welsh their own 'Basis, Purposes, and Rules of the Societies or Private Meetings which have lately started coming together in Wales' in 1742; and William Williams's fuller treatment in Welsh, 'The Experience Meeting', in 1777 (published in English under that title in 1973). They were clearly convinced that these fellowship meetings were vital and had 'unspeakable advantages' for the spiritual progress of believers.

Hardly a month passed before Whitefield visited Wales a second time. On this occasion, his ministry took him to Gwent, the southeastern corner of Wales. There was pleasure in meeting new friends, and pain at opposition to the gospel. One friend was Thomas Jones who had been since 1719 the curate of Cwm-iou near Abergavenny.[19] Accompanied by 'about forty on horseback', Whitefield travelled to his parish on April 5th, 'the church not being quite large enough to hold the congregation, I preached from the cross in the churchyard.' It was a joyous occasion when 'the Word came with power', and Whitefield confessed, 'Did not God call me elsewhere, I could spend some months in Wales very profitably. The longer I am in it, the more I like it.' Whitefield's companion, William Seward, afterwards arranged for 150 copies of Whitefield's sermons and one of his *Journal* to be sent to Jones. For his part, Jones wrote later to Whitefield: 'I rarely meet with a brother of the same Communion who so exactly corresponds with me in principles . . . Yours is the good old Puritan doctrine that, to my great concern, I thought had quite forsaken the land till about 14 months ago I met with some of your sermons.' When Harris had to appear before the magistrates at Monmouth for preaching at Pontypool in June, it was Jones who provided him with a testimonial that helped secure his acquittal. It was to Cwm-iou that Harris and many others went for spiritual nourishment and guidance during the early years of the Revival.

Opposition demanded both grace and wisdom, lest the Revival

should be discredited in its most vulnerable phase and by its leading figures. As Whitefield and Harris travelled through Gwent they found that 'a public motion' had been made at the previous Monmouth Assizes to stop them 'from going about teaching the people'. Consequently, at Usk permission to speak in the church was refused, and Whitefield 'preached upon a table under a large tree to some hundreds'. At Abergavenny the next day, he 'expected much opposition', but in the event 'not any dared to utter a word.' The following day, to crowds now numbering thousands, he preached at Caerleon where Harris had been bitterly opposed in the past, 'but God suffered them not to move a tongue now'. In the evening at Trelech, Whitefield was denied the use of the church, and so 'stood upon the horse-block before the inn, and preached from thence for about three-quarters of an hour.'[20]

In print, too, there was mounting opposition to the emerging Methodist movement.[21] What may be regarded as 'the most authoritative and serious' appeared in the summer of 1739 from the pen of Edmund Gibson, Bishop of London. It bore the title *A Pastoral Letter by Way of Caution against Lukewarmness on the One Hand and Enthusiasm on the Other,* and Whitefield realised that a quick 'Answer' was necessary. Both 'Letter' and 'Answer' were translated into Welsh and published the following year. The bishop's main charges were levelled against Methodism as a whole as much as against Whitefield in particular. Under the disapprovingly emotive word 'enthusiasm', the bishop censured them for claiming immediate inspiration, for introducing new doctrine (regeneration), and for 'casting unworthy reflections' upon the clergy. Whitefield's point-by-point answer was respectful, claiming that the bishop had misrepresented vital, personal experience of the truth as 'inspiration', and had failed to recognise that regeneration was both scriptural and Anglican teaching. He hoped the bishop would not defend the neglect and pleasure-seeking which characterised so many clergymen of the day. For Whitefield, it was always important to reflect Christ-like attitudes, and to conform as closely as possible to biblical standards of belief and behaviour.

Whitefield's second visit to America lasted from October 1739 to January 1741. Such was his concern for the Welsh brethren that he had written them letters of advice and affection. He spoke of Rowlands as 'a Boanerges in the Church of God', and reminded him that 'experience of God's work upon our own souls is the best qualification to preach it effectually to others'. He added, 'I would expect to suffer in the flesh for what had been done already; but what have we to do with the consequences of performing our duty? Leave them to God.' He urged Harris to 'speak every time as if it was your last', and added, 'O Wales, thou art dear to my soul!'[22]

The closing two months of 1741 saw Whitefield back in Wales. On November 14th he married a widow from Abergavenny, Elizabeth James, who had been 'for three years last past, a despised follower of the Lamb of God'. He described her as being 'of about thirty-six years of age . . . neither rich in fortune, nor beautiful as to her person'. He claimed that marriage had not hindered his preaching, and had done 'much good' to his soul. Harris saw in her a 'true inward concern for the glory of God', and affirmed, 'what a true, inward, broken spirit, truly humble, she has.' John Wesley regarded her as 'a woman of candour and humanity'. She bore Whitefield a son, who died in infancy, and suffered four miscarriages. At her funeral in August 1768, Whitefield reminded his London congregation of a particular incident in his early ministry among them to illustrate the support she had given him:

Do you remember my preaching in those fields by the old stump of a tree? The multitude was great, and many were disposed to be riotous. At first, I addressed them firmly, but when a desperate gang drew near with the most ferocious and horrid imprecations and menaces, my courage began to fail. My wife was then standing behind me as I stood on the table. I think I hear her now. She pulled my gown, and, looking up, said, 'George, play the man for your God'. My confidence returned. I spoke to the multitude with boldness and affection. They became still, and many were deeply affected.[23]

Labourers in the spiritual harvest were not exempt from adversity and grief. No small part of the provision the leaders made for people in such circumstances lay in directing them to the strengthening consolations of God's Word and Spirit.

There were problems within Methodism as well as opposition from without. When Whitefield left for America in August 1739 he had entrusted the work to John Wesley. In his preaching Wesley increasingly emphasised his convictions on grace and on the sinlessness of believers. For him, salvation was a matter of co-operation between God and the sinner, the former offering grace, and the latter receiving it as a matter of unfettered choice. This was in direct conflict with Whitefield's view on God's sovereign initiative in bestowing salvation and man's inherent disinclination to receiving it. Furthermore, Whitefield could not subscribe to the perfectionism suggested by Wesley as attainable in the believer's lifetime. Both John and Charles had been invited to Wales by Harris, and they had advocated their distinctive tenets there as well, much to the Welsh leaders' disapproval. Two of Whitefield's letters about this controversy will serve to clarify his position. The first was written from Boston, America, in September 1740:

Sinless perfection, I think, is unattainable in this life. Show me a man that could ever justly say, 'I am perfect' . . . Indwelling sin remains till death, even in the regenerate, as the article of the church expresses it. There is no man that liveth and sinneth not in thought, word, and deed. However, to affirm such a thing as perfection, and to deny final perseverance, what an absurdity is this? To be incapable of sinning, and capable of being finally damned, is a contradiction in terms . . . this is sorry divinity.[24]

The second letter was written to John Wesley in October 1741, after Harris had spoken to the two brothers. 'Though I hold particular election, yet I offer Jesus freely to every individual soul. You may carry sanctification to what degrees you will, only I cannot agree that the in-being of sin is to be destroyed in this life.'[25] Welsh Methodism was carefully nurtured by Rowland and Harris, and graciously confirmed by Whitefield, along these lines.

Another issue which might have altered the character, if not disintegrated, the Revival, was the dilemma which faced the converts with regard to their ecclesiastical affiliation. The leaders were Anglican to a man, but Anglican churches and clergy were largely hostile. Sympathetic clergymen were few and far between, and under the blessing of God the need for labourers in the spiritual harvest was great. The Welsh leaders had arranged to meet in formal 'Association' on 8th January 1742, and Whitefield wrote in good time a letter of far-reaching consequences for the occasion.

The affairs you meet about are affairs of the utmost importance. You had need to watch close, and be instant in prayer. For you need much of the wisdom which cometh from above . . . One great matter then is rightly to know to what particular part Jesus Christ has called each of you. For I take it for granted, none of you will presume to run before you are called or have evidence of your conversion. Different persons have different gifts and graces. Some are called to awaken, others to establish and build up. Some have popular gifts for large auditories, others move best in a contracted sphere, and may be exceeding useful in the private societies . . . Some of you are ministers of the Church of England. But if you are faithful, I cannot think you will continue in it long. However, do not go out till you are cast out, and when cast out for Jesus Christ's sake, be not afraid to preach in the fields. And while you remain in, oh! let not the other children of God starve for the want of the Sacrament, though they may belong to another parish . . . As for those who are not ordained, I cannot say much, only pray that each may take his proper place . . . I wish also you could meet monthly, if not all together, yet in little bodies, as you lie nearest to each other . . . All this may be done without formal separation from the Established Church, which I cannot think God calls for as yet.[26]

As a result, the affairs of the Welsh Methodists were 'settled according to Mr Whitefield's letter'. They would do their utmost to avoid separation or any appearance of being a sect, and they rejoiced that the problems they faced were such as always attend life and growth. Rowland, who presided over the meeting, could have spoken of the ninety or so who attended a society in his parish of Llangeitho, who 'never come together without meeting God, and most of them return home ravished by His love.' Harris wrote exuberantly to Whitefield afterwards, 'Everyone agreed with your thoughts, we had much union, sweetness, concord and brotherly love together.'[27]

It was not always sweetness, though. Harris felt that there were occasions when both Whitefield and Rowland were guilty of levity and legalism. Whitefield rebuked Harris on at least one occasion for his selfish ambition and domineering attitude, writing in November 1741:

The Lord keep you and me, my dear brother from a hot, rash, positive, overbearing temper. This I think is the predominant failing in my dear brother Harris. I think you do not deal gently enough . . . it is a meet thing to give reproof in a proper manner . . . with the utmost gentleness and love. Ministers must not be wolves to worry the sheep, but shepherds to lead them and feed them. Tender souls are not to be used like obstinate, unawakened sinners . . . Let us therefore, my dear brother, pray for more of the mind of Christ. And the more we drink into His Spirit, the more tenderly and lovingly shall we deal with those under our care.[28]

The humility and love required to offer and suffer reproof were in themselves graces for which the Methodists looked and desired.

This is not to portray their fellowship meetings as opportunities for mutual criticism, but rather as disciplined occasions for self-examination, self-denial, and spiritual progress.

Another year was to elapse before Whitefield's next visit. Meanwhile, Harris had been to London, persuading Whitefield to resume relationships with John Wesley. He also had an opportunity of observing Whitefield's supervision of the work in the metropolis. 'I was stunned . . . to see his amazing wisdom . . . to manage the church, doing all calmly, humbly, wisely . . . following the Lord, waiting [to see] how He points the way before him.'[29] That wisdom would be needed to deal with an urgent matter, raised by Rowland in a letter to Harris in London. It concerned excommunication from the Anglican Church of Rowland's followers in Montgomeryshire, an area under the jurisdiction of the Bishop of Bangor. Whitefield was consulted, and urged the bishop to consider the consequences of such a policy: 'These persons thus indicted . . . are loyal to his Majesty, and true friends to, and attendant upon, the Church of England service . . . if those acts ... were put in execution against them . . . they must be obliged to declare themselves Dissenters. I assure your Lordship, it is a critical time in Wales. Hundreds, if not thousands, will go in a body from the Church, if such proceedings are countenanced.'[30] Already English and Welsh Calvinistic Methodism were making a common cause of propagating the gospel, a fact that was soon to be given formal expression: Whitefield was appointed 'Moderator' of the Welsh Association.

This Association took place on January 5th, 1743 at Watford, near Caerphilly, the home of a leading Methodist. It was the occasion of Rowlands's first meeting Whitefield, and it is depicted in an imaginary painting of 1912 as 'The First Association'. Three main decisions were taken:

That the brethren who had scruples about receiving the Sacrament in the church on account of the ungodliness of the ministers, and receiving with the Dissenters on account of their lukewarmness, should continue to receive in the Church, till the Lord should open a plain door for leaving her communion; that no exhorters should be reckoned one of us but what was tried and approved, and that no one should go beyond his prescribed limits without previous advice and consultation; that each private exhorter should bring an account of his respective societies and of those who would be admitted into fellowship to the next Association.

In effect, this Association regulated the Revival's organization in Wales, and settled its affiliation to the Church of England for some time to come. As Harris reported to Griffith Jones afterwards, 'All are brought under discipline . . . All should continue in the Established Church as before'. Whitefield remained Moderator of the Welsh Association until August 1748, a figure-head that provided stability, unity, and leadership. His preaching at this time, too, was 'with great power'.[31]

The character of Whitefield's future visits to Wales reflected the conditions prevailing at the time. Pre-eminently, Whitefield's preaching profoundly influenced the Welsh Methodists, by its power, instruction, and example. The crowds that flocked to hear him were astonishing, his success, in terms of lives changed by the grace of God, significant. There was a deepening of Revival experiences as well. Rowland was able to report to Whitefield in February 1743, that there was 'a general stirring afresh everywhere . . . such power I never felt in preaching and administering the Sacrament . . . The convictions now are more deep and solid than formerly.' His regular Sunday congregations were to be numbered in hundreds. At Carmarthen in April 1743 one of those converted under Whitefield's ministry was Peter Williams, whose commentary on the Bible in later years was to become a household possession.[32] Harris's 'observations' after the Watford Association of January 1744, over which Whitefield again presided, summarised the character and progress of their formal meetings:

Everything was settled so that hitherto the Lord visibly blesses, leads, and unites us. He shows each his place, and gives us fellowship together, and gives His presence in our meetings. He also comes as a prophet among us, and countenances our order. We are enabled to wait for Him to point out our way for us, and so to follow Him . . . We write nothing here down of our doctrine, because in a wonderful manner we are led in the same light, speaking the same things, agreeing in general with the Reformers and Puritans . . . It is about three years since we began to assemble, some of us seeing it necessary to prevent confusion and lest wicked persons should go out in our names and do mischief. But we were not come to a fixed, determined plan till this time twelve month, when we unanimously called Mr Whitefield among us. Since that time we have been coming to order, those of public and private gifts, and now all in general are solid, the believers everywhere assenting.[33]

A decision 'that there is to be preaching at every Quarterly Association', was taken the following April. Both Whitefield and Rowlands preached on this occasion, and preaching became part of Association arrangements on subsequent occasions.

In August 1744, Whitefield and his wife left for America. On his return four years later, Whitefield felt compelled 'to go about preaching the Gospel to every creature', a statement that had far-reaching implications. It meant that he could no longer serve as Moderator of Welsh Calvinistic Methodism, nor could he concentrate his energies on providing leadership to that Methodism in England. As far as he was concerned, however, where his gift lay, there his labour should be, and that was clearly in preaching.

It was chiefly in this capacity that Whitefield visited Wales after 1748. He managed two days' rest at his wife's house in Abergavenny in May 1749, a welcome respite. 'It has been sweet, yes, very sweet, so sweet that I should be glad never to be heard of again', he confessed in a letter to the Countess of Huntingdon. 'But this must not be', he adds, 'a necessity is laid upon me, and woe is me if I do not preach the Gospel of Christ'. From Abergavenny he travelled to West Wales, covering several hundred miles, with congregations growing 'larger and larger', and opposition diminishing, so that he could say, 'not a dog stirs a tongue'. For the converts there was an emerging identity: 'Such an honour God put upon the Methodists, that whoever renounces the world and takes up Christ's cross, and believes and lives the doctrines of grace, must be styled "a Methodist" whether he will or not. Formerly it was "You are a Puritan", now it is "You are a Methodist".'[34] The year 1750 saw the tragic withdrawal of Harris from the work in Wales. The reasons were theological as well as temperamental. However great the loss, other leaders, gifted and experienced, were by this time available to help Rowland shoulder the burden, William Williams of Pantycelyn, and Howel Davies of Pembrokeshire among them. Whitefield fully supported Rowland, and 'these apostolic labourers' preached together at Bristol 'to vast multitudes'. The Countess of Huntingdon reported that they were 'greatly owned and honoured of the Lord in the conversion of notorious profligates and self-righteous formalists.'[35]

Whitefield administered the Lord's Supper in the spring of 1751 at Woodstock Chapel in Pembrokeshire, newly opened for the Methodists by Howel Davies, whom Whitefield esteemed as 'that good soldier of Jesus Christ'. A year later, Whitefield was 'carried through' Pembrokeshire 'in peace and comfort', with 'almost incredible' numbers attending his preaching.[36] In 1753, he returned to the same area, and 'a gracious melting seemed to be among the people', while at Wrexham in North Wales later in the year, he 'met with a little rough treatment'. 'What have pilgrims to expect better', he asked, 'in their journeying through the wide and howling wilderness of this noisy and troublesome world?' His preaching tour through South Wales in 1758 'was one of the most prosperous' he ever took, in terms of power and fruit, with 'near fifteen thousand' people attending at Haverfordwest. 'The Lord Jesus seemed to ride in triumph . . . Tears flowed like water from the stony rock. The cup of God's people quite runs over.' However, both journey and preaching took their toll: 'the Welsh roads have almost demolished my open one-horse chaise, as well as me . . . how low I have been in body, scarce even lower.'[37]

An unusual preaching opportunity offered itself to Whitefield at Abergavenny in June 1760 when he was asked to preach to some twenty-eight Army officers at their dinner. In passing he commended Harris and the twenty-four other Trefeca men, who together had volunteered for military service, for their 'zeal and good behaviour'. His main purpose, as ever, was 'inviting souls to come to Christ'.[38]

Whitefield's last preaching opportunity in Wales, however, had an added purpose: to open Trefeca College for the training of ministers for the Countess of Huntingdon's churches. It was an impressive occasion on account of both the people present and the preaching sessions they enjoyed. The Countess of Huntingdon, together with four Ladies arrived at Trefeca on July 29, 1768, and stayed for over two months. The College was opened on her birthday, 24 August, and Whitefield later spoke of being 'favoured with glorious Gospel-gales' for the opening of that 'place of pious education in Wales.' His text was Exodus 20:24, 'In all places where I record my name, I will come unto thee, and I will bless thee'. Whitefield's record continues: 'August 25. Gave an exhortation to the students in the College chapel, from Luke 1:15, 'He shall be great in the sight of the Lord'; Sunday, August 28. Preached in the court before the college, (the congregation consisting of some thousands) from 1 Cor 3:11, 'Other foundation can no man lay, than that which is laid, which is Jesus Christ'.' The project had been conceived jointly by Harris and the

Countess, Harris having nurtured in his heart from as early as 1740 the prospect of 'a School of the Prophets'.[39] Although the college provided preachers mainly for England, its existence on Welsh soil was an indication of the bond that existed between English and Welsh Calvinistic Methodism. It was also a testimony to the commitment of the leaders to the consolidation and expansion of the gospel harvest which God had granted through their labours.

In summary, then, it is clear that the leaders of the revival recognised certain priorities in the work as it unfolded. No work of God is without its attendant difficulties, and this is true of revival as well. Identifying priorities and resolving difficulties call for great wisdom, especially in the midst of ever-changing scenes and profound experiences. Some things, however, remain the same, and these abiding, foundational principles for every work of God are found in the Scriptures. While the leaders may not always have been successful in discerning, or consistent in applying, those principles, they were at least aware of the need to do so. As the Revival unfolded, therefore, they sought to match each need with God's provision.

Preaching had unquestioned and sustained prominence among the Methodists. Nothing was allowed to unnerve them in their conviction of its relevance, importance, and absolute necessity. However elevated the experiences of those around them, however intimidating the opposition of their enemies, preaching remained constantly to the fore. This was the means by which sinners were brought to saving faith: 'faith comes by hearing, and hearing by the word of God'; 'it pleased God through the foolishness of the message preached to save those who believe' (Romans 10:17; 1 Cor 1:21). Nothing was allowed to deflect them from this single-minded purpose, since preaching was God's ordinance. No gospel work would prosper without it, neither the evangelism of the lost, nor the disciplining and teaching of the saints. In all their public meetings the Methodists insisted on the preaching of God's Word.

From the beginning of his ministry, Whitefield spent much time in prayer, whether on his knees or 'in the fields'. Regarding such 'retirement', he thought much of Matthew Henry's saying, 'The mower loses no time whilst he is whetting his scythe'. For the fruit of their labours the Methodists depended utterly upon the power and activity of the Holy Spirit. It was the Spirit's prerogative to impart life, authority, and liberty in preaching the message. He alone could

awaken those that were 'dead in trespasses and sins', remove blind
prejudice, undermine a false self-righteousness, portray Christ vivid-
ly before the soul, and settle a soul's salvation. A transforming sense
of God's presence, majesty, and holiness, and of the reality of spiritual things and of eternity, could only come from the Holy Spirit.
Planting grace and faith in the soul, working repentance and new
obedience, self-denial, humility, heavenly-mindedness, and a thirst
for God, all stemmed from the same source. This is why private
devotions, fellowship and association meetings, and solemn public
fasts all turned around prayer.[40]

Fellowship meetings were, perhaps, the most distinctive Methodist outcome of the Revival. Scriptural warrant for them was drawn
from Malachi 3:16, 'then those who feared the Lord spoke to one
another . . . ', and from Hebrews 10:25, 'not forsaking the assembling of ourselves together'. They were a vital part of the Revival,
safeguarding its fruit, and promoting its character. It was important
that genuine Christian experience should be clearly understood. True
profession of faith had to be distinguished from false, since the
enemy invariably sowed tares wherever there was wheat (Matthew
13:28). The magicians of Egypt could imitate by their enchantments
what Moses and Aaron did at the command of God (Exodus 7:10-
11). By means of the questions that were put to the converts, their
experiences, motives, attitudes and progress were all tested. Appropriate reproof or consolation was offered, exhortation and encouragement administered. Healthy growing in grace, and progress in disci-
pleship were vigorously promoted. Familiar scriptural images of the
Christian life were kept before believers. Whitefield was fond of
speaking of himself as a 'pilgrim', of others as 'soldiers', and exhorting all to keep 'looking unto Jesus and running in our Christian
race'. Christian experience and Revival manifestations, then, were
always subject to scrutiny and review in the light of scripture teaching. What was spurious and harmful was to be shunned. But those
seasons of refreshing from the presence of the Lord, whether to the
soul in personal revival and restoration, or descending on a whole
community as water on a parched land, were to be both sought and
enjoyed.

'Methodism' was synonymous with order, and consequently the
regulation of personal life and public ministry soon characterised the
movement in Wales. At the fellowship meetings, or 'societies', as

well as at the monthly and quarterly 'Associations', a disciplined, structured view of the Christian life prevailed. In this way those who owned allegiance to these respective bodies signified their submission to each other, and bore one another's burdens, too, in the spirit of Romans 12 and Galatians 6:2. But this conformity to an agreed standard was not a new legalism, which led people into bondage and quenched the Spirit. Its intention was quite different. It fostered mutual concern and joint endeavour, and reflected the very nature of the truth which governed it. Truth is exclusive and demanding, as well as productive and liberating. Thus the Methodists earnestly contended 'for the faith which was once for all delivered to the saints' (Jude 3), by conforming their preaching, writing, and daily living to it. Their aim was to reproduce consistent New Testament Christianity in the people of their own day.

The powerful movements of revival which God sent in eighteenth century Wales stirred the whole nation. What appeared unthinkable and impossible in 1735 had in fifty years been marvellously realised. The lives of vast numbers of spiritually indifferent people were transformed, new churches emerged, and society was challenged by biblical standards and values. But God had also raised godly, responsible leaders. Their determined efforts to safeguard and consolidate those heavenly visitations ensured for posterity a powerful, solid, and lasting legacy.

REFERENCES

1. *George Whitefield's Journals*, 1960, pp.60-63. Henceforth GWJ with page number(s).
2. *Select Sermons of George Whitefield*, 1959, p.117.
3. GWJ 197; *A Select Collection of Letters of . . . George Whitefield*, vol.i, 1772, p.47. Henceforth GWL with volume and page number, *Cylchgrawn Hanes (Journal of the Historical Society of the Presbyterian Church of Wales)*, 1980, p.26. Henceforth CH.
4. GWJ 67; GWL i.13; Mary Clement (ed), *Correspondence and Minutes of the SPCK Relating to Wales 1699-1740*, 1952, p.175, abstract 13,813, and n.349; Luke Tyerman, *The Life of the Rev George Whitefield*, vol.i, 1890, pp.56,57. Henceforth Tyerman with volume and page number. For Sir John, see *Dictionary of Welsh Biography Down to 1940*, 1959.
5. See chapter 4, 'Spirituality Before the Great Awakening'.
6. Ibid.
7. GWJ 181,220; For an account of Charity Schools and SPCK activities in Ireland, see M. G. Jones, *The Charity School Movement*, Cambridge, 1938, Chapter VII.
8. GWJ 88; Howel Harris's Diary in the National Library of Wales, Calvinistic

Methodist Archives; Arnold Dallimore, *George Whitefield*, vol.i, 1970, pp.233-5, 249,256. Henceforth Dallimore with volume and page number. The second volume appeared in 1980.

9. GWJ 228; Tyerman i.188; Dallimore i.264; CH xxiv.7; xxxi.36; xlv.17,52; Eifion Evans, *Daniel Rowland and the Great Evangelical Awakening in Wales*, 1985, pp.83-5. Henceforth DR.

10. DR 84,n.

11. See DR chapter 8 'A Great Revival'.

12. *A Brief Account of the Life of Howell Harris, Esq.*, Trevecka, 1791, pp.19-20.

13. London Moravian Church Archives Box a/3, Letter of William Seward to James Hutton, March 14, 1739, Postscript by George Whitefield.

14. GWJ 86,81.

15. CH xxiv.7-14. This is a full transcript of Harris's Diary for March 9-14, 1739.

16. GWL i.87.

17. Tyerman i.95.

18. See the chapter on 'Adding to the Church—in the teaching of the Welsh Calvinistic Methodists'.

19. For Thomas Jones, see Eifion Evans, 'Thomas Jones, Cwmiou (1689-1772)' in CH 1984, pp.24-30.

20. GWJ 244-7.

21. See the chapter 'Early Methodist Apologetic'.

22. GWL i.60,149,87,220.

23. Tyerman i.531; *Proceedings* of the Wesley Historical Society, vol.x (1916); Tom Beynon, *Howell Harris, Reformer and Soldier*, 1958, p.32; Tyerman ii.554-5; see also CH xxviii.10-22 for an article on 'Mrs James, Abergavenny'.

24. GWL i.209.

25. GWL i.331.

26. GWL i.347; D E Jenkins, *Calvinistic Methodist Holy Orders,* 1911, pp.52-4; *The Evangelical Magazine*, 1826, pp.469-70.

27. DR 176-180.

28. *Proceedings* of the Wesley Historical Society, vol.x (1916), p.24.

29. D. E. Jenkins, op. cit, pp.83-4.

30. GWL i.463.

31. CH xlviii; Gomer M. Roberts (ed) *Selected Trevecka Letters (1742-1747)*, pp.73-4,94.

32. National Library of Wales, Calvinistic Methodist Archives, Trefeca Letter No. 792; Gomer M. Roberts, *Bywyd a Gwaith Peter Williams*, 1943, 15f, 62.

33. CH xlviii.69-70.

34. GWL ii.257,262,263.

35. [A. C. H. Seymour] *The Life and Times of Selina Countess of Huntingdon*, vol.i, 1844, p.177.

36. Gomer M. Roberts (gol) *Hanes Methodistiaeth Galfinaidd Cymru,* cyf.i. 1973, p.384; GWL ii.409; John Gillies *Memoirs of . . . George Whitefield*, 1811, Appendix, p.lxiii; GWL ii.439.

37. GWL ii.439; iii 14-15,35,36; 234,236.

38. Tom Beynon, op cit, p.72; Tom Beynon, *Howell Harris's Visits to London,* 1960, p.19; GWL iii.262.

39. John Gillies, op. cit, p.225; Eifion Evans' *Howell Harris Evangelist 1714-1773,* Cardiff, 1974, pp.62-3.

40. GWJ 61, 169; and see DR 256-8.

7

ADDING TO THE CHURCH—
In the Teaching of the Welsh
Calvinistic Methodists

Welsh Calvinistic Methodism was at once a part and a product of the Great Awakening of the eighteenth century. From the fiery experiences of the powerful revivals of the period there emerged in Wales a strong, spiritual movement as widespread as it was indigenous, culminating in the formation of a new religious denomination. From its earliest days the movement was characterised by a vigorous spiritual life. Its preaching was unashamedly scriptural and evangelical, authoritative and urgent. Its fellowship was heavenly and disciplined, jealously guarded and nurtured, fruitful and lasting. Its distinguishing marks were a Calvinistic theology and an experimental spirituality.

In it people at large felt that God was doing something new, that here was no hybrid religion, but a distinctive strain of piety brought into being by the sovereign creativity of God. For those involved in this upsurge of spiritual energy, the outcome was not so much a novelty as a fresh manifestation of genuine Christianity, a living reproduction of the New Testament Church.

Nearly a century was to pass before the movement was to settle into visible ecclesiastical form. The mutation from spontaneous, lively fellowships of believers, into a legalized religious body complete with its own ordination and confession took Welsh Calvinistic Methodism into the nineteenth century. In time this new denomination came to be known as 'The Calvinistic Methodist or Presbyterian Church of Wales'.

The Beginnings of the Movement

The earliest leaders of the movement, Daniel Rowland and Howel Harris, remained, in affiliation if not in attitude, faithfully Anglican until their death. To all intents and purposes the determinative principles which regulated the life of Calvinistic Methodism were established during their lifetime. Early in its history those principles received universal recognition as scriptural and valid. With very little modification they were incorporated into the official constitution of the Calvinistic Methodist Church of Wales. In breaking from Anglicanism the second-generation Calvinist Methodists found no necessity for severing their continuity with the teaching and practice of their apostolic predecessors. Time was to vindicate their judgment of those principles, for they proved an effective bulwark against ecclesiastical degeneration until the end of the century.

The beginnings of the Welsh Calvinistic Methodist movement can be traced to the conversion in 1735 of both Rowland and Harris. Its growth was due in large measure to the astonishing success which attended their labours. Rowland's ministry at Llangeitho for over fifty years was phenomenal in terms of powerful preaching, sustained lively impressions, heavenly communion seasons, large crowds, and deep spiritual experiences. Harris was the indefatigable evangelist of the movement, a man of intense solemnity and fervent godliness, justly famed for his unflinching zeal, organizing genius and ecumenical spirit. Complementing one another in gifts, they imparted to the movement soundness and stability, Rowland by the authority and orthodoxy of his preaching, Harris by the unction of his personality and depth of his pastoral concern.

From the outset, stability and identity were crucial issues to the converts of the Awakening. In the matter of stability, there was the need for a charitable and scriptural assessment of the validity of a person's experience of the gospel. Coupled with this was the clear obligation to provide for the care and oversight of those who showed some evidence of grace and a genuine longing for godliness. These factors in turn precipitated a crisis of identity.

Neither the Anglican nor the Nonconformist churches could offer a home to the converts which provided exact or even proximate spiritual kinship to them. The ethos of the Awakening, its mould, its atmosphere, was peculiarly original, or so it seemed to those who experienced its power. God was creating a spiritual culture which found no parallel in the ecclesiastical forms which already existed. In each of them there were kindred elements, but in none of them was there that precise expression of Christianity which gloried in a sublimely personal and practical experience of the truth. For this new wine the old bottles were patently inadequate.

Consequently, the fellowships, or societies, of young believers which shared such unprecedented experiences were happy to be called 'The Society People'. Gradually, imperceptibly, but justifiably and correctly they were called 'Methodists'. On account of their Calvinistic interpretation of the 39 Articles which they avowed from conviction to be their theology, they came to be specifically identified as 'Calvinistic Methodists'.

Harris felt keenly this crisis of identity as early as 1737. He writes:

Behold . . . iniquities here in the Anglican Church, and there [Nonconformity] too much rigidity. Oh! Lord! where shall I go? I am tossed to and fro by people of different views. Behold me at Thy feet to be guided; place me where Thou wilt . . . On reflection, I never saw anything lacking in the Church of England, except these three things: 1. A privilege of meeting together as a Society to consult about points of salvation, self-examination. 2. More home pressing the necessity of regeneration in the pulpit, with familiar teaching, catechizing and instructing privately in families, and in public; an inspection of the life of every communicant. The reason of their absenting to be taken by some set apart for that business, deacons, etc. with an examination on the Saturday before, public, ere they are admitted to Christ's Table, and to have the sacrament monthly. 3. More familiarity between the Pastor and the sheep.[1]

He tried to eliminate the factors within Anglicanism which might have created problems: 'her doctrine seems to me to be wholesome', he says in 1737. By 1742 all possibility of integrating the societies within the Church of England was exhausted: 'For my part I have gone toward reforming all as far as I think I am called and commissioned of the Lord'.[2] The statement applied equally to the Nonconformists, and the conclusion was inescapable: 'The Society People' could not be accommodated in any existing religious denomination. They must meanwhile belong to one by way of formal connection, but they must renounce all for the sake of mutual fellowship.

Others recognized his dilemma, as, for instance, William Herbert, a Baptist. At the beginning of 1737 he wrote to Harris:

I know you are carrying on the essence of religion, not regarding much the circumstances of it . . . Now I shall put myself in your place and deal with myself accordingly. Have I been labouring and toiling night and day to reduce and reclaim those that were like sheep going astray? Did not the Lord bless my endeavours so far as to prevail with a great many to become

religious? . . . Now, how do I serve these? Do not I in effect tell them to
continue where they were before, when I send them to such a public house
which is open to all comers? . . . have not I been labouring hard to cure
many scabby sheep of the rot, and when I made them almost well, did I
not turn them to a field full of scabby ones which made them as rot and
scabby as ever? Should not I turn them rather to some enclosure by themselves, or to such as were sound and healthy . . . you may tell me, that
there are some faithful shepherds belonging to that common that I send
them to; true, but not in that part of it I send my sheep to . . . Should I not
rather continue to be their leader, as well as continue to be the shepherd of
my sheep?[3]

Thus Herbert advocated separation from the Established Church,
which Harris resolutely resisted.

There was another way open for the converts. For the time being
the society was to constitute their spiritual life-line. They would
avoid all appearance of separation by maintaining intact their sacramental link with whatever denomination they chose. As time passed
this strategy was repeatedly called in question, and the minutes of
their Association testify to the delicacy of the theological and
ecclesiastical balance of the Calvinistic Methodist position:

(3 May 1744) we agreed . . . as far as we can remove stumbling-blocks, to
communicate in the parish churches, and to advise the people to do so, in
order to prevent our appearing like a sect (having before agreed not to call
our Societies Churches, but Societies in the Established Church, and not to
call the exhorters ministers) . . . (25 April 1745) In discoursing with the
brethren I declared I differed with them in 3 things. (1) That I never looked
on the Societies as Churches, but little branches of a Church. (2) The
exhorters never as ministers to dispense ordinances, nor, many of them,
even the Word, by way of preaching, but by way of exhorting. (3) On us
never as a sect, but a people in the Church, called to reform till either we
should be heard, or turned out; and that whoever is called to labour as a
reformer must have strong love to bear much.[4]

Harris's refusal to separate from the Church of England was a matter
of conviction as well as of expediency and experience. So long as
the Church of England held to its 39 Articles and suffered the
Methodists, he would avoid division. He conceded that the initiative
in the matter should lie with the Anglican authorities. As his experience had taught him, sacramental efficacy was guaranteed by God's
Word rather than by clerical integrity. For the faithful preaching of

that Word Harris had no compunction in turning elsewhere if the Anglican Church failed in its responsibility.

All this he makes clear in a letter to Griffith Jones, written in 1742:

I have been a constant communicant in our Church . . . and I trust I can in truth say, that I have never been there without meeting the Lord, more or less everywhere I received, and I found no great difference, but that I had most good when I went most poor in spirit, labouring and self emptied, looking most to Christ and least to the man administering, or the element administered; and that I had least when I went most full there, or expecting much because administered by such a man, etc. So while I met the Lord in the Ordinance, I thought it my duty to join in that, though I could not benefit by the preaching, because many of them preach the law more than the Gospel, and many neither law nor Gospel, but confusing both, and neither light for a poor soul to see where he was, nor any power to attend it; and so was obliged to seek out for the most heart searching and powerful preaching of the Word, wherever I could find it.[5]

Such considerations merely confirmed Harris's view of the absolute necessity for the societies as the means of 'strengthening the small beginnings of grace and gracious dispositions in any to know, love and fear the Lord', and ideally suited to 'examine the state of each other's souls every meeting'.[6]

These sentiments summarize the original intention behind the establishment of the societies, independently and spontaneously commenced by Rowland and Harris. From Harris's diaries and letters it is possible to trace their development and some of the movements which might have influenced the Methodists in their thinking and planning for them. Their contribution to the success of the Awakening in Wales was pivotal, and the late Dr M. H. Jones rightly concluded, 'If it had not been for these Societies, the Methodist Movement in England and Wales would have been a rope of sand'.[7]

The Aims of the Society Meetings

The principal aims of a society meeting were, the sharing of Christian experience, submission to the discipline of God's Word and people, growth in the knowledge of the truth, and advancing the cause of holiness in the life of the believer. The attainment of these ends hinged on one thing: opening the heart to fellow believers in the context of mutual concern and commitment. 'Let none neglect private bands to meet to open their hearts,' counsels Harris, adding with conviction, 'Sure this is of God. O that we should all lie low at Christ's feet, then everything would not offend us so easily.' During one of the most powerful revivals at Llangeitho, Harris could testify to Whitefield about some of 'the unspeakable advantages' of the societies in this way: 'Such is the power among them in prayer often that they are struck with awful silence, and often the speaker has his voice drowned by the cries of the broken hearts . . . sometimes they go to say grace before meat, the Spirit of prayer falls upon them one after another, so that they are kept in prayer near three hours.'[8]

Early in 1742 Harris had written to the Tabernacle Society about Christian unity, advocating mutual charity, recognition and co-operation between believers in each denomination. He added his ideas about church membership:

requiring no other qualification . . . but proofs of a saving acquaintance with the Lord Jesus, by a lively faith productive of holiness in heart and life, making itself more visible by its growth . . . Was I called to take the care of a particular congregation, I should think it my duty to receive all to my communion that I could find sufficient proof to hope were born of God, though they could not agree with me in my judgment about some externals.

While on a visit to London in 1748 he 'showed the qualifications of one to come to our societies, either to be acquainted with the Lord Jesus, or else to be so deeply sensible of their need for Him as to seek Him in earnest'.[9]

Apart from such general statements relating to membership of the societies, Harris began to formulate rules for them as early as 1738.[10] At that time there was very little material available, even if he could have had access to it, to provide guidelines for the regulation of such groups. Josiah Woodward's *Account of the Religious Societies,* first published in 1697, met a different need.

Nevertheless, Harris may have become acquainted with its main ideas through Griffith Jones as early as 1736, but he did not own a copy until early in 1739. Later in his life, he 'opened of Woodward's societies, and how from these I took the plan of societies in Wales first'. In his autobiography he recounted his debt to Woodward's work in this way: 'I began in imitation of the societies which Dr Woodward gave an account of, in a little Treatise he wrote on

that head. There being as yet no other societies of the kind in
England or Wales. The English Methodists not being as yet heard of,
though the Lord was now, as I found afterward, working on some of
them in Oxford, and elsewhere'. A Welsh translation of Woodward's rules appeared in 1740 as an anonymous publication.[11]

Harris's rules of 1738 have been lost. They preceded by over a
year Whitefield's *Letter to the Religious Societies*. Whitefield's aim
was partly apologetic, and it serves to indicate the point of departure
between the Methodist societies and those of Woodward.

The only end which I hope you all propose by your assembling yourselves
together, is the renewing of your depraved natures, and promoting the hidden life of Jesus Christ in your souls . . . Content not yourselves with reading, singing, and praying together; but set some time apart to confess your
faults, and to communicate your experience one to another. For want of this,
(which I take to be one chief design of private meetings), most of the old
Societies in London, I fear, are sunk into a dead formality, and have only a
name to live . . . they have only the form of godliness left amongst them,
and continue utter strangers to the state of one another's hearts. My
brethren, let not your coming together be thus altogether in vain, but plainly
and freely tell one another what God has done for your souls.[12]

Later Welsh Methodist rules, published successively in 1740, 1741,
and 1742, developed Whitefield's experimental emphasis, omitting
the apologetic altogether.

Subsequent developments in Welsh Calvinistic Methodism produced two more major works on the societies. William Williams, the
hymn-writer, was the most skilful of the leaders in conducting a
society meeting. His book, *Templum Experientiae apertum, neu,
Ddrws y Society Profiad*, translated into English under the title *The
Experience Meeting*, was originally published in 1777. It is undoubtedly the classic statement on the nurturing of spiritual experience in
the fellowship of believers. The second major work appeared in
Welsh in 1801, and in English the following year under the title *The
Rules and the Design of the Religious Societies*, the joint work of
Thomas Charles of Bala and Thomas Jones of Denbigh. This was
adopted by the Calvinistic Methodists as their 'Rules of Discipline',
and was published with the newly formulated Confession of Faith in
1823.

An examination of these rules gives an indication of some of the
things involved in joining the society. These included doctrinal,

experimental, covenantal, and ethical requirements. Doctrinal orthodoxy was demanded, particular attention being paid to the Trinity,
election, original sin, justification by faith, and perseverance in
grace. Self-examination was expected, as well as openness within
the fellowship regarding God's dealings with the soul from time to
time. Mutual confidence, love and respect even to the point of secre-
cy was stipulated. Each society was to give every encouragement to
its members to live a life of practical godliness and good works,
avoiding the social evils as well as the more blatant sins of the day.

The realization of Harris's ideal of 'opening the heart' is constantly in focus in these rules. He had once said, 'That is the purpose
of our societies, and to this end I was called, and through the power
of grace I will set up such discipline that no hypocrite will be able to
bear it'.[13] Consecutive sets of rules bring out this important and distinguishing aspect of careful examination.

(1740) We, who have received God's mercy and grace to become the disciples of Christ, to be shepherded and protected by Him, after making a definite profession of our faith in Him, do firstly submit ourselves to Christ,
and then to confide in one another in the fear of God as one Body in Christ
. . . We meet to examine our faith and conduct, to glorify God thereby, to
confirm our privileges in Christ, and to foster discipline, peace, purity and
protection amongst ourselves . . . each one is to magnify peace and purity,
avoid blasphemy and idle words, and never to disclose the secret confes-
sions of the Society.

The 1741 'Basis and Rules of a Society' is a Llangeitho manuscript,
and may reflect Rowland's thoughts and influence.

(a) That we are to reveal our whole heart to one another in simplicity of
faith like little children and that we hide not the evil of which we are conscious within . . . so that we can thereby strengthen our love towards one
another and learn the deceitfulness of the heart, the wiles of Satan, and the
operations of grace upon our lives.

(b) That we, according to the advice of our Saviour, shall be vigilant over
one another's tempers and behaviour, and with gentleness exhort one
another . . .

(c) That we shall allow ourselves to be examined by one another in relation to our motives, choice and principles in all things; and by so doing,
recognize that our souls and bodies, talents and knowledge, memory and
understanding, time and wealth, strength and opportunity to labour are not
our own possessions but the gifts of God.[14]

Some of the Dangers

The seventh dialogue of Williams' work seeks to safeguard against an unhealthy repetition of those things which must not be related to the society. These included such things as blasphemous thoughts, wild wandering thoughts, sudden temptations which agitate the passions, waywardness before conversion, and the faults and weaknesses of others.

There lay some of the dangers. But the advantages, for Williams, far outweighed them, as he makes clear in *The Experience Meeting*'s second dialogue:

First . . . they are a means of keeping up this same warmth and liveliness that was ours at the beginning . . . second . . . this kind of fellowship is profitable to unravel the various nets and hidden snares woven by Satan to catch the simple believer on his own ground . . . Many young saints are like lambs, that run after the dogs instead of after their mothers; imagining that some sins are no sins, but grace; that the breezes of nature are the breath of heaven; that the spirit of melancholy is a truly broken heart; and pride, envy, and prejudice are a sign of zeal for God; and it is necessary for the godly to gather together to extricate weak Christians from these snares, and to direct those who have lost the right way back into it again. Thirdly, these special meetings are good at forestalling contentions, suspicions, prejudices, discords, jealousies and all uncharitableness . . . fourth . . . that we may look after and watch over each other's lives, lest any should fall into loose living and turn the grace of God into lasciviousness . . . fifth . . . bearing one another's burdens . . . sixth . . . to declare the work of God on our souls . . . lastly . . . for strengthening ourselves against all our spiritual enemies, and for praying together as one man against them all . . .

Behind the Methodist leaders' comprehensive arguments and directions lay the concern for maintaining life and purity in the fellowship. There was ample encouragement for any to join who felt some measure of the Holy Spirit's activity in his soul, especially if there was a willingness to submit to the mutual examination and admonition of others of like mind. In effect, the marks of a true fellowship were distilled from the New Testament epistles and used as requisite pointers to godliness among those who desired a place in the Methodist Zion.

Leadership

Admission into membership of the societies was regulated by these rules. Each society was led by one or more 'stewards'. Such leaders were responsible to Harris as 'superintendent', who, together with the Ministers at an 'Association' would receive detailed reports of the spiritual state of each member. In each fellowship there was a general society and, for more mature members, a private society. This division was a recognition of the distinction drawn in Scripture between those who are 'babes' and those who are 'teachers', between those who take 'milk' and those who could take 'strong meat'.

Anyone desirous of joining the general society would need to give his name to the stewards beforehand. They examined his spiritual experience and understanding of gospel truth, and made enquiries among his neighbours as to the uprightness of his life. This could last for a month or more, during which time he was reckoned to be 'on trial'. If he met with the approval of the stewards he was required to present himself before the members of the society to be questioned along lines suggested in the rules. With the entire society's approval, the candidate was then solemnly charged and encouraged to maintain scriptural standards of behaviour within the society and outside it.

The 1740 rules specified that 'special care be taken to refuse no one however weak, provided there are tokens of his acceptance by Christ'. Williams for his part cautioned, 'You must not expect as much light of faith and assurance in those newly received into membership as in those already in, who have long enjoyed the visitations of the Lord'. 'With regard to a flat rejection' of an applicant for admission, Williams added, 'we have no basis in Scripture for doing so, unless it is obvious that his life is unworthy and reveals that the truth is not in him; or it transpires that it is for some false purpose that he wants to come into the fellowship; or that he only attends the means of grace in fits and starts, under the turbulent convictions of natural conscience . . . no one, in the person of a seeker, and with a true desire for eternal life, should be shut out, however faint may be the revelations and visitations of God to him'. Expulsion from a society was a matter of delicacy, and judgment was to be generously tempered with mercy. Scriptural guidelines were to be strictly observed in the conviction that the cause of purity was not hindered by the demands of charity.

During the thirty or so formative years of Calvinistic Methodism the questions put to candidates for membership of the societies were those outlined in the 'official' publication of 1742. Here is a summary of them:

Are you convinced of sin? 1 Tim.3:15; Have you been awakened by God's grace? Job 11:12; Do you admit your moral inability to do good in and of yourself? Eph.2:1; Do you accept the imputed righteousness of Christ in Salvation, and that God's Spirit alone is the author of that faith whereby you believe? Rom.3:24; Have you felt the Spirit of God inclining you to forsake sin to embrace Christ? Luke 18:28-30; Have you counted the cost of following Christ? Mark 8:35; Though you have not yet received the witness of the Spirit, do you prove in your heart that you desire God with your whole heart, and that you will not rest until you have Him? Rom.8:16; Are you unwilling to rest until you know that you believe, and truly hate all sin, until you have received the Spirit of adoption within you? Rom.8:15, Isa.56:5; Do you accept and assent to the fundamental truths of the Trinity, Election, Original Sin, Justification by Faith, and Perseverance in Grace, as taught in the 39 Articles? Gal.1:6; Is it the love of Christ that constrains you to join our society, and are you prepared to abide by these rules? Gal.5:6.

Williams, at least, was aware of the danger of making hard and fast rules, and counselled wisdom and charity in the use of such questions. 'I know of many mistaken ideas about this—some catechizing in an obscure way, a hard way; some asking totally irrelevant questions, some so entangling and confusing the man being questioned that he has nothing to say, and some doing all the talking, so that the man they are questioning can hardly get a word in.' He laid the responsibility for taking a compassionate and understanding approach squarely on the shoulders of the stewards. 'We must understand that we should not be putting the same questions to everyone—not the same question, for instance, to a beginner in Christ as to an older Christian; not the same one to the doubting as to the one enjoying assurance, to the one suffering onslaughts of trials and temptation as to the one dwelling in the bosom of the Lord.'

The rigidity with which the questions were interpreted, together with the spiritual sensitivity of the steward were evidently important factors in the reception of new members. This accounts for the substantial variation in the experiences of those who sought admission. John Thomas, who later became an Independent minister, sought that privilege in 1744 when he was 14 years of age. He did so with some measure of spiritual understanding and experience in the things of God. 'I did not know much about the plague of my heart,

my misery by nature, my fall in the first Adam,' he says, 'and the
Lord Jesus was but a little Saviour in my sight . . . About this time I
joined a small company of godly people . . . who, when they examined me, received me lovingly, wondering at the Lord who had visited me as it were in the days of my infancy.'

Thomas Williams, a hymn-writer, faced a severe examiner in the
society. The year was 1771, and he was a mere 10 years old. The
steward would have refused and reprimanded him, but the members
of the society prevailed with a more charitable judgment which time
and Williams's hymns amply vindicated.

Hesitancy in Seeking Membership

It is not surprising, therefore, to find considerable diffidence, if not
reluctance, in seeking membership among the societies. Edward
Jones, another hymn-writer, was 26 in 1787 when he came under
strong spiritual impressions. He considered himself too great a sinner to join the society, and the local stewards gave him little encouragement. On offering himself in the usual manner he was nevertheless received, in spite of some trepidation among the members
lest his poetic gifts should be used to deride their piety.

John Elias of Anglesey was terrified lest the stewards should be
harsh in their examination. But his fears were unfounded, and at 19
years of age, in 1793, he was admitted to the society in a very gracious and gentle manner. Robert Ellis, later a preacher with the
Calvinistic Methodists, was kept 'on trial' for some months. At his
first appearance before the members his whole body trembled and
he was nearly speechless. He was finally received into membership
on a Saturday evening in 1829, and admitted to the Lord's Table the
next day.[15] Evidently by this latter date, the Calvinistic Methodists
were finding it necessary to follow general denominational practice
in aligning membership of the church with admission to the Lord's
Table.

Sixty years later the Welsh General Assembly advised a more
lenient interpretation of the rules of admission. In 1882 the question
had been asked, 'whether it would not be wise under the existing circumstances, when many of our hearers, out of delicate feeling,
experience great difficulty to break through to make their appearance for the first time in the church meeting, and there publicly

express their religious feeling and their desire to become members, to devise some method by which such persons could converse privately with the office-bearers in this matter?' In the course of discussion 'the sacredness that belongs to religious convictions' was emphasised, 'and that it would be a great loss to the church not to have it related at our church meetings, but to bear in mind that every one who has a profound feeling is not ready to express it in public'. Accordingly, in 1889 the General Assembly allowed candidates to be examined by the elders, who should then convey the substance of their findings to the congregation when proposing their acceptance.[16]

Assurance of Salvation

More serious than the matter of diffidence was the question of assurance of salvation. Admission to the general society was allowed to those who were still seeking assurance. Significantly, the first set of questions to be asked on admission to the private society was to be along the following lines:

Do you know that you believe? 1 Jn.5:10,13; that you have faith? 2 Cor.13:5; and that your sins are forgiven? Ps.32:5; and that Christ has died for you in particular? Gal.2:20; and by His Spirit now dwells in you? 2 Cor.13:5; and that God has loved you with an everlasting love? Jer.31:3; Does God's spirit continually bear witness with your spirit, that you are a child of God? Rom.8:16. (1742 rules)

An affirmative answer was expected, an indication that progress in Christian experience for the Methodists involved, among other things, a conscious enjoyment of the assurance of salvation in the different ways signified by the questions.

The private society received addition from those in the public society who 'had been attending for some time, had behaved worthily, and could answer the questions' on assurance, and others as indicated by the following:

Do you prove in your heart more sympathy with those who are tempted? Rom.12:15; Do you prove more spiritual light within, revealing more and more of God's holiness and purity, and the spirituality of His law? Jn.8:12; Is your conscience more sensitive to convict you at the first beginnings of sin in the mind? Prov.22:8; What lesson has the Lord taught you since we last met? Isa.48:17 Are you more and more amazed at God's love for you in particular? Gal.2:20; Do you find that your souls are being more and more grounded and established in love? 1 Peter 4:8; Can you say, through more intimate acquaintance on account of the testimony of the water and the blood, (1 Jn.5:5), that your names are written in the Book of Life? Rev.21:27. (1742 rules)

Clearly the societies were totally committed to advancing the cause of spiritual and doctrinal maturity.

Reports to the Association of the state of members of the societies included such remarks as the following: 'There is still considerable darkness in them regarding their justifiction, but their souls thirst after God'; or, 'these have not yet had a full sight of their justification'; or, 'under the law'; 'under the spirit of bondage'. Comments like these referred to persons in the general society. They were intended to convey a lack of assurance in them, that they did not yet enjoy the liberty and joy of an acquitted conscience, and that the terrors of the law and its condemnation still held them in bondage. Such people were encouraged to seek a fuller view of Christ's merit, and a fuller experience of Christ's Spirit in the terms of Rom.8:14-16. A soul culture like this, so characteristic of the Methodist movements in both England and Wales, whether Calvinistic or Arminian in theology, repeatedly insisted that conversion was not merely a decisive step of faith. Conversion involved that and much more besides. It was nothing less than a progressive work of the Holy Spirit, in which, by spiritual discipline, the smallest beginnings of grace in the sinner were to be carefully analysed and nurtured.

The distinction between weak and mature Christians was repeatedly drawn by the Methodists. Put in another way it was the distinction between those who lacked, and those who possessed, assurance. Williams of Pantycelyn gives their respective characteristics in the 'address to the reader' which prefaces collections of hymns issued in 1758 and 1762.

I acknowledge that there are some of these first hymns—on the assurance of faith, longing to be dissolved, spiritual joy, together with triumph over enemies—which weak Christians cannot easily sing; this happened not so much because the Lord kept my own soul in good spirits at the time, but chiefly because the Spirit had been so plentifully poured out on those godly people for whom they were written . . . I am constrained to give a little advice to those who give out these hymns . . . some give out verses full of assurance and delight to a congregation that denies the first and has not experienced the second . . . others give out verses of complaint and questioning to a people who have been elevated to the heavenlies, and who feel life in their faith and Satan under their feet, as if to urge people to sing about the cold of winter while the sun blazes in hottest summer. (1758)

Here there is merely a selection of hymns which the weakest in the Church can sing, since they are either in the form of a prayer for some of the gifts of the New Covenant, or grief because of sin; whereas many of the first ones cannot be sung by some, on account of the full assurance of faith regarding eternal life that is in them. (1762)

On the issue of assurance, Rowland agreed with Williams, but Harris differed from them, partly because of his own experience. He had forfeited his early assurance of salvation by showing deference to one he considered an advanced Christian, lest he should be judged guilty of disrespect.

Later, when his assurance had been restored, Harris taught that assurance was inseparable from saving faith. Writing to John Wesley in 1741, he complained of Jeremy Taylor's book, *Holy Living,* in which assurance was disowned as presumption. He continues with a word of personal experience:

When any would ask, 'How is it with your soul?' my cry was like the rest of such as I conversed with, 'I am up and down; I have great cause to doubt'. And so I passed for an humble Christian, till the Lord sent Brother Whitefield about 2½ years ago and the first question he asked me was, 'Do you know that your sins are forgiven you?' and the question astonished me, having never heard the like before. I could not say they were, being in great bondage under the law . . . then I began to groan for liberty, using one means after another to bring me out of myself to Christ . . . a word that Brother Whitefield said was of great use to me and conveyed much light to my soul. Talking once in company he said, 'As yet he is only working for life and not from life'. There came such a conviction to show the difference between a man under the law and under grace, the first doing all good in order to have life, and the other doing good out of gratitude because he had life.

He met Whitefield in March 1739, and by 1740 Harris's view of assurance was unambiguous and dogmatic: 'We can't pass from death to life, from being children of wrath to be made children of God, from being blind to come to see . . . unknown to us; the work of the devil can't be destroyed by the Son of God in us and we not know it, no it is impossible'.[17]

Controversy about assurance between Rowland and Harris came
to a head in the spring of 1742. 'There arose a dispute that held to
midnight,' says Harris, 'about our knowing our interest in Christ,
between me and Brother Rowland . . . what I was afraid of in him
was his feeding hypocrites; and what he feared in me was my over-
throwing weak ones.' A week later he wrote: 'had still on me a conviction that Brother Rowland is wrong, and I can't agree when he is
dabbling so much with saying we may be in Christ and not know it.
None can be disciples till they are made willing to leave their lives,
and this is common work, nor is it wrought till we have the Holy
Ghost'. Another week passed before he wrote to Whitefield, 'I
believe the doctrine of assurance is what is needed. It would be to
God's glory and the present good of the church. If you should be
called of the Lord to write a discourse upon it, we should translate it
into Welsh. Indeed it is much wanting'.[18]

Harris came into conflict with others, too, about the doctrine of
assurance. 'Griffith Jones having been this way to preach,' he
records in his diary for 5th March 1741, '1. That a man may be converted and not know it. 2. That there is no assurance. 3. That we
should not speak our assurances. I showed the necessity of assurance
from Gal.4:24,29; and Rom.8:9.' But Harris's chief antagonists were
the Dissenters.

4 Dec. 1740 . . . to Mr Evan Davies, Dissenting Minister, where he objected
. . . to my saying that a man can't be in Christ without knowing it. He said I
wounded those that God would not have to be wounded, that many have
only a hope. I said there was no hope without faith, and no faith without a
witness. There are two degrees of knowledge, the first will admit of doubts,
but even he is restless till he has the full assurance.

The Nonconformist case regarding assurance was very ably argued
by David Williams in a letter sent to Harris towards the end of 1740:

I did not mean that it was so absolutely necessary to salvation, that I
believed many are gone to heaven who obtained not a full assurance thereof
here, but none without being in Christ. And he that is in Christ is a new
creature. There are in Christ babes, young men, and fathers. There is a weak
faith, a strong faith, and a full assurance of faith. It is the duty of all Christians to be very constant and close in self-examination, in order to know the
state and condition of their souls. Yet I cannot pronounce concerning those
that have not come to a full persuasion of knowledge, that they are not in
Christ; or, supposing they should die so, that they will be sent to hell. I

know that no impenitent believer shall be saved. I know that no penitent believer, though he has not attained to an absolute full assurance free from doubts and suspicions concerning himself, shall be damned.[19]

The rules of the societies indicate that Rowland and Williams prevailed over Harris in the matter of assurance as it affected the societies. While the terms of admission were exacting, they were not at this point prohibitive.

The Criticism of the Dissenters

The Dissenters also took issue with the Methodists over their most distinctive features: the searching of the heart and the sharing of Christian experience. Some Dissenters envied the Methodists this aspect of church life, but they were few. Most of them criticized the Methodists for lack of discipline, but this was hardly the case. The truth of the matter lay in the fact that Methodist discipline was of a different kind. The Dissenters looked for a measure of moral integrity and doctrinal competence as the prerequisite to admission to the Lord's Table. Sacramental fitness was not at issue in the Methodist ranks, at least not until they had ordained their own ministers in 1811. Discipline within Methodism was a matter of assessing the validity and maturity of spiritual experience.

Harris countered the charge of the Dissenters regarding discipline with a statement, as he saw it, of the weakness of their position:

They come to have no real spiritual discipline at all, for all their examination . . . in receiving a church member in, is to examine the orthodoxy of their principles, and about the morality of their lives, of a common change, which many hypocrites have tasted more, and then, calling them God's people, build them up on the sand. And so the love of the world and unbelief, and habitual lukewarmness and carnal conversation, in public and private, becomes the course of their lives, being strong enemies to assurance, and to opening the heart.

Three months later, in another letter to Whitefield, Harris complains of the Dissenters drawing away converts from the Methodist ranks:

When they go, as there are few of them that lead them on from grace to grace, and build them up, but in head knowledge, so most that go do visibly grow more careless in their walk, selfish in their spirit, lukewarm as to the power of godliness, and become zealous for their party, losing their love to those they dissent from disputing, etc . . . others preaching against some

Rules we wrote to the societies, making that their chief objection because we directed according to the liberty given to open the whole heart, the good and evil.

Dissenters and Methodists parted company on this issue, and Harris crystallized the differences between them in this way:

We preach chiefly to the heart and spirit, and we pierce them, wounding the flesh and making it uncomfortable. We emphasise faith in the heart rather than light in the head. Their light comes from the head and puts the soul at ease, but it does not strengthen faith. We disturb the soul to its depths, taking conviction to the very bottom, giving a more extensive knowledge of Christ by the Spirit; they leave the soul in peace, undisturbed. They do not search the heart . . . [20]

The excellent benefits of searching the heart, in the opinion of the Methodists, made its absence or forfeiture intolerable. Methodism could never have been absorbed into Dissent.

Later, however, there were to be prudent concessions to the Nonconformist 'image' of strict moral standards. While the second generation Methodists followed the method and experimental attitude of their predecessors in adding to church membership, the 1801 Rules do show a shift of emphasis. There is no mention of assurance or the witness of the Spirit, and the majority of the rules have a more legalistic outlook. Here are a few instances:

XII.   They must avoid all those modes and fashions of dress which tend to foster pride, wantonness, or extravagance . . .
XIV.   That they be men of few words in buying and selling . . .
XV.   That they do not make it their business to buy or sell running (i.e. smuggled) goods . . .
XXII. They must on no account use enchantment or witchcraft . . .
XXIII It is required of all that live near the sea, to show kindness to those whom they may see in danger . . .

Slander and persecution against the Methodists account partly for the exact morality of these rules, but there is also the implicit assumption that the societies were already, in practice if not in reality, churches. There are references to 'elders' and 'the church meeting', and the distinction between general and private societies is no longer sustained.

The pattern which the Methodists developed was determined by several factors. The spontaneity and intensity of the revival experiences demanded a substantial measure of discernment and discipline along experimental lines which neither Anglicanism nor Dissent could offer. When the Methodists had to justify their principles they invariably claimed scriptural warrant for them.

They sought to hold certain emphases in balance, namely a vigorous spiritual experience, a well-founded and increasing understanding of the truth, a careful and charitable discipline, and a progressive holiness of life. This Calvinistic Methodist culture faithfully reflected the characteristics of the powerful revival movements which brought it into existence. Whatever its shortcomings, it endeavoured to be true to Scripture, true to its vision of life and power, and true to the spiritual harvest of the Awakening.

Safeguarding the life of God within, preserving the purity of the fellowship, keeping the heart aflame for God, had been the great triple vision which the early leaders so zealously sought to achieve through the societies. For many years their efforts were eminently fruitful, and even in times of spiritual declension the discipline which they advocated carried with it the promise, and on occasions, the foretaste of glory.

REFERENCES

1   Diary No 23 (March 18, 1737), Calvinistic Methodist Archives, National Library of Wales; Richard Bennett, *The Early Life of Howell Harris*, 1962, pp.105f.
2   Bennett, p.149; Gomer M. Roberts, *Selected Trevecka Letters (1742-1747)*, 1956, p.51.
3   *Journal of the Historical Society of the Presbyterian Church of Wales*, MS Supplement, i.108-109.
4   D. E. Jenkins, *Calvinistic Methodist Holy Orders*, 1911, pp.100,114-115.
5   Roberts, p.24.
6   M. H. Jones, *The Trevecka Letters*, 1932, pp.234,235.
7   Ibid., p.222.
8   Roberts, pp.41,66,68.
9   *Journal*, MS Supplement, ii., p.219; Tom Beynon, *Howell Harris's Visits to London*, 1960, p.197.
10 *Journal*, MS Supplement, i., pp.121,130.
11 Tom Beynon, *Howell Harris, Reformer and Soldier*, 1958, pp.90,95,130; *A Brief Account of the Life of Howell Harries*, 1791, p.24; M. H. Jones, pp.248-9.
12 Tyerman, pp.318,319.
13 Bennett, p.80.
14 M. H. Jones, pp.246,247; 250-1.
15 Ioan Thomas, *Rhad Ras*, 1949, p.44; Gomer M. Roberts, *Emynwyr Bethesda'r Fro*, 1967, p.16; J. E. Caerwyn Williams, *Edward Jones, Maes-y-plwm*, 1962,

p.15; J. O. Jones, *Cofiant a Gweithiau y Parch Robert Ellis, Ysgoldy*, 1883, pp.13-14.

16 Minutes of the Llangefni Quarterly Association, 28-30 June, 1882; Cylchlythyrau ac Adroddiadau Cymanfaol y Methodistiaid Calfinaidd am y flwyddyn 1889, p.25.

17 *Journal,* MS Supplement, ii. 145-6; 6-7.

18 Jenkins, p.64; *Journal*, vol.xxxiv, 79; *Journal*, MS Supplement, ii, 242.

19 Tom Beynon, *Howell Harris's Visits to Pembrokeshire,* 1966, pp.52,40; *Journal*, MS Supplement, ii. 11.

20 John Morgan Jones and William Morgan, *Y Tadau Methodistaidd*, vol. i, 1895, p.334; Roberts, pp.12-13, 32; cf. Jenkins, 75.

8
EARLY METHODIST
APOLOGETIC
Explaining and Defending Revival

From its earliest appearance Methodism in Wales had to contend with opposition. Some indication of the extent of that opposition is given in the literature of the period. Howel Harris received a fore-taste of what was to come in a letter from his brother, Joseph, as early as January 1736 when he was cautioned, 'beware of enthusiasm.'[1] A month later a letter from Price Davies, the Vicar of Talgarth, had amplified the word 'enthusiasm', and the word of caution had become an indictment. He spoke of 'those who audaciously presumed to invade the office ministerial . . . a factious zeal, and a puritanical sanctity . . . fanaticism and hypocrisy.'[2]

The offending aspect of Harris's activities lay in his ecclesiastical irregularities, authoritative preaching and irrepressible zeal. They caused great consternation to 'regular' clergymen like John Tilsley of Llandinam who wrote to Harris in August 1739 expostulating against 'This Licentious way of exercising ye Spirit':

If you think you are under a divine impulse, take care of an illusion, and that the broad seal of heaven which you may think you carry about with you, is not controlled by that grand deceiver . . . The regard I have to the eternal welfare of my parishioners oblige me to desire you in an amicable way not to sound your trumpet in so unwarrantable a manner, both contrary to the laws of God and man, any more in my parish; assuring you that the rigid way of exhorting, and of pouring out the vials of God's wrath so peremptorily upon your ignorant hearers, with your extempore effusions, has not only seduced several . . . to live, and end their days . . . under the guilt of schism . . . you have left several in a state of despair or with little hope of mercy.[3]

The laws of God and man were evoked often enough against the Methodists, and Harris was never one to evade an issue, especially when it gave him the opportunity to witness to a wider audience. His appearance in court at Llanbryn-mair in February 1740 gives a typical example of his defence against such charges:

The Justice said I was a mixture between ye Presbyter and Quaker. I said I
was a member of ye church of England and was in Church twice yesterday,
they said that was only a Pretence, that I belonged to that Gr. Jones and ye
Methodists. Asked me if I had used ye Prayer of ye Church there. I said I
thought they were not be used but in Church. Aye, you pretend to ye Spirit.
I then said I hope you don't make a Jest of ye Spirit of God, that ye and I
must have ye Spirit of God. I told him he charged me with bringing false
doctrines, that I never said one word agt. ye articles of our Church. He said I
broke ye Law. I asked him what Law, that it had been searched for in
London and they could find no Law agt. me ... [4]

From this and other accounts of Harris's appearance before his
accusers, legal and ecclesiastical, it is hard to escape the conclusion
that judge and defendant had changed places. Harris's apologetic
was neither timid nor indecisive, but another tool for confident,
aggressive evangelism.

   In one form or another the allegations faced by Harris continued
throughout the eighteenth century. The *Gentleman's Magazine* at the
turn of the century carried a correspondence charging the Methodists
with 'a style of worship so dissonant to the form of the Established
Church of England' referring to the practice of 'jumping', and to the
Methodists as 'the religious sect . . . called Jumpers' under the leadership of a 'poor ignorant fellow, devoid of education, and devoid of
sense.' Another writer charged the Methodists with disseminating
revolution ('instruments of Jacobinism') and atheism ('Paine's
works . . . translated into Welsh, and secretly distributed about by
the leaders of this sect'). Thomas Charles replied, pointing out that
monoglot Englishmen on tour through the Principality were hardly
in a position to judge the educational achievement of a preacher or
the edifying value of his discourse when the service was conducted
entirely in Welsh! He proceeded to deny the charges with rational
argument and convincing proofs, adding,

They believe the Bible, and bow implicitly to its divine authority: in the best
of books they are enjoined to fear God, and honour the King; nor do they
believe the first can subsist in the mind, without the other being a fruit of it
. . . The doctrines preached, the morality inculcated, by the Methodists, are
drawn from the pure fountain of inspiration; and are in exact conformity
with the articles of the Established Church . . . The Bible is familiar to them,
and understood in no other light than that in which our great Reformers
explained it. Bodily agitations in their assemblies constitute no essential part

of their religion. When the mind is affected by the various and contrary sensations of joy and sorrow, correspondent bodily effects (such is the wonderful connexion between them) will, in more or less degree, be expressed; and, even when these strong feelings of the mind are sanctified and attended with evident reformation of morals, and true diligent attention to religious duties both public and private, I dare not utterly condemn them . . .

Two hostile pamphlets appeared in 1801, one in English and the other in Welsh virtually amplifying the criticisms voiced in the *Gentleman's Magazine*. In them the Methodists were charged with dishonesty, immorality, conceit, and hatred of the clergy; they were labelled sectarians, schismatics, enthusiasts, fanatics and traitors. The Association asked Thomas Charles to reply, which he did in 1802 under the title *The Welsh Methodists Vindicated*, affirming their doctrinal and moral integrity, their loyalty to Church and State, and the scriptural order of their worship and practice.[5]

Between the spontaneous, militant response of Harris to his detractors and the more considered apologetic of Thomas Charles lay an extensive battleground of controversies. The Methodists not only fought unbelief and ignorance, they also had to open a 'second front' and wage warfare against prejudice, misrepresentation and libel. This 'second front' of apologetic was no less costly in terms of time and effort than their primary purpose of evangelism. The very magnitude of the opposition voiced against them demanded the attention of the Methodists.

According to Luke Tyerman, of some fifty pamphlets issued in 1739 about Methodism, principally about George Whitefield, almost all were hostile.[6] Albert M. Lyles reckoned that 'of 200 anti-Methodist publications . . . issued during 1739 and 1740, 154 were aimed at Whitefield.'[7] Another spate of critical, often scurrilous literature appeared between 1760 and 1762. Richard Green in his *Anti-Methodist Publications Issued During the Eighteenth Century*, published in 1902, listed 606 such works. With regard to the Welsh scene, Gomer M. Roberts's invaluable treatment of the subject surveys ballads and poems as well as pamphlets and books.[8] He rightly concludes that ordinary people were not deceived by the malicious propaganda of those who opposed the Methodists. 'Another literature appeared, a new dynamic which spread throughout the land in the spiritual power released through the agency of the Methodist revivalists. And it was this, in the end, which conquered.'

Even the name 'Methodist' proved to be controversial. Howel Harris was not particularly fond of it: 'About not taking the name Methodist. The name I had and do take still is 'exhorter', and the people in Wales were called 'the Society People'.'[9] In spite of his strictures the name persisted. Whitefield had recognized its significance in 1748: 'The Methodists are now as it were a skreen for others. Formerly, if a person was serious, or preached CHRIST, he was termed a Puritan, now he is a Methodist.' From Llandovery a year later he wrote in the same strain: 'blessed be God, such an honour has he put upon the Methodists, that whoever renounces the world and takes up CHRIST's cross, and believes and lives the doctrines of Grace, must be stiled a Methodist whether he will or not. Formerly it was 'You are a Puritan', now it is, 'You are a Methodist'.'[10]

At about the same time in Yorkshire William Grimshaw was answering a Sermon against the Methodists in this way:

Methodism, so call'd by Way of Reproach, is a compleat System of Gospel-Truths, and a perfect Summary of Reformation-Principles . . . It ascribes the Total of Man's Salvation, to the mere free Grace of God, the sole merits of Christ, and the Operation of the Holy Ghost. It makes Faith the Instrument, Jesus's Blood the Cause, and the Spirit the Discoverer of our Justification. It attributes our Sanctification wholly to this Heavenly Paraclete. It makes Christ the Alpha and Omega, the Author and Finisher of our Faith . . . It holds forth, not the Form merely, but the Life and Power of Godliness also.[11]

'Not the Form merely, but the Life and Power of Godliness also;' this was the keynote of Methodism, a refrain taken up by John Wesley in describing the Yorkshire societies in 1751:

I found them all alive, strong, vigorous of soul, blessing, loving and praising God their Saviour . . . From the beginning they had been taught both the law and the gospel. 'God loves you: therefore love and obey Him. Christ died for you: therefore die to sin. Christ is arisen: therefore rise in the image of God. Christ liveth evermore: therefore live to God, till you live with him in glory.' So we preached; and so you believed. This is the Scriptural way, the Methodist way, the true way. God grant we may never turn from it, to the right hand or to the left.[12]

To the Methodists religion was nothing if it was not vigorous, personal and powerful.

In 1768 when seven undergraduates were expelled from St. Edmund Hall, Oxford, it was for 'holding Methodistical tenets, and taking upon them to pray, read, and expound the Scriptures, and singing hymns in private houses,' what a contemporary periodical termed 'having too much religion.'[13] This action prompted Whitefield to write to the University's Vice-Chancellor in their defence. He offered 'the true portrait of a Methodist, drawn at full length, drawn to the very life . . . by those good old skilful scriptural limners, Cranmer, Latimer, Ridley, in the seventeenth article of our church,' adding, 'Methodism . . . is no more nor less than "Faith working by Love. A holy method of living and dying, to the glory of God" '.[14]

A similar apologetic purpose was claimed by John Davies for translating Daniel Rowland's Eight Sermons in 1774: 'as the Methodists in Wales have been represented as a set of ignorant, hot-headed Enthusiasts, the public may now form some judgment of their understanding as well as of their principles, from the writings of one, who hath presided among them for such a length of time, with unblemished reputation, and may be supposed from the nature of his connexions, to express the sentiments of the whole fraternity.' The sermons themselves showed that the Methodist mind was cast into the mould of historic, biblical Christianity: the Christianity of the Reformers and Puritans. It was a Christianity opposed to ignorance and formality, and its greatness lay in its combination of doctrinal orthodoxy with experimental devotion and goodness.

To some of their opponents, however, the Methodists were mindless: 'a weak illiterate crowd . . . bold visionary rustics'; 'illiterate mechanics, much fitter to make a pulpit than to get into one'; 'blind guides and either too proud, or too lazy to follow their lawful callings, and think it better to ramble about the country than to mend shoes, or repair old clothes at home.'[15] To others the Methodists were hypocrites, and their preaching was sheer emotionalism. 'In the early stages of Methodism,' says T. B. Shepherd, 'the references in contemporary verse were nearly all hostile, and the poets simply looked back to the Puritans of the previous century and transferred the insults hurled at them to the Methodists. The preachers were all hypocrites, probably cobblers or tailors; they spoke with a nasal twang and ranted "enthusiasm"; and their stands or pulpits were always called "tubs".' So Whitefield was caricatured in contemporary plays as an actor, a hypocrite, and in one of them he is made to say

'The Passions alone, I find fit for my trade,
The Passions are nat'ral, but morals were made.'[16]

As early as 1743 John Wesley encountered in Newcastle 'a Farce, called TRICK UPON TRICK, or METHODISM DISPLAYED', presented by the Edinburgh Company of Comedians.[17]

This insinuation, that the Methodists were not what they claimed to be, was often linked to their insistence on faith rather than works as the means of salvation. Their emphasis on the initiative of grace was regarded as an invitation to licence; their teaching on justification by faith only was misrepresented as antinomianism, a total disregard for moral standards and restraints. Hence in 1760 a play called ' The Minor', produced at the Haymarket Theatre, London, caricatured one of Whitefield's 'converts' at the Tabernacle as a procuress. She justifies her profession by quoting his sermons, claiming that it is faith and not works that matters. Other immoral activies are justified on the same ground in a novel by Richard Graves, *Spiritual Quixote*, in 1772: 'Yes, yes, faith's all; our good works are no better than "filthy rags" in the sight of God.'[18]

Justification by faith is one of the issues debated in *An Earnest and Affectionate Address to the People Called Methodists,* published by the S.P.C.K. in 1745 and translated into Welsh in 1765.[19] In reply the Methodists had only to refer to the Eleventh, Twelfth, and Thirteenth of the 39 Articles to demonstrate their doctrinal integrity. The two other issues raised in the *Address* were regeneration, and the working of the Holy Spirit. One of Whitefield's earliest sermons, that on 'The New Birth', had brought forth *A Letter* in 1739 in which the claim was made that the Church of England taught baptismal regeneration. This the Methodists vigorously denied.[20] Theophilus Evans in his *History of Modern Enthusiasm*, published in 1752, lists several Methodist doctrines which he found objectionable, including, 'The Sudden Expectation of the Millenium . . . The presumptuous Doctrine of the Assurance of Pardon . . . The gross Antinomian Doctrine . . . Their depreciating Good works, and teaching Justification by Faith alone.' These were similar to the charges brought against Whitefield in 1739 by Edmund Gibson, the Bishop of London, in his *Pastoral Letter to the People of his Diocese . . . by way of Caution, against Lukewarmness on One hand, and Enthusiasm on the other.*

Another bishop, George Lavington of Exeter, published anonymously in 1749, *The Enthusiasm of Methodists and Papists compared*. The charge of popery was a convenient stick with which to beat the Methodists, often used and widely recognised as seriously damaging to their cause. In his answer to the bishop, Whitefield claims for the teaching of the Methodists: 'These are doctrines as diametrically opposite to the Church of Rome, as light to darkness. They are the very doctrines for which Ridley, Latimer, Cranmer, and so many of our first reformers burnt at the stake.' His reply also distilled the essence of Methodism:

To awaken a drowsy world; to rouse them out of their formality as well as profaneness, and put them upon seeking after a present and great salvation; to point out to them a glorious rest, which not only remains for the people of God hereafter, but which, by a living faith, the very chief of sinners may enter into even here, and without which the most blazing profession is nothing worth—is, as far as I know, the one thing—the grand and common point, in which all the Methodists' endeavours centre. This is what some of all denominations want to be reminded of; and to stir them up to seek after the life and power of godliness, that they may be Christians, not only in word and profession, but in spirit and in truth, is, and through Jesus Christ strengthening me, shall be the one sole business of my life.[21]

The whole thrust of the Methodist movement is epitomized in the words 'awaken', 'living faith', 'in spirit and in truth'.

Such emphases, in the face of Prayer Book order within the Established Church and doctrinal orthodoxy within Nonconformity, raised the issue of ecclesiastical identity. The Methodists, with their societies, lay preachers and extra-parochial ministerial activities, claimed a kind of ecclesiastical dual-nationality: Episcopal and Methodist. The leaders often vigorously denied any hint of separation or schism, and held to that position throughout their lives, exercising their freedom within the Church of England to practise their Methodism. 'I am now, and have been from my youth a member and minister of the Church of England', says John Wesley as late as 1786, adding, 'I have no desire to separate from it till my soul separates from my body'.[22] But this attitude left the Methodists in a dilemma: where was the unity of the Church, and the visible expression of that unity? For the Welsh Methodists, these questions were not to be resolved until another century had dawned.

By far the greatest point of the controversy relating to Methodism had to do with the question of genuine Christian experience. Indeed it could be justifiably argued that the single most important contribution to the eighteenth century Awakening was to highlight this very issue. For the Methodists, as has been indicated, life, authority, and power were more important than rules, rubrics, or canons. In the eyes of the ecclesiastical authorities, however, Methodist zeal was 'enthusiasm', excess, fanaticism even, and it was dangerously schismatic. Consequently they were charged with claiming inspiration of apostolic proportions, and with being the religious charismatics of their day. By contrast, 'orthodoxy' insisted that true religion was reasonable and orderly, regulated rather than spontaneous, dignified rather than inspired.

One of the earliest opponents of Methodism, Joseph Trapp, wrote in 1739, 'By Enthusiasm is meant a Person's having a strong, but false Persuasion, that he is divinely inspired; or at least, that he has the Spirit of God some way or other; and this made known to him in a particular and extraordinary manner.' It was seen as something which 'not only tends to the confusion of society, but to undermine the foundation of all religion, and introduce, in the end, scepticism of opinion, and licentiousness of practice.'[23] From that kind of conviction it is hardly surprising that Methodism faced a storm of protest as to its understanding of genuine religious experience.

Methodist apologetic showed a scriptural emphasis at this point and made a lasting contribution to the true understanding of the subject. Jonathan Edwards blazed the trail with his classic literary contributions forged as a direct result of the Great Awakening in America and his first-hand involvement in it. Edwards recognized that realities were only truly grasped when the emotions and will were involved, as well as the mind or intellect. Nowhere was this insight more valuable than in the realm of religious experience, dealing as it does with eternal realities. These are unseen and inaccessible to the physical senses, but they are gloriously responsible to the 'spiritual sense of the heart', and only then genuinely influential on the physical faculties and moral conduct. Perry Miller's study of this aspect of Edwards's contribution to the Great Awakening speaks of 'Edwards's great discovery' as 'his assertion that an idea in the mind is not only a form of perception but is also a determination of love and hate. To apprehend things only by their signs or by words is not to apprehend them at all; but to apprehend them by their ideas is to comprehend them not only intellectually but passionately. For Edwards . . . an idea became not merely a concept but an emotion.'[24]

The fruits of this 'great discovery' included, in 1741, *The Distinguishing Marks of a Work of the Spirit of God*; in 1743, *Some Thoughts Concerning the Present Revival*; and in 1746, *The Religious Affections*. The first of these was printed in Edinburgh in 1743 and came to the notice of Howel Harris and William Williams. It gave Williams the theological confidence he needed to write his own treatises on the revival. *Golwg ar Deyrnas Crist*, published in 1756, gave expression to the Calvinism of the Welsh Methodists and provided the theological base for what followed. *Theomemphus*, in 1764, depicted the personal experience of a typical convert in the revival. *Llythyr Martha Philopur at Philo Evangelius* of 1762 together with *Ateb Philo Evangelius* of 1763 made out a convincing case for the scriptural validity of revival experiences. His crowning achievement was *Drws y Society Profiad*, published in 1777.

Both Edwards and Williams argued their positions from Scripture. The former went as far as to say:

I have mentioned but a few texts, out of an innumerable multitude, all over the Scripture, which place religion very much in the affections. But what has been observed may be sufficient to show that they who would deny that much of true religion lies in the affections, and maintain the contrary, must throw away what we have been wont to own for our Bible, and get some other rule to judge of the nature of religion.[25]

Edwards also answered those who objected to the seeming confusion which characterised the Great Awakening in a passage which Williams translated in *Ateb Philo Evangelius*:

Some say, God cannot be the author of it; because he is the God of order, not of confusion. But let it be considered what is the proper notion of confusion, but the breaking that order of things whereby they are properly disposed, and duly directed to their end, so that the order and due connection of means being broken they fail their end. Now the conviction of sinners for their conversion is the obtaining of the end of religious means . . . But if God is pleased to convince the consciences of persons, so that they cannot avoid great outward manifestations, even to interrupting and breaking off those public means they were attending, I do not think this is confusion . . . nay more than if a company should meet on the field to pray for rain, and should be broken off from their exercise by a plentiful shower . . . He who is going to fetch a treasure need not be sorry that he is stopped by meeting the treasure in the midst of his journey.[26]

For Williams, the opposition which Methodism met with was in itself a token of the authenticity of the work of God in their midst. 'Persecution is a sure inheritance for those who follow true religion,' he warns. 'And who suffer persecution in these days? those who are zealous to hear often, to sing, to pray for hours on end, to cry out that God is good . . . and for what reason is this persecution? Because they follow the Lord with all their heart.' By the same token, those who opposed the Methodists did so 'because their religion is only in their understanding, and that it had never risen in their hearts.'[27]

Methodism was Christianity restored and renewed to its apostolic purity and power. In their defence the Methodists contented themselves with scripture warrant and experimental evidence. The truth felt in the heart and obeyed in practice was the sum of their apologetic. It was also their most effective vindication.

REFERENCES

1 *Cylchgrawn Hanes y Methodistiaid Calfinaidd.* Manuscripts Supplement First Series, p.68. Henceforth shortened to CH and CHMS.
2 CHMS. i. 69,70.
3 CHMS. MS. i. 202.
4 CHMS. MS. i. 421.
5 For details of this controversy see D. E. Jenkins, *The Life of the Rev Thomas Charles B.A. of Bala*, 1908, vol.ii, pp.360,ff.
6 *The Life of the Rev George Whitefield*, 1890, vol.i. pp.283,ff.
7 *Methodism Mocked*, 1960, p.127.
8 *Hanes Methodistiaeth Galfinaidd Cymru,* cyf. 1 'Y Deffroad Mawr', 1973, tt.430,ff. This contribution is supplemented in CH v. 62,ff. 'Llenyddiaeth Wrth-Fethodistaidd a Dadleuol', and by E. G. Millward's articles 'Rhai Agweddau ar Lenyddiaeth Wrth-Fethodistaidd y Ddeunawfed Ganrif' in CH. lx. 1,ff; 52ff. G. T. Roberts's study, *Dadleuon Methodistiaeth Gynnar*, 1970, deals with issues which became matters in dispute between the various branches of Methodism.
9 Tom Beynon, *Howell Harris, Reformer and Soldier*, 1958, p.210.
10 *A Select Collection of Letters*, vol. ii, 1772, pp.212,263.
11 Frank Baker, *William Grimshaw*, 1963, pp.141,142.
12 Quoted in G. R. Cragg, *The Church and the Age of Reason 1648-1789*, (The Pelican History of the Church), 1970, p.152.
13 Geoffrey F. Nuttall, *The Significance of Trevecca College 1768-91*, 1969, pp.3,4.
14 John Gillies, *Memoirs of . . . George Whitefield,* 1811, pp.223,224 n.
15 Quoted in Richard Green, *Anti-Methodist Publications,* 1902, pp.56,100,65.

16 *Methodism in the Literature of the Eighteenth Century*, 1940, pp.235,194.

17 *The Journal of . . . John Wesley*, ed. Nehemiah Curnock, vol. iii, 1938, p.110.

18 See T. B. Shepherd, op. cit, pp.197,212,f. The title Spiritual Quixote may have been inspired by an allegation against Griffith Jones for 'putting a windmill into Whitefield's head and sending him Quioting up and down the world.' (Richard Green, op. cit .,p.60).

19 See Luke Tyerman, *The Life and Times of . . . John Wesley*, vol. 1, 1878, pp.475-6; *Hanes Methodistiaeth Galfinaidd Cymru*, cyf. 2 'Cynnydd y Corff', gol. Gomer Morgan Roberts, 1978, tt.28-29.

20 Richard Green, op. cit . p.4.

21 Luke Tyerman, *The Life of . . . George Whitefield*, vol. ii, 1890, p.221.

22 Quoted in Frank Baker, *John Wesley and the Church of England,* 1970, p.286.

23 Albert M. Lyles, op. cit . pp.33-4.

24 *Errand into the Wilderness* (Harper Torchbooks), 1956, p.179.

25 *Select Works of Jonathan Edwards*, vol. iii, 1961, p.35.

26 *Select Works of Jonathan Edwards*, vol. i, 1965, pp.126, 127.

27 *Gweithiau William Williams Pantycelyn,* cyf. ii. Gol. Garfield H. Hughes, 1967, tt.29,21.

9
DAVID JONES OF LLAN-GAN
Consolidating a Work of God

The events of July 1736 displayed in embryo some of the most prominent features of the eighteenth-century evangelical awakening. George Whitefield had been converted for nearly a year, had recently been ordained and preached his first sermon, and graduated B.A. at Oxford. He would shortly prove in London that the doctrine of the new birth and justification by faith in Jesus Christ, which he preached plainly and powerfully, 'made its way like lightning into the hearers' consciences.' His whole time, apart from preaching and necessary refreshment, would be 'wholly occupied in talking with people under religious concern'.[1]

For John Wesley it was a month of disillusionment. The full impact of its incidents were to come upon him only later: 'I went to America, to convert the Indians; but oh, who shall convert me? who, what is he that will deliver me from this evil heart of unbelief? I have a fair summer religion. I can talk well; nay, and believe myself, while no danger is near. But let death look me in the face, and my spirit is troubled.' And on July 10, 1736, he had looked death in the face, the death of a young lady who had been full of promise. In the evening of that day there had been an unparalleled storm of thunder and lightning which John Wesley felt was the voice of God which, in his own words, 'told me I was not fit to die, since I was afraid rather than desirous of it.'[2]

His brother, Charles, was just as frustrated with missionary endeavour in the New World. Temperamentally he was not fitted for the secretarial duties of his employment, physically his body could not stand the pace, and spiritually he was disqualified for those very duties to which he most aspired, being then a stranger to the saving faith of the gospel. It was no surprise, therefore, that July 1736 saw his resignation, and his departure from Savannah, never to return.

In Wales by that time both Daniel Rowland and Howel Harris, like Whitefield, had been converted for a year. By the end of July

Harris had both sought ordination from the Bishop of St. David's and been refused it, on the ground of his activities in lay evangelism within his own parish and beyond it. Before the end of the year, in spite of the Bishop's prejudice and censure, he was to preach in the open air, and group the young converts into 'societies' where they would find fellowship, encouragement and edification.

It was in this same month, on the tenth to be exact, that David Jones was born. He was to be in Glamorganshire what Rowland was in Cardiganshire and Howel Davies in Pembrokeshire, a key figure in the growing Methodist ranks, with his own parish church of Llan-gan the centre of tremendous spiritual activity. David Jones's father was a farmer at Aberceiliog, in the parish of Llanllwni, on the Carmarthenshire-Cardiganshire border. His grandfather on his mother's side had been vicar of Llandysul, and it is interesting to note that David Jones had Jewish blood in him, the vicar's wife being a rich Jewish lady.

Educated at Carmarthen Grammar School, he was ordained deacon in 1758 and priest in 1760 by the Bishop of St David's. He served several curacies before his settlement at Llan-gan, near Bridgend, in Glamorganshire: in North Wales, Breconshire, Monmouthshire, near Bristol, and in Wiltshire. In this way God was preparing him for the extensive travel he would undertake in later years, preaching the gospel of Christ. It was only when he removed to Trefethin and Caldicott, Monmouthshire, in 1761, that he came face to face with the doctrines of grace, and proved for himself the power of God in the gospel. The instrument of his conversion was the reading of John Flavell's works, loaned or given to him by a godly Methodist doctor, William Read, a close friend of William Williams, Pantycelyn. David Jones's life and ministry were transformed, and on his removal to a curacy near Bristol, and subsequently to Crudwell, Wiltshire, he came to the notice of the Countess of Huntingdon. It was through her influence that he was presented to the living at Llan-gan by the patroness of the parish, Lady Charlotte Edwin, and duly instituted on April 16, 1767.

It was inevitable that the new vicar should soon give evidence of 'Methodist' tendencies. He had derived a great deal of benefit from their fellowship at Trefethin, and his contact with the Countess had firmly established in his mind the necessity for an uncompromising stand with regard to the preaching of Christ crucified. In any case, it is important to note that organised Methodism of the Wesleyan variety was at that time unrecognisable in South Wales, and evangelical clergymen unaligned with the Calvinistic Methodists were few in number and limited in influence. Things like extempore preaching, preaching itineraries, open-air preaching, which the bishops cavilled at, were the very marrow of the evangelical clergy's ministries, and David Jones was no exception.

The quality of his personal faith, the biblical emphasis of his preaching, and the vigour of his evangelical activities clearly marked his affinities with men like Rowland, Harris and Williams. Sufficient evidence of this is to be found in the Deeds of a chapel built for him at a nearby village called Pen-coed in 1775, as a meeting place for the Methodists of the area. According to those Deeds, the Trustees 'shall permit and suffer [the Chapel] for the use of the said Protestants called Methodists and wherein such Teachers or Ministers only are to be admitted as shall preach and embrace the Doctrine of Salvation contained in the 9, 10, 11, 12, 13, 15, 17 and 18 Articles of the Church of England.'[3] These declare unequivocally the doctrines of original sin, the bondage of the will, justification by faith only; the place of good works, and of works before justification; Christ's atonement for sin; predestination and election, and that eternal salvation is to be obtained only by the Name of Christ. This was evidently considered to be a sufficient confession of faith for the regulation of the Methodist society, its members and leaders alike. It was also, by the same token, a summary of David Jones's personal beliefs.

In one of his last letters he says, 'I am now endeavouring to reduce all my religion to one point—Christ is ALL, and in all my salvation . . . Confidence in Jesus is the marrow of faith. We can never trust Him too much. He is able to save to the uttermost, and will not disappoint us.'[4] While Christ's sufficiency gave him a confident faith, Christ's love gave him the deepest joy in his heart and the strongest motive in his ministry:

I hope you are all happy in the love and fulness of Jesus—and there you cannot be poor. Could we but live upon Him, then the important matter is settled. But my legality is my bane. Sometimes I think I am safe because I love Him, then I am surrounded with an army more numerous than the French, and I know not what to do: but when I can tell them He loves me, then they will vanish. O sweet Saviour, Thou art far more precious to me than all the treasures of Snowdon, and than all the Snowdons in the world. In Thee is my life and my all.'[5]

It was this personal, living faith in Christ together with an almost overpowering sense of His love which constrained David Jones to 'fulfil his ministry' in the face of staggering difficulties and trials. For all that, indeed because of it, he gloried in the cross of Christ and in the tribulations which arose because of it: 'Well may I, of all men, say, "It is of the Lord's goodness that I am not consumed." Tribulations are my lot; and I find they do me good. I am too much wedded to this world, and it is a great work of divine grace to wean me from its allurements.'[6]

Reference to the chapel at Pen-coed requires a little explanation. The Methodist policy with regard to the Established Church was one of accommodation and reformation. It was a supplementary and complementary task which the 'societies' performed, supplying a serious, but not in the Methodist view disqualifying, deficiency in the Church and in far too many of its clergy. Furthermore, Methodist societies were not Anglican societies, even though essentially orientated to the Anglican framework of Church order, ministry, and sacrament. Consequently many of the Dissenters enjoyed fellowship within the Methodist societies. For a sound ministry of the Word, and a disciplined administration of the Sacraments, the societies were dependent on the availability of Methodist clergymen and consecrated buildings.

During the early years of the awakening extensive use was made in Wales of 'chapels of ease', buildings belonging to the Established Church which, because of an isolated position or sheer neglect, were sometimes dilapidated in condition, but generally available for use by those duly ordained. The gradual provision of separate buildings explicitly for the use of the Methodists could never be more than a stop-gap, and the more serious issues of separation from the Established Church were raised in several quarters from as early as the 1740s. In any case their legal position was hard to define while they remained neither consecrated buildings of the Established Church nor yet independent of it as were the Dissenting Meeting Houses. In practice, however, they were referred to as 'Tŷ Cwrdd' or Meeting House, placing them in the eyes of the public on the same footing, if not for exactly the same purpose, as those of the Dissenters.

So far as the exposition of Scripture was concerned the societies were provided for by laymen showing aptitude in 'rightly dividing the word of truth', called 'exhorters'. Even though many of these were qualified by spiritual experience and ministerial gifts, increasingly as time went on they were being refused ordination through prejudice against their Methodism. By 1745 several of them were constrained to address the Welsh Methodist leaders on this issue, pressing the clergymen to take the decisive step of ordaining them, not merely on the considerations of expediency, but in the light of Scripture precedent (quoting in particular Acts 6:6):

We are of the opinion that you are too much attached to the Established Church. We think that if you received ordination in the Church of England, as also you expect, that would not suffice to set at rest numerous brethren and sisters in the country; because what they require is a number of men to minister the Word and ordinances to them regularly; to undertake their oversight as shepherds over flocks; or remain as we are, and to this we cannot think of consenting. We have placed our case in God's hand, hoping that, if you fail in compassion for us, God will open for us a way to a better order ... [then follows Acts 6:6]. Therefore we pray you to do what they did; by so doing, you cannot offend any man who takes God's Word as the guiding rule of his life; then we may expect the same effects, increasing our number, and strengthening such as are already called.

This request was not granted, Howel Harris being especially allergic to any talk of separation, while the clergymen (in spite of repeated rebuff and spasmodic persecution on the part of the bishops) likewise fought shy of becoming a distinct party outside Anglicanism. It is no surprise, therefore, that when the matter was discussed by the leaders at their 'Association', Howel Harris was adamant and inflexible:

In discoursing with the brethren I declared I differed with them in three things. (1) That I never looked on the Societies as Churches, but little branches of a Church. (2) The exhorters never as ministers to dispense ordinances, nor, many of them, even the Word, by way of preaching, but by way of exhorting. (3) On us never as a sect, but a people in the Church, called to reform till either we should be heard, or turned out; and that whoever is called to labour as a reformer must have strong love to bear much.[7]

His distinction between preaching (the activity usually associated with the word, exercised by ordained men) and exhorting (the term he used for a similar task performed by laymen), while useful as a diplomatic measure to avoid technical difficulties over his own early lay activity, [he had written in 1736, 'calling my work exhorting, not preaching, was a means of blinding the eyes of my opposers'8] had become so rigid in his mind as to pass from the realm of expediency to that of validity.

Furthermore, the recognition that discipline on the basis of Scripture truth was only possible in the context of a spiritual fellowship of the regenerate was not forthcoming while Harris looked on the episcopal system (or any other) with uncritical eyes. Neither he nor his contemporary Methodist clergymen had a doctrine of the Church developed solely along scriptural lines. They accepted without reservation the status quo of the Establishment. Their peculiarly Methodist organisation was conceived for spiritual ends, certainly, but on purely pragmatic considerations. Chapels such as Salem Pencoed, then, gave them a pulpit over which no bishop had any control whatsoever. It also provided them with a meeting house where they could exercise their own discipline—and David Jones regularly met the society for this purpose on a Saturday afternoon—a work which they saw to be necessary but impossible within the framework of Anglicanism.

In a reference to David Jones, William Williams of Pantycelyn speaks of him as a true and tender evangelist, one whose warm compassion moved the stiff-necked and indifferent alike. Another of his fellow-workers, Christopher Bassett (who had been a curate to William Romaine at Blackfriars) gave this testimony of him: 'I consider his style of preaching as "peculiarly" evangelical. I have never seen one who appeared in the pulpit imbued to such a degree with the spirit of the gospel. His ministry seemed to me singularly adapted to conciliate enemies to the truth, to strengthen the weak, and to decide the wavering. He was well skilled in administering the "Balm of Gilead" to the wounded conscience.' A contemporary witness described the scene at Llan-gan church in this way: 'The church was so crowded that to find a vacant seat was out of the question . . . I see him now . . . in his gown, with his fine commanding countenance, and drops of perspiration, and sometimes the trickling tear, running down his face, commending most earnestly Jesus Christ to the chief of sinners, but telling them at the same time to go and sin no more. And with what reverence did he speak of the love and sufferings of Christ; and how sublime was his language! Oh, how dignified and noble was his countenance when bathed in tears, as was often the case with him in the pulpit.'[9]

His preaching was both powerful and melting, having what could only be called the unction of the Holy Spirit in it, and as a result the effects were truly spiritual and lasting. One who experienced those powerful influences could not easily forget them:

> I well remember the precise spot on which I stood when such a thorough sense of my sinful, depraved, and lost state filled my soul, under his ministry, that I trembled in intense agony, lest the paving on which I stood should sink under the weight of my innumerable sins, and consign me to the bottomless pit, as unworthy of a place on earth. In this (terrified) state I looked wildly around, and happened to observe that a man of whose piety I had the best opinion, was standing on the same flag as myself, which induced a hope in my despairing mind that I might thus be spared for his sake.[10]

Powerful influences of this kind continued unabated at Llan-gan for more than forty years, at times being intensified, so that it was said that during his ministry five revivals broke out at Llan-gan, the first in 1773 and the last in 1805. In 1790, for example, he could report: 'There is a greater call for the gospel sound in this neighbourhood than I have known since I came to this part of the world. It is a blessed sowing time, and I verily believe there will be a glorious harvest of souls to the eternal glory of our dear Lord, when He appears to bring home His redeemed ones.'[11]

The year 1799 may well have been another of those seasons of refreshing from the presence of the Lord, for he could write: 'We had a shower of divine blessing within the last eight months . . . God has discovered the wonders of His grace to multitudes of our poor fellow-creatures, particularly to young persons about fifteen years of age.'[12]

Scenes similar to these had been witnessed at Llangeitho where Daniel Rowland ministered for over fifty years until his death in 1790. The crowds flocking in from all parts of the Principality to a communion Sunday at Llangeitho in Rowland's time would have been numbered in tens of thousands. What Llangeitho was to the Methodists in mid and North Wales, Llan-gan must have been for the South, especially Glamorganshire and Monmouthshire. There was no 'problem of communication' when the Spirit worked so mightily, and the eternal blessings received through the preaching of

God's Word were publicity enough to attract men in such a way that no obstacle of distance or inclemency of weather could daunt their determination to attend the ministry of these men of God:

The travellers increased all the way as we went until we arrived at Llan-gan, about eleven miles distant; and many coming from a greater distance overtook us on the road. Such was our desire for spiritual food, that we could not be prevented by any weather, however severe. I well remember that the roads were so slippery in the winter on account of the ice, that it was dangerous to go on horseback, and consequently we were frequently obliged to dismount and walk.[13]

That souls were satisfied under his ministry is no wonder since, according to William Williams, Christ the Bread of Life was so eminently set forth, 'Christ the text, and Christ the sermon; Christ the end of the law, and Christ the object of faith.'

A sermon in cold print can hardly do justice to the 'unction' of the preaching, but it does help to give an impression of the emphases of the preacher. Something of the pathos of David Jones's preaching comes through in the sermon he delivered at the funeral of the Countess of Huntingdon in 1791 on Genesis 50:24:

You will say, we have a great mother in Israel; but the God of Israel lives. If He take away a Moses, He will give a Joshua; there is no loss at the hands of our God . . . Indeed, were we to judge according to human wisdom, that was the greatest loss that ever happened under the sun, when the presence of God in the flesh upon earth was taken away. But was it so? He says, It is expedient for you that I go away. If so, all is for the best: for now God, by His Spirit, comes among His people. Let us always remember this truth, that God's Spirit will exalt Jesus Christ more in the Church than any instrument whatever; and this the blessed Spirit will do when priests and prophets are no more.[14]

Under the title 'Great Effects from Feeble Means', he preached on Judges 7:2 before the London Missionary Society in 1796. Having in mind the great missionary task that lay ahead and the limited resources of the Society, he encouraged them to 'have faith in God':

The Lord will take care of His own glory. God is sometimes ready to complain of too much help, but never of too little . . . That ardour, and zeal, which at present seem to engage your hearts in the work, can hardly be sufficiently admired, yet it is a patient looking up to God, and waiting in the dust for His blessing, that must crown the work . . . you must have faith for the work. We ought not to be too much elevated by human probabilities; and, as Christians, we ought not to be dismayed at improbabilities. It is the work of faith to overcome all these as we go on . . . There is never any danger in trusting God, with weak and improbable means. Here the danger lies, in the bias of the human heart to look more to great means than to the great God . . . I must allow that at times the eye of faith hath its motes in the best of saints, and these intercept the light of the sun . . . We read of a large mote in the eye of Elijah's faith—that wicked Jezebel, the fear of whom caused him to fly for his life . . . Faith, when the eye is clear, will do wonders.[15]

Finally, extracts from two sermons which are preserved in manuscript, the one on 1 Peter 2:7 in English speaks of Christ's excellence, and the other, in Welsh, on Luke 14:22 deals with the gratuitous nature of the gospel offer. Here are the chief points of the former:

Christ is precious: 1. In Himself, in the glory of His Person . . . in the glory of His qualification and endowments, and in the worth of His sufferings. 2. He is precious in the account of the Father. 3. In the esteem of angels. 4. In the esteem of the saints . . . Let us try whether Christ be precious to us? 1. Are you willing to part with everything you have that you may enjoy Christ? 2. What desire have you of fellowship with Christ? He who esteems Christ precious indeed thinks he hath never enough of Christ. 3. Is everything of Christ precious to you? His holy life, promises, precepts, His death? 4. What opinion have you of those who follow Christ? Whatever hath reference to Christ let it be precious to us—precious faith, precious ordinances, precious blood, precious grace, precious glory.[16]

The latter sermon is an exposition of the parable of the great Supper:

I. Where is there room? 1. There is yet room in God's mercy. 2. In Christ's merit for all who return to the Lord. 3. There is room by virtue of the power and efficacy of the Holy Spirit. 4. In the Covenant of grace, the gift of pardon and life through Christ to every one that repents and believes. 5. In the household of faith, that is, in God's church for sinners to come and be saved. II. For whom is there room? For the chief of sinners and the most indifferent in the world—the poor, maimed, halt, blind, the afflicted. To those who have long opposed, neglected, and despised the invitation sent to them, if they but come now. Behold now is the accepted time . . . There is room for those who have backslidden and have fallen shamefully . . . for the chief of sinners. There is yet room in the kingdom of grace and glory. But remember, there is room in the grave and in hell as well, and how many have descended to them while they put off their repentance and neglected their salvation. Be wise in time, and strive to enter the narrow gate, lest you should come at the last bitterly weeping after the door is closed.[17]

Both in manner and matter David Jones's preaching showed how indebted he was to the Puritans, and this was equally true of the other Welsh Methodists of his day. From Daniel Rowland's sermons, Howel Harris's reading matter, Williams Pantycelyn's hymns and poems, to Thomas Charles's 'Scripture Dictionary' and John Elias's contribution to the Calvinistic Methodist Confession of Faith, it is quite evident that their theology owed much to such men as Sibbes, Charnock, Owen, Goodwin and Manton. In this respect David Jones was a typical Welsh Methodist.

Apart from the two sermons noted above, David Jones also published a brief biography of Christopher Bassett on his death in 1784, and printed at Trefeca. Two years previously the Welsh Methodists had urged Jones and Daniel Rowland's son, Nathaniel, to seek the printing of a 'small pocket Bible', but nothing came of it. Nevertheless he was a supporter of the Bible Society, requesting in 1807 a supply of Welsh Testaments, and by October three hundred and seventy-five had been sent to him. He was also one of the London Missionary Society directors in 1797, 1799 and 1800.[18] It was as a preacher of the gospel, however, that he excelled, and the lasting monument of David Jones's ministry was to be found at Llan-gan.

It was axiomatic for Jones, as for the other Methodists, that preaching the gospel could not be confined to one parish. So it was that he was 'in journeyings oft' for his Master, facing not only the hazards of the weather, but also persecution, danger, and most threatening of all, the displeasure of his bishop. His travels took him from Monmouthshire to Anglesey, from Bristol to London. In the metropolis he often used to supply the Countess of Huntingdon's Chapel at Spa Fields for periods of several weeks, when many thousands would crowd to hear the Word of God. During these intervals away from Llan-gan his pulpit would be supplied by other Methodist clergymen. In addition to Llan-gan, Jones preached in nearby Coity, where a Methodist sympathiser, Thomas Davies, had obtained a living by the same means as himself. In fact, David Jones and Thomas Davies supplied each other's pulpits in this way whenever occasion arose and in spite of the bishop's interference.[19]

From the time of his installation at Llan-gan to the year of his death the calls for his ministry were numerous and pressing, witness the following letters. 'I have had a long journey in the North. I was out no less than six weeks. I met with many rough storms, but, blessed be our dear Lord and Master, I had some very bright and shining days indeed.' That was in 1778; by 1800 he was itinerating for most of the summer months from May to November: 'I hope to meet my brethren there [the Trecastle, Breconshire Association], and to go from thence through Cardiganshire and Pembrokeshire, and then back to this country by the end of June; and if I can, I will . . . pay you a short visit in Monmouthshire . . . early in June I shall . . . set out on my North Wales round, and go as far as Chester, Liverpool, and Anglesea, before my return. And if I am able, I shall go to London for the month of October and November.' There was still no sparing of his energies in 1804, even though he was beyond 'retiring age'; 'I cannot tell you how I am hurried from place to place . . . I am very seldom two days together at home'; and the pace was by no means retarded in 1810. When he had but a few months to live, he wrote, 'I am still hurried from place to place.'[20]

Although he had no financial difficulties, there were many trials in his home, his two sons particularly causing him much concern. That which grieved him more than all else, however, was the sight of sinners rejecting the gospel of God's grace. The sense of sorrow and pain he experienced over such is evident in a letter written in his last year:

In the latter end of last year, the Lord enabled me to travel many hundred miles, in endeavouring to exhibit my blessed Master's matchless treasures of love to the best advantage that I could. And although I told poor mortals that these vast treasures were all freely bestowed, yet after all my toil and labour, there were very few indeed that would stop and receive them. Many would come and offer some dunghill rags for pearls of more value than all the mines of India. But some poor, ruined, guilty creatures here and there in my round, would draw near and cry 'Oh the depth of infinite love! that I who have deserved nothing but Hell should be so freely and so fully enriched with such treasures.' . . . Had there been a penny to pay, such poor creatures added, we could have no hopes, for we are nothing but poverty itself . . . .[21]

Even as Christ's righteousness was the central theme of his preaching, so it was the rock on which his hope was founded, and his supreme comfort in the face of death. Two days before he died he recorded in his diary, 'Had a sweet promise this morning, that Jesus will be my righteousness.'[22] With this note of lively hope his life ended on August 12, 1810, almost exactly a year before the Welsh Calvinistic Methodists became a separated body by ordaining men for the first time into the ministry of the gospel.

REFERENCES

1   *George Whitefield's Journals*, 1960, p.81
2   *The Journal of the Rev John Wesley*, Standard Edition, 1938, vol.i, pp.418,246
3   *Journal of the Historical Society of the Presbyterian Church of Wales*, vol.xl, pp.42-3 [abbreviated to *Journal*]
4   E. Morgan, *A Brief Account . . . of . . . D Jones*, 2nd edn, 1864, p.92 [abbreviated to *Morgan*]
5   *Journal* xl. 38-9
6   *Morgan* 43-4
7   D. E. Jenkins, *Calvinistic Methodist Holy Orders*, 1911, pp.104-05,114-15
8   Richard Bennett, *The Early Life of Howel Harris*, 1962, p.83
9   *Morgan* 60,57
10 *Morgan* 83
11 National Library of Wales, MS 893 C
12 *Morgan* 87
13 *Journal* xx. 99
14 [A. C. H. Seymour] *The Life and Times of Selina, Countess of Huntingdon*, 1844, vol.ii, 504-5
15 *Morgan* 105, 106
16 National Library of Wales, Calvinistic Methodist Archives, MS 12760
17 Cardiff Public Library, MS 1.127
18 D. E. Jenkins, *The Life of the Rev Thomas Charles of Bala*, 1908, vol.iii, pp.83,92; vol.ii, pp.186,196
19 *Journal* xlvi.3, 39,41
20 *Morgan* 15, 16, 24, 92
21 National Library of Wales MS 1093A
22 *Journal* xxxiii. 52

10

THE BIBLE AND
THE GREAT AWAKENING

In every genuine revival of religion the Bible has a prominent and crucial place. As a result of revival, whether individual or general, people often say that for them the Bible is a new book. It has 'come alive' in such a way that the study of the Bible becomes a passion, and not just a pastime. Bible sales soar, Bible conferences multiply, and the demand for biblical exposition in preaching or through books is well nigh insatiable.

Nor is this heightened interest merely academic or 'historical', as though the subject matter was a purely cultural or antiquarian exercise. The Bible is now sought and studied for its teaching on what is true and false, as well as for its guidance on what is good and bad. Since all things come within the scope of its pages, it is consulted with commitment as well as application, and its precepts for this world and the next are deemed both solemn and binding.

Consequently, an evaluation of the way in which the Bible is seen and used during revival may serve as an index of its true value. Given that times of revival are times of great spiritual earnestness as well as activity, we may well feel that revival insights and practice with regard to the Bible are a measure of its character and worth for Christians at all times. For this reason, we shall explore the views of leading Calvinistic Methodists in the period of the Great Awakening's creative years in Wales.

A letter published some years ago in a leading Welsh newspaper, *The Western Mail*, provides a convenient starting point. The letter claims that Daniel Rowland, the curate at Llangeitho, discovered a copy of the 1588 edition of the Welsh Bible in the church's old chest. It was in a bad state of repair, and much of the book of Genesis was missing. It was said that Rowland wrote out the missing passages, and stitched the new pages on to the old Bible.[1] The anecdote portrays Rowland as a man of diligence, with a deep respect for the Scriptures.

Later in his life, a copy of another edition of the Bible, that of 1621, came into his possession, and beside his signature it bears the date '1754' on the title-page of the New Testament.[2] Rowland's high estimate of these Bibles certainly did not stem from a historical or antiquarian interest. He was a man of strong convictions, and among them he believed the Bible to be the Word of God.

Proof of this is the fact that early on in his ministry, in 1739, Rowland had translated and published a sermon by one of the Puritans bearing the title 'Spiritual Milk'. The text was 1 Peter 2:2, and the purpose was to exhort Welsh people to thirst for this 'Spiritual Milk', the Word of God. In his preface he addresses his readers in this way:

Some go as far as to make of Holy Scripture a kind of Fairy-tale, and others use all the ingenuity at their disposal to discredit and resist God's truth. But their folly is as great as it would be if they should try to devise a means of darkening the sun so that it no longer shone; for Almighty God so preserves His Word of truth, that not all the powers of darkness (neither evil men nor devils) can purpose to destroy it, but they shall know that heaven and earth shall pass away before God's Word will fail.

With this conviction in mind, Rowland proceeds:

Therefore let every Christian, that earnestly seeks to fulfil the purpose of his existence by glorifying God and saving his soul, embrace and follow God's Word and Law. This is the sincere, precious light by which we are to be guided through the darkness and ignorance of this present state and world. Know . . . that life, assurance, and comfort are to be had from God in Christ through the Word of Truth.

His appeal to the readers closes with 'The Testimony of the Godly with regard to these things',

where they claim that God's Word quickens the soul; that it is sweeter to them than honey, more precious than gold, more desirable than necessary food . . . Let not the foolishness of wicked men, nor your cares, nor your own worldly pleasures, ever cause you to devalue God's Word, which is the food of the soul.[3]

We shall see shortly that this conviction was shared by all the leaders of the Great Awakening in Wales.

But how could anyone obtain a copy of the Bible in Welsh in the eighteenth century? It is true that the philanthropic activity of the half-century to 1730 had secured 40,000 copies of the Welsh Bible.[4]

However, the question must be asked, was this fact sufficient to motivate people to read and believe the Bible, and to ensure its application to everyday life? Hardly, since such a response presupposes an inner, spiritual transformation. And to realise this in personal experience required anointed preaching and an accompanying ministry of the Holy Spirit.

By the time of George Whitefield's first visit to Wales in 1739, that creative, spiritual awakening had begun. It is not surprising, therefore, that one of Whitefield's companions on the memorable journey, William Seward, felt keenly the scarcity and high cost of Welsh Bibles. ''Tis thought the greatest service to be done for Wales is to have an edition printed', he says in a letter to his friend in London, the printer James Hutton. With typical generosity, Seward was prepared to finance such a venture, while Howel Harris and his fellow-workers were to enlist subscribers.[5]

A thirst for God's Word was a direct consequence of the Great Awakening. This accounts for the increasing demand for Bibles: for 15,000 in 1743, for 20,000 in 1769, for example, but all of them printed outside Wales. Between these two dates, in 1749, Thomas Broughton, the secretary for the agency responsible (the Society for Promoting Christian Knowledge) testified to the 'extraordinary and universal demand' for Welsh Bibles.[6] By 1770 the work of publishing Peter Williams's 'Great Bible' was complete, the first Bible to be printed in Wales.[7] Its appearance, if controversial on doctrinal grounds, at least demonstrated a staggering demand for Bibles.

In a letter of 1787 Thomas Charles of Bala complained of the scarcity of cheap Welsh Bibles, even though a second edition of Peter Williams's Bible had appeared by that date.[8] From that time, procuring Bibles for his poor countrymen remained for Charles a clear vision and a vigorous crusade. Dr R. Tudur Jones summarises his contribution in this way: 'When we consider the public ministry of Thomas Charles, it is immediately apparent that his varied projects centre around the Bible. He belonged to a generation of religious leaders who shared with him the same ideals, and between them they were responsible for weaving the Bible in a new way to the life and culture of the Welsh people . . . More than anything else he desired that the Welsh way of life should be rooted in Scripture.'[9]

What, then, were those ideals which the Great Awakening's leaders shared in common? How did the Bible come to have such a deep influence on the life of Wales, an influence that persisted for at least another century? In reply to these questions our discussion can be conveniently arranged around the convictions they held regarding the Bible as revelation, message and promise.

We begin with the idea of the Bible as God's revelation. At the outset of Howel Harris's spiritual pilgrimage, he decided to read three chapters of the Bible every day, preceded and followed by prayer. In 1739 he felt great love for the Bible as God's Word, and 'hugged it' in his arms. He looked on it as the soul's beneficiary: 'O when shall I be fishing in this pond, and sailing in this sea, and trading in this market.'[10] On another occasion he sets out his convictions more fully:

The glory of the sun is nothing compared to this precious treasure. This alone is God's mouth, and this alone bears God's image drawn by Himself. It is a book which He has made a standard, touchstone, and rule by which even His own works are measured; by which the church's life, its teachings, ministry, and discipline—all faith, love, truth, and obedience—are tested . . . This is the seed by which the church and her faith are begotten, and in it she is purified and nourished; this is the Christian's armour; herein is the incomparable light of the world . . . Without it there is no faith or salvation. By the Word we know what cannot be known by any other means or way, and that with the fullest assurance, with regard to God and ourselves, to this life and the one to come. Apart from the Word all is uncertain, and thick darkness. The Word alone speaks infallibly, and demands unshakeable faith to believe it . . . Without the Word we are without hope, without knowledge of our misery or our salvation.[11]

In the context of eighteenth-century religion, Harris's statement has particular significance. When he says 'By the Word we know what cannot be known by any other means or way', and 'Apart from the Word all is uncertain and thick darkness', he comes into direct conflict with the fashionable Deism of his day. For the Deists, man's reason defined what was true or false in both spiritual and secular realms, and their influence was all-pervasive.

William Williams brings the issue into focus when dealing with the relationship between reason and the gospel:

What good Apologetics, to buttress Gospel grace,
To rout the Deists' reasoning, and cause them to lose face?
Their genius lies in reasoning, by this they conquer all,
And with that selfsame weapon, the Gospel will but fall.

Heaven is the source of power, authority, and might,
By which the Gospel breaches the dragon's castles quite;
Along with Christ's atonement, the victory He wrought,
No need to borrow reasons, the fruit of human thought.[12]

The truth of the matter is that the natural man is most reluctant to admit that his intellectual and moral capability is shrouded by a fog of sin. And to dispel that fog requires nothing less than the sun of divine revelation and the powerful winds of the Holy Spirit. Herein lies Williams' thrust in another place:[13]

Since man with guilt is loaded,
  He no way can find out
With only earthly wisdom,
  What saving grace's about;
Except the Great Creator
  Revealed His grace with light,
It would, both now and ever,
  Be hidden from his sight.

And so, henceforth, I'm singing
  Of a far clearer art,
Which sets forth the compassion
  That lies within His heart.
Towards poor, guilty sinners,
  Who've wholly lost their way,
And by the light of nature
  Can only go astray.

Within the Holy Scripture
  Shine truths that hitherto,
Unfathomed were by angels,
  Not even by a few;
Great mysteries now appear,
  Revealed by grace sublime,
The theme of songs and praises
  Beyond all age and time.

How greater is the privilege
  By heavenly grace bestowed
Upon each true believer,

> Than Adam was endowed;
> The Holy Bible's fuller
>   Of heaven's pure light,
> Than all the light of nature
>   Which gave to Adam sight.

With this belief, that the Bible was God's revealed Word, and was therefore an objective and decisive truth, the Methodists overcame many difficulties.

For one thing, there was no need any more to choose between natural reason and no reason at all. In the eighteenth century the Methodists were accused of being unreasonable, because they accepted literally the supernatural and other-worldly in Scripture. But for them there was a reason other than natural reason, namely Christian reason, the reason which thinks of everything in line with, and subject to, God's revelation. The intellectual framework of the Great Awakening was thoroughly biblical, and to it the believer's intellect conformed and intertwined with harmony. The believer, then, has a Christian mind, founded on revealed truth, of relevance to a temporal world in its every aspect, and yet stretching effectively and without mutation to the very bowels of eternity. Herein lies the Bible's excellence: it sets everything in complete perspective and unites all knowledge and experience.

As a result, the dichotomy between 'sacred' and 'secular' is unnecessary. This explains the vast range of Williams Pantycelyn's literary output. He can be as much at home discussing the planets of the universe, as he is in an experience meeting probing the subtleties of corruption in the hearts of the saints, or giving advice on marriage to young Christians:

> I study all of nature, above, below, around;
> The sky, the earth, the oceans, whatever in them's found;
> And scan the moons of Saturn, with interest and joy,
> So long as for this knowledge God's grace can find employ.

So it follows:

> I praise all feats of knowledge, each one's the gift of heaven,
> All biblical translation by this fair means is given;
> And O! that every Welshman, before his hair goes grey
> Might search each tree of knowledge, in such a godly way.[14]

Here, then, is a healthy union of knowledge and gifts, woven together in proving God's Word in personal experience and behaviour. The Bible's supernatural origin and comprehensive scope were twin pillars in the mind-set of the Great Awakening's subjects.

Another aspect which followed acceptance of the Bible as divine revelation was the safeguarding of standards and balance in religion. We are now in the realm of biblical authority. The man, more than any other, who consistently sought to apply biblical authority in the midst of the Great Awakening's fervour, was Griffith Jones, Llanddowror. 'The Holy Bible', he said in 1737, 'has the Holy Ghost for its author, infallible truth for its subject-matter, and eternal life for its end.' It followed that reading, hearing, searching the Scriptures were an unavoidable obligation to any who desired to be saved. God is 'their author', he claimed, 'since they were all given by His inspiration; they are the infallible Rule which came from the mouth of the Most High Himself'. Furthermore, 'the grand purpose for which the Scriptures were given to us', is 'to teach us the way to heaven, and to make us wise to salvation; that we may know God's will, and what is good, and acceptable, and perfect in His sight'. To crown everything, God's Word 'is the perfect yardstick by which all doctrine is to be measured'.[15]

Griffith Jones had to remind the Welsh Methodists of the Bible's authority on more than one occasion. Here ar two examples, recorded in Howel Harris's Diary:

10 May 1741. Heard Mr Jones preaching on the disciples calling fire from heaven. He shewed the spirit of error, 1. When we lean on our experiences before the Word. 2. On our own understanding to read and apply the Word above the judgment of others. 3. When we set up little things or even greater truths further than they affect us.

13 October 1745. He was offended with the screaming and crying out under the Word. I said that I heard Mr Rowland reproving [those] as cried [out of] themselves, but that many I believe could not help it, and that I had rather see them cry than gape . . . He said we were charged as going to Quakerism and all errors, and to leave the Bible and to follow our experiences. I said that was not true, but what is the Bible but a dead letter to us till we do experience the work of the Spirit in us, not one or the other separately, but both together.[16]

This was timely reproof on the part of the seasoned campaigner of Llanddowror, one that touched the most sensitive nerve of the

Methodists. Yet it was of the utmost importance in safeguarding the Great Awakening from any strange fire that threatened to engulf it.

On a more positive note, the Welsh Methodists did not always fail to give biblical authority its rightful place. Take, for example, Martha Philopur, one of Williams Pantycelyn's most ardent imaginary converts. Where did she look for peace of mind regarding the validity of her spiritual experiences? 'I searched the Holy Scripture', she says, 'and I was reassured.'[17] In reply, her teacher emphasises that 'everything under the sun is mixed . . . The feelings and passions of true believers co-mingle with the pure enjoyment of God's Spirit. Natural love often insists on claiming its place in that heart where God's love has been kindled.' Even so, her teacher admits that 'the Scriptures, as you observe, are clear enough in confirming that this late work is of God.'[18]

The experience or society meetings were measured by the same yardstick. If finding 'a foundation in God's Word' had not been the easiest of tasks, Williams would not have acknowledged or nurtured them by writing *Drws y Society Profiad* (The Door to the Experience Society or Meeting). He refers to the Bible as a 'brilliant sun', 'which turns night into day', and 'the charter which safeguards all the principles of faith'. this is 'the point and compass' which unerringly shows the way; in it are found the 'most precious promises of all time', and 'statutes', 'the sweetest wine', and 'heavenly manna'. For such reasons, Williams can sing of the Bible as,

> The full and precious parchment where safely lies impressed
> The plan of God's salvation, before the world was blessed.'[19]

Again, where did Williams find the metaphors and imagery for his hymns, unless they were drawn from the Bible? His characters have a scriptural feel about them, whether it is Theomemphus, Avaritius, Fidelius, or Orthocephalus. Some of them may possibly have been drawn before in the homespun materials of John Bunyan, but what does it matter? The original pattern for their outline and form was in the Bible; now they bear the characteristic imprint of a Methodist ethos, an ethos which Williams himself partakes of, as well as his readers.

What, then, of biblical interpretation? In Williams's *Pantheologia*, we find Eusebius confessing his handicap in this important discipline without the learning and counsel of his teacher, Apodemus.

After all, the histories, shadows, customs, and culture of the various biblical periods are foreign to him. But Apodemus reminds him of God's activity to help him:

> An expert in all the arts, a good historian, familiarity with all the customs and principles of the religions of mankind: in and of themselves, none of these achievements will be of much help to open the Scriptures or to edify others. It is the Spirit of God alone, not anything else, opens His Word, and applies it to the heart . . . However, every means put at the disposal of that glorious Spirit is glorious. Just as the proper stewardship of wealth brings its owner to the kingdom of heaven, so also learning, when sanctified by the Word of God and prayer, is a means of throwing light on the Word, and makes the humble man more useful to God's people.[20]

When difficulties arise, the believer has faith in the heart as a partner to the Bible in his hand. 'When one Scripture apparently contradicts another', says Williams, 'understand that it is the darkness of our minds that accounts for this, and that there is no inconsistency in Holy Scripture. The only way to proceed when something seems dark, is to seek the Lord for heavenly light for only the Spirit who wrote it can open the Word that He gave as a pillar of fire and cloud to lead us to eternal life.'[21] Here again we see that natural reason must serve Christian reason, and learning becomes the handmaiden of grace:

> To understand the Scripture, mere intellect will not do,
> It takes the Holy Spirit, God's grace experienced, too;
> The Spirit Who first wrote it, His pencil and His pen,
> Must open and apply it, interpret it to men.[22]

For the Welsh Methodists, biblical interpretation was a responsible discipline, but also a spiritual discipline, bringing to the Bible that Christian reason which we have already discussed. Hence, while they were trying to interpret words written by men, chiefly they endeavoured to understand God's revelation, and this second consideration predominated. The idea can be compared to the mystery that belongs to the Person of Christ, where two natures are found in one divine Person. Equally, in the Holy Scriptures there is a union without mixture, this time of human words and divine revelation, with the latter having priority and ultimate significance. This explains the deep respect for the Bible that characterised the Great Awakening.

To close our survey of the Bible as revelation, we turn to a chapter in Williams's *Golwg ar Deyrnas Crist* [A View of Christ's King-dom], which bears the title 'Christ's Statute Book, or, Christ all things in the Bible'. God's verbal revelation has for us a special purpose:

> Christ is the Bible's marrow, each chapter in it's found,
> In greater, lesser measure, Christ's praises to resound;
> He was the Great Testator, His testament supreme
> From first to last displaying salvation as its theme.

Here is a book for man to know himself by; here he finds every law and rule, warning, promise, command, and doctrine necessary for man's salvation. In the Old Testament Christ's pre-incarnation appearances are recorded, there are prophecies relating to Him, and shadowy representations of Him. And in the New?

> Each word foretold by prophets, since time and space appeared,
> Regarding Christ the Saviour, each word will be fulfilled,
> Within the former Test'ment, in New without a loss,
> His Person and His passion, the anguish of the cross.
>
> Both Testaments agreeing, in harmony as one,
> To trace our full salvation to Christ, God's only Son;
> And here revealed in splendour, authentic and divine,
> Lies God's pure will and purpose, to your view and to mine.

Not one iota of this will be lost. By this every man will be judged, and on this man's eternal bliss depends. In the light of this view of the Bible, only one response is worthy:

> O! precious, golden volume, believe it O my soul,
> And each iota of it, spread through a heart made whole;
> Herein no line or letter, no word will go astray,
> It gives profoundest pleasure, to my soul night and day.[23]

The Bible, then, was the object of faith and great delight in the Great Awakening, to be approached with personal humility, and to be applied with diligence in every area of life.

We come now to the second aspect, that of the Bible as God's message. Even though reading the Bible is a means of grace, God's instrument in man's salvation is usually the preaching of the Word. In the time of William Morgan, the great translator of the Bible into

Welsh, the man who campaigned bravely for preaching in Wales was John Penry. 'Preaching be granted necessary, and the word read no means to salvation', was his watchword in that struggle.[24] A generation before the Great Awakening, Thomas Gouge, renowned for his generosity to Welsh religious causes, had highlighted the same need: 'The Word is made effectual through preaching. By this means it works on the affections, and makes a greater impact on men's minds. Although many in private reading of the Word have some sweet breathings of God's Spirit, there is in the public ministry of the Word a greater measure of the grace of God's Spirit comes upon the elect, Acts 10:44.'[25] The Welsh Methodists never made a clearer declaration than that.

Regrettably, it must be admitted that the quality of preaching varied considerably, as Williams's hero, Theomemphus, found. The preacher Orthocephalus, for example, demanded strictly, 'sound doctrine must be believed',

> And knowledge was the mother, of all religion true,
> And this the one foundation, on which is built all new.

Theomemphus found such preaching unedifying, but that of Schematicus was no better for all its narrow party spirit:

> It set men's thoughts in turmoil, divisions followed fast,
> The church split into parties, for union could not last;
> Zeal for obscure issues, a zeal both hot and blind,
> One pulpit 'anathema' shunned by the other kind.

While some were trapped by such preaching, it pained the heart of Theomemphus 'to hear true words from a powerless pulpit'. Having the Bible in Welsh together with orthodox preaching in and of themselves did not guarantee spiritual life and blessing. The essence of the Great Awakening lay in having heat as well as light, life as well as truth, the power of grace attending the means of grace, personal experience as well as public privileges:

> 'Tis nought to hear of doctrine, though clear to the mind,
> 'Tis heaven's power only, no less, that I must find;
> Base error and true teaching, to me are both the same
> While I beneath sin's burden still grovel in my shame.

But oh! it profits nothing, to know truth in the head,
Mere knowing may not influence, the heart is still not fed;
To prove it all is different, a taste of pardoning grace,
Would make my life most blessed, my home the happiest place.

O! holy, heavenly Spirit, before my life will cease,
Through wholesome, powerful doctrine, O let me prove true peace;
Forgiveness, oh! forgiveness, forgiveness whole and free
Is what I first desire, by grace, from Calvary.

It was only in men like Boanerges and Evangelius that Theomemphus found the anointed preaching and powerful impressions that he longed for. And if you want a living example of this, what about Dafydd John, the lay preacher, from Pwll-y-march?

Who so simple among preachers?
    Who so honest, who so clear?
Who so humble, who so earnest?
    Who so sweet, and who so dear?
Who without much education
    Preached with eyes fixed up not down;
Yield, all ministers, acknowledge,
    Pwll-y-march has won the crown.

Feeling was his life and power
    Heaven's breeze his hidden strength;
For without the Spirit's blowing
    His boat moved not one length;
No wooden oar did he possess,
    By God's sweet breeze alone, to bring
The saints, with triumph and with joy,
    To shores of endless spring.

Williams is writing an elegy for a Methodist lay-preacher or 'exhorter', one who is no 'professional', either as a student or clergyman, describing his lack of formal, academic attainments in poetic terms as 'no wooden oar did he possess'. But don't misunderstand Williams. The secret of Dafydd John and others like him was this: they possessed that Christian mind which rests on God's Word and the anointing of the Holy Spirit for authority and success. From 1749 onwards they were provided with some education, arranged by the Methodist leadership, but this was never the source of their confidence, nor their boast.[26]

It was preaching of this kind that shook Ioan Thomas to the depths of his being, and brought him to deep conviction of sin. At the time he was listening to Howel Harris, another exhorter without theological training: 'He was preaching the law with great severity; among other things, I remember him saying something like this, "Perhaps you have turned the pages of the Bible often for forty years, and yet you don't know more of God than a dog, or a pig . . ." Now as I reflected on these words, I realised that I was the man . . .'[27] And he was not the only one. Here are the words of an Anglesey man this time, defending his faith to an Anglican: 'Indeed I read the Holy Scripture many times without being enlightened, as you do now, but what benefit did I have from it? Precious little or nothing.' As Derek Llwyd Morgan remarks, 'It was unusual preaching, rather than ordinary reading, that converted people' during the Great Awakening.[28]

It is not necessary to labour the point that preaching was the hallmark of Welsh Methodism. The leaders were preachers, and it was under powerful preaching that men and women came to such elevated experiences that characterised the Revival. 'I have done nothing but preach the Bible', claimed Howel Harris, and in particular 'the preaching of Christ crucified is preaching all the truth.'[29] If the Bible was the source of the message they proclaimed, it was the anointing of the Spirit that accounts for the fruit that followed.

We are now in a position to see how the Bible, the verbal revelation and saving message of God, gave such powerful succour to the converts of the Revival. For, not the least of the Bible's offices to the believer is that it includes promises to lean on and to hope by. Their value to the Christian is demonstrated by our hymn-writers, since so many of the promises have been powerfully and ingeniously woven into their hymns. To one, the promises are 'unchangeable', to another 'immutable', to yet another 'unconditional', sufficient proof of the high regard in which the authors held God's words.[30] Here is an extract from a hymn by Williams, bearing the title 'The confidence of faith in times of distress':

> All your words are true and faithful
> Vows of great solemnity,

By your holiness you've sworn them,
Vows to greater could not be.

You'll not let a single accent
Of your promise to get lost . . .

Williams's favourite adjectives in describing the promises are 'pure'
and 'precious': 'Some precious promises . . . have been sealed to
me'; 'I wait on your pure promise'. We are given an exposition of
the former concept in a hymn from his *Gloria in Excelsis*:

I know that firm and faithful stands
Each word that came from God's own hands,
    Yea and Amen each one;
Of sovereign grace the whole design,
Confirmed by blood that was divine,
    I triumph through the Son.

And with regard to the other statement, regarding the purity of the
promises, their origin is in heaven: 'Vast power and light lie in
heaven's blessed words'; 'the blessed words of heaven . . . from His
own lips are given'; 'Not amiss His promise, Those it speaks of,
shall find bliss'; 'My fullest trust henceforth alway, Shall be in
God's Word night and day.'[31]

Let us remain with this point for a short time, and develop it a little further. For one thing, by God's Word being sealed to the heart a
sinner is brought to salvation. By this means, God's promise
becomes a matter of personal, living, decisive experience for the
soul. The classical example of this, perhaps, is again Williams's
Theomemphus. Here is the description of his effectual calling:

Convictions well nigh triumphed, he hardly could bear more,
The heat of accusation, the pain of guilt was sore;
A Word was sent from heaven, a word to heed and heal
Far greater than creation, and bearing heaven's seal.

He must be found or perish, in time God's word then came,
'Son! all thy sin's forgiven, its guiltiness and shame,
A ransom was forthcoming, atonement has been done,
And payment has been rendered, no debt is left, not one.'

Before the promise reached him, he heard a soft breeze blow,
It whispered in the branches, as stirring leaves did show;
The air itself was churning with heavenly influence,
The placid quiet water with blessed turbulence.

And then within him silence, like an eternal rest,
'This peace', said Theomemphus, 'must bring to me God's best;
'T will come, 't will come', he murmured, ''t will come of that
    I'm sure,
It even then descended, I felt it strong and pure'.

No sooner had he spoken, a force from heaven's store
Came, like a gushing river, to flood his soul with more
Than he before had dreamt of, or understood, or knew,
That now he felt within him, and realised was true.

And so he leapt to safety . . .

So much for the commencement of Theomemphus's Christian pilgrimage. It is hardly surprising, therefore, that immediately he sings, and loves, and shouts, and remembers, for 'the power of heaven came down to burst asunder his strong chains'.[32] And lest anyone should put all this down to poetic licence, listen to Thomas Jones of Denbigh in his autobiography recalling his own conversion:

One day when I was reflecting on my state, desiring to know what foundation my weak, troubled soul could rest on, and to be settled on that rock, this word sprang to mind with light and power, 'when he had made peace by the blood of his cross', Col.1:20; and again, this word, 'being justified freely by his grace through the redemption that is in Christ Jesus', Rom.3:24. These brought light to my spirit, so that I saw clearly that in Christ alone is there perfect righteousness, freely offered and given to make such a sinner as I blameless before God. I returned to my room with great joy and surprise; and shortly opened my Bible, intending to read a portion of it. The word which first came to my attention was this, 'No weapon that is formed against thee shall prosper; and every tongue that shall rise against thee in judgment thou shalt condemn. This is the heritage of the servants of the Lord, and their righteousness is of me, saith the Lord.' Isa.54:17. I did not wish to use the words of the Bible in a superstitious way; but the subject matter was sufficient for me, and its echo filled my soul. My heart was enlarged, and I was enabled to prove a little of the joy of salvation. I bowed before the Lord, thanking him; and I told him that I ventured my all for eternity on the righteousness of Emmanuel, God with us; seeking God's grace to exalt him in heart and life, and to walk in His ways as long as I live.

Not that this kept Thomas Jones in a perpetual state of comfort and ease. Doubts disturbed him from time to time, but he was not bereft of all help:

In such circumstances, I had occasional visitations of support and consolation by various means of grace. One time, this word in particular. 'The covenant of my peace shall not be removed' (Isa.54:10) was especially effective to dispel grave fears and doubts, and to fill me with joy and thanksgiving. Briefly, in those days, something of the glory, certainty, and fitness of the promises, together with my claim in them, was, I thought, being jointly sealed to my spirit. To refuse God's promises, and the gracious treasures of His covenant, would be too hard for me. Despite my strong, ingrained unbelief, it was too hard for me to doubt.[33]

Without realising it, Thomas Jones has drawn attention to the principles of eighteenth-century Methodism.

For it had two poles: a covenantal relationship and covenantal promises, the one answering to the other. The eternal covenant that God made with His Son secured the salvation of all who were brought into a relationship with Christ through grace and by faith. The relationship is sure and steadfast because it is a covenant relationship. The believer, in an uncertain world, realises and enjoys that relationship on the basis of the covenantal words that God has spoken in the Bible, both Old and New Testament.

Listen to another of the Great Awakening's famous converts, Thomas Charles of Bala: 'when his great and precious promises meets with firm faith in us, we can do all things. The coming together of faith and promise is invincible, and they are more than conquerors over sin, Satan, death and hell. There is omnipotence in the promise; and when faith grasps it, it embraces endless power and strength. Thus all things are possible to him that believes.'[34]

As in every biblical covenant there are obligations as well as privileges, even so in the Bible there are commandments as well as promises. Listen again to Thomas Charles:

O blessed Saviour! Since you have given us such holy and spiritual commandments, and also such great and precious promises, I hope to be unflagging until my soul, through fulfilment of the latter, is conformed to the former. Your promises and commandmnents are intimately joined together, and let them never be severed in my experience or practice. Rather, let me, while leaning in my heart on the promises, walk constantly in conformity to your commandments. The one is as precious as the other; my soul loves them. The commandment on its own, separated from the promise, is nothing more than a dead letter to us sinners, because it does not meet with power within us to keep it, it is 'weak through the flesh'. But the promise, when it meets with faith in the heart, gives it life and power; the commandment becomes the delight of the soul, and obedience to it is easy, comforting, and pleasant. This is the work and life of faith, to unite the commandment to the promise.[35]

Now we are ready to come back to Theomemphus, to see how crucial God's word was to his spiritual pilgrimage.

During a period of backsliding Theomemphus felt the constraints of love for Philomela, but the conviction that his love was carnal was gradually brought home to him. While he was 'yet in confusion and deep sadness . . . at one time striving to part, but at another the fire of love kindling fleshly passion', what was it that gave him the victory at last, but 'a great messenger from heaven':

> When Theomemphus slumbered, and all was dark and still,
> One word came down from heaven, 'twas not of human will.
>
> 'Love God with all your senses, with soul and body, too,
> Each passion, gift, and member, give Him a love that's true . . .
>
> The words directed to him from heaven's eternal throne,
> With sweet and stirring breezes, effectively were borne . . .

Then follows his farewell to Philomela, and his 'parting song' to her demonstrates the victory of grace in his life.

What Theomemphus felt for Iratus the persecutor was quite different: 'malice, jealousy, anger, and revenge'. It was necessary to conquer these, too. But how? When he was about to call 'fire from heaven' upon the object of his wrath,

> The voice came to him clearly, a voice both small and still,
> The words were full of power, like this straight to his will:
> 'It's not for Theomemphus full vengeance to demand,
> This right belongs entirely to the Almighty's hand.'
>
> In this way heaven's power by secret words made known,
> While Theomemphus listened a gracious seed was sown;
> He felt his heart was melting at such authority,
> And anger had to crumble, gone its tenacity.

Theomemphus was subdued, and as a result of his compassionate witness, Iratus was won for Christ.

Allow me one more reference to Theomemphus. He is now facing the last enemy, death. In the same breath he speaks of his chief bequest to his family and the chief comfort to his own soul:

> I leave with you my family, the Bible's words as well
> As promises in thousands, which India's wealth excel . . .
>
> That God is true and faithful, this, then, is my sole base,
> The words that He has spoken, these nothing can erase;
> In Christ there's resurrection, His death and purity;
> In God my satisfaction, for all eternity.[36]

If the Welsh Methodists had a high opinion of the Bible, it was no dry, barren conviction for them. Covenantal words become covenantal experiences because of the relationship between the people of the Covenant and the Bible's author.

We see, then, that the purpose of the promises, the Word, the scriptural words, was not merely to give knowledge, but also an acquaintance, not merely an acquaintance even, but an *enjoyment*, a personal and blessed enjoyment of God. This was the chief bliss this side of glory, even though transient, yet of the same kind as the everlasting enjoyment of God, and a sure earnest of it.

In 1759 Williams Pantycelyn translated a sermon of the Scotsman, Ebenezer Erskine, under the title *Siccrwydd Ffydd (The Assurance of Faith Opened and Applied*, Heb.10:22), because it crystallised this very truth. A second edition was called for within a year, and the book was recommended in this way:

The best Book printed in Welsh for these days, when some think of believing as feeling some breezes of joy and pleasure in the service of God, and when they have lost them, there is nothing left but to return to the same place to seek them, or to suffer in unbelief; others, on the other hand, claim that believing is merely grasping with the mind the letter of the Bible, and thus make of it a dry, dead faith, unfruitful, unpleasant, impotent, not much different in virtue, if at all, from that possessed by the devil.

The Methodists were straining for a balanced religion, for an expression of a 'felt, experimental faith that is the mother of all good fruit, and virtuous living.' Here is a paragraph from the work which is relevant to our discussion:

The object of the assurance of faith is Christ, promised, revealed, and offered in the Word; the object of the assurance of feeling, is Christ formed in us by the Holy Spirit. The assurance of faith is the cause, that of feeling is the effect; the former is the root, the latter is the fruit . . . By the assurance of faith Abraham believed he would have a son in his old age, because God, who cannot lie, had promised, but through the assurance of feeling, he believed when he had Isaac in his arms.

The great passion of the saints of the Great Awakening was to press nearer to God, to have more of God, and a clearer sight of His countenance. While the majority of their religious contemporaries were satisfied with reading, and hearing, and understanding the words, they longed for the Presence who dwelt within the veil. And on what ground could they venture into that holiest place? Here is Erskine's answer: 'the nearest and most immediate ground of faith, or the assurance of it, in approaching God, is God's own promise of acceptance through Jesus Christ; of which promises the Word from cover to cover is full, Isa.40:7; 56:7; Mk.9:24; Mt.7:7; Jn.14:13-14.' Here lay the strength of the promises, a strength which provided a far superior foundation than any sign or dream:

Now God has condescended to commit the word of His promise to a Book, yes, he has placed it deliberately in the Remembrance Book of the Scriptures of Truth, and is not this a signal indication of God's faithfulness? Perhaps you think that if you could have voices, or visions, or immediate revelations from heaven, then you would believe; but I can assure you in God's Name that the Bible, God's Book, which you have in your hands, is far better, and a far superior ground of faith and trust, than anything of that nature . . . 2 Pet.1:17.[37]

The purpose of the promises was to bring the believer not only to an enjoyment of God's covenant—that was the assurance of faith—but also to enjoy the *God* of the covenant, which was the assurance of feeling and experience. And every earnest Methodist set his sights on the personal *realisation* of the promises. Just like Mr Ready-to-halt in Bunyan's *Pilgrim's Progress*, it was on their crutches ('that is, the promises' says Bunyan), that the Methodists went to glory. Furthermore, on occasions, just like that famous character, they, too, though frail and limping, could dance and rejoice as they felt the undergirding of God's promises beneath them.

Another such was Williams's character, 'Fidelius the Christian' in

Hanes Bywyd a Marwolaeth Tri Wyr o Sodom a'r Aifft (The Life and Death of Three Men from Sodom and Egypt). Williams's portrayal of him shall close our discussion. He was a man who read 'God's Word frequently and diligently'; 'believing the Word along with the father of the faithful [Abraham] only because God had spoken it, allowing the One who had spoken it to harmonise one part with another. The Bible was Fidelius's Body of Divinity, and in it he meditated day and night.' On occasions, 'heaven bestowed on him the spirit of power and strength'; 'confirmation of all the truths of Holy Scripture; every promise, warning, word, and syllable, that all would come to pass that God ever spoke.' thus, 'the pure promises of the Bible were his sharpest swords in the face of death'.[38]

The Great Awakening gave to the Bible, in its entirety and veracity, as revelation, message, and promise, its proper place. With this historical example before us, we too, although in a very different situation, may renew faith to see the Bible once again the instrument to change a whole nation, and to take individuals victoriously to glory.

REFERENCES

1 *Y Cylchgrawn Hanes* [*Journal of the Historical Society of the Presbyterian Church of Wales*] cyf.liii.62-3. Henceforth shortened to CH.

2. Charles Ashton, *Bywyd ac Amserau yr Esgob Morgan*, 1891, p.338.

3. *Y Llaeth Ysbrydol neu Bregeth; yn dangos mawr hiraeth y ffyddloniaid am laeth y gair ynghyd â'r ffordd i mae cynyddy trwyddo*, 1739, 'Rhagymadrodd'. The original sermon was by Henry Smith, and is included in volume one of the 1866 edition of his *Works*, pp.485-500.

4. See Geraint H. Jenkins, *Hanes Cymru yn y Cyfnod Modern Cynnar 1530-1760*, 1988, p.284.

5. Moravian Archives, London, Box A/3, 'Original Letter, John and Charles Wesley, 1735-1774', William Seward to James Hutton, from New Passage, Bristol Side, March 6th, 1739.

6. Lewis F. Lupton, *A History of the Geneva Bible*, vol.xiii, 1981, 'Index', 43,48.

7. Gomer M. Roberts, *Bywyd a Gwaith Peter Williams*, 1943, 67; Lewis F. Lupton, op. cit , 53,54.

8. D. E. Jenkins, *The Life of the Rev Thomas Charles . . .* , vol.i, 1908, 567.

9. *Thomas Charles o'r Bala*, 1979, 21,38.

10. CH September 1917 (Manuscript Supplement) i.16; Tom Beynon, *Howell Harris's Visits to Pembrokeshire*, 1966, 5 (Henceforth shortened to HVP).

11. CH xxviii.91-2.

12. *Gweithiau William Williams Pantycelyn*, gol. Gomer Morgan Roberts, cyf.i, 1964, 380-81. Henceforth shortened to GWP. The second volume, edited by Garfield H. Hughes, appeared in 1967.

13. J. R. Kilsby Jones, *Holl Weithiau . . . William Williams*, 1867, 773. Henceforth

shortened to Kilsby.

14. GWP i.383,385.
15. *Letters of the Rev Griffith Jones*, ed Edw Morgan, 1832, 217; *Selections from The Welch Piety,* 1938, 103,23; *Hyfforddiant i Wybodaeth Jachusol . . .* Y Rhan Gyntaf, 1763, v; *Galwad at Orseddfainc y Gras*, 1738, 9, 11.
16. HVP 118,119.
17. GWP ii.5.
18. GWP ii.13,19.
19. At the end of *Byrr Hanes . . . James Albert*, 1779. Stephen J. Turner in his 1982 M.Th (Wales) Thesis, 'Theological Themes in the English Works of Williams Pantycelyn', discusses Williams's views of Scripture.
20. Kilsby 512.
21. GWP ii.224-5.
22. GWP i.380.
23. GWP i.121,139,140.
24. John Penry, *Three Treatises Concerning Wales*, 1960, 37.
25. *Gwyddorion y Grefydd Gristianogol*, 1679, 167.
26. GWP i.226-34, 223; N. Cynhafal Jones, *Gweithiau Williams Pant-y-celyn*, cyf.i, 1887, 508, 'Marwnad Dafydd John, o Bwll-y-march . . . 1776'. Henceforth shortened to CYN. For details of the education provided for the exhorters, see Eifion Evans, *Daniel Rowland and the Great Evangelical Awakening in Wales,* 1985, 266-7.
27. *Rhad Ras*, gol. J. Dyfnallt Owen, 1949, 28-9.
28. *Y Diwygiad Mawr*, 1981, 39,38, quoting from *Ymddiddanion cyfeillgar rhwng Gwr or Eglwys Loegr, ac Ymneillduwr neu Un o'r Grefydd Newydd a elwir Methodistiaid* [7].
29. HVP 214; Tom Beynon, *Howell Harris, Reformer and Soldier,* 1958,164.
30. *Llyfr emynau y Methodistiaid Calfinaidd a Wesleaidd*, [1927], Rhif 690 (David Williams, 1712-94); Rhif 618 (Thomas Charles, 1755-1814); Rhif 338 (Ann Griffiths, 1776-1805).
31. CYN cyf.ii.1891, Emynau 313(1),(4); 818(2); 797(1); 826(4); 796(1); 809(1); 810(2); 815(4).
32. GWP i.252.
33. *Hunangofiant y Parch Thomas Jones,* 1937,20-21,22.
34. *Cofiant . . . Y Parch Thomas Charles*, 1816-89. For a discussion of covenantal words see Meredith G. Kline, *The Structure of Biblical Authority*, Grand Rapids, 1972, especially the second chapter, 'Covenantal Bible'.
35. Cofiant . . . , 92-3; For a discussion of the relationship between promise and obligation in God's Covenant see John Bright, *Covenant and Promise*, 1977, especially pp.196-8; and R. E. Clements, *Prophecy and Covenant*, 1965.
36. GWP i.336,366,368,398.
37. *Sicrwydd Ffydd, wedi ei agoryd a'i gymhwyso . . .* , 1759, 41,66,76; Gomer M. Roberts, *Y Per Ganiedydd*, cyf.ii.1958, 240.
38. GWP ii.148,154-5,157.

11
JOHN DAVIES, TAHITI

In these days of fast communications and reduced travelling hazards it is hard to envisage or appreciate the adventurous nature of a journey to the other side of the world in 1800. John Davies, born in an isolated Welsh village and with little enough knowledge of the wide world, was called upon in that year to blaze the trail as a Christian missionary to Tahiti and to pioneer, with a handful of fellow-workers, the London Missionary Society's outpost in that remote island. With no more qualification than a constraint to do God's will; with no more training than that of a village schoolmaster, and with no higher ideal than the glory of God in the salvation of the heathen, he was thrust by the call of God into an utterly pagan society, illiterate, unregenerate, barbaric, and backward. Yet in the midst of the most alarming opposition, against tremendous odds, often well-nigh overcome by discouragements, this man of God fulfilled a mammoth task of evangelization and education. His achievement, by God's grace, ranks high indeed among the annals of missionary endeavour and conquest.

Born in 1772 on the small farm of Pendugwm in the parish of Llanfihangel-yng-Ngwynfa, Montgomeryshire, the son of a weaver, his early prospects—educational, social, and religious—were limited indeed. However, through the legacy of Griffith Jones's Charity Schools he was educated at a 'circulating school' and became himself, through aptitude and diligence, one of the schoolteachers itinerating under this singularly useful arrangement, by that time under the supervision of the Rev. Thomas Charles of Bala. Eventually, he came as a schoolmaster to Machynlleth and joined the Calvinistic Methodist 'society' or fellowship meeting there.

This in itself was indicative of a genuine work of grace in his heart, for the searching questions which he would have to answer with conviction and feeling before the fellowship were of a personal and spiritual nature. Witness some of them:

Have you seen your own misery and enmity to God, resulting in eternal ruin

167

except the Lord have mercy upon you; and that of yourself you deserve God's wrath? Have you seen yourself as the chief of sinners, and your sin more heinous, more aggravating in God's sight than that of others? Have you realized the darkness of your own mind in spiritual things, and that without the supernatural illumination of the Holy Spirit you can never savingly know the Father or His Son? Have you realized your utter impotence to think or do anything that is good in God's sight, and that you cannot in any way save yourself, and will remain therein until God Himself undertakes to save you? Have you seen the need for Christ's righteousness to cover you in God's sight, and do you forsake your own righteousness for His? Have you seen the need for faith more than any other grace, and that it is faith which receives Christ in all His offices, and that this faith is not a human product, but a gift of the Holy Spirit? Have you counted the cost of suffering shame, persecution, etc., for Christ's sake and the Gospel's, and are you willing to give your life in His service if need be? Do you earnestly seek God Himself, and intimate heart-communion with Him? Are you content with anything short of true knowledge of Christ in your heart, and of His supreme satisfaction on your behalf as the spring of all your affections and obedience to Christ?[1]

Questions such as these were designed to maintain, as far as was humanly possible, the integrity and intensity of the spiritual fellowship, and in the prevailing religious decadence of those times they proved invaluable to many otherwise orphaned and isolated believers.

It was during his stay at Machynlleth that John Davies was led to believe that God had laid His hand upon him for service overseas in the kingdom of Christ. This call of God came to him at a time when the London Missionary Society was preparing a second vessel for taking missionaries to the South Sea Islands of Polynesia; the first, famous ship, *The Duff*, was to be followed by *The Royal Admiral*, and Thomas Haweis, 'the Father of the South Sea Mission' as he has been called, was in correspondence with Thomas Charles of Bala, one of the Society's Directors, on this very matter:

I have the pleasure now of informing you, that in the fullest meeting of Directors we have yet seen, it was unanimously voted to accept the offer of the owners of *The Royal Admiral* to carry out Missionaries. We are seeking 30 within the course of the next month: and hope some of your Congregations will contribute to our supply men of true grace—tried, good spirits to live in union with their Brethren, willing to endure hardness as good soldiers of Jesus Christ . . . Who do not expect to become preachers, gentlemen, or idle, but active labourers, and examples to the Heathen of purity and industry. We look to you Brother to be active in your inquiries respecting such as you know we want, and your mountains, I think, can supply. Examine them, and state to me their qualities, age, and occupation, that these may come before the Committee, and such a selection made as may give glory to God, and accomplish the great end we have in view of Heathen conversion. Meekness and humility are among the first qualifications.[2]

How sure, though secret, is the working of God's providence! For at that very time God had wrought in John Davies's heart a strong constraint and inclination for the mission field:

Missionary work was first laid upon my heart chiefly through reading about the Moravians in Greenland, and Mr Thomas and Mr Carey going to India, and through reading *The Evangelical Magazine*. When I was in Machynlleth I wrote to the late Rev Mr Charles of Bala regarding my state of mind to seek his advice. I was a long while awaiting an answer, and feared that all was in vain, but eventually I received a letter from him to inform me that he had written to Dr Haweis and others of my case, urging me to go to London, and that Dr Haweis was eager that I should go there.[3]

In 1799 an issue of *The Evangelical Magazine* had included the principles of the London Missionary Society together with the character required of their missionary candidates, and it is reasonable to suppose that John Davies had found these acceptable and compelling.

Certainly his experience and knowledge was such that Thomas Charles had no hesitation in recommending him as a suitable candidate, and on this he was in due course accepted. Consequently John Davies proceeded to London, carrying with him Thomas Charles's recommendation to Thomas Haweis. It was with mixed feelings that Thomas Charles saw him go:

The Bearer of this is John Davies, whom I recommended and you accepted last summer for a Missionary. He continues steady in his resolution, and comes up to London according to your request to be disposed of in the great missionary cause according to your wishes. I trust the Lord disposes his mind to the arduous and important work to answer some useful purpose. I still heartily recommend him as a young man who has been useful as a teacher in our circulating schools and has hitherto honoured his profession by a consistent walk and conversation. It is with regret that I part with him, though, when I consider the vast importance of your undertaking, and the noble end you have in view, I wish I had many more to recommend to you . . .[4]

If such were Thomas Charles's sentiments, who can measure those of John Davies himself, leaving family, friends, country, all that had been familiar, for the uncertainty of a long sea voyage to an inhospitable and uncongenial environment. How easy it would have been to remain at his teaching post at Machynlleth with no other hazards than the occasionally inclement weather, or an unfriendly community, or unruly children. But he cannot be a 'good soldier of Jesus Christ' who is not prepared to 'endure hardness' (2 Timothy 2:3).

So John Davies duly arrived safely in the metropolis having seen the last of Wales, for he would never return. In one letter he wrote some twenty years later he acknowledges that oftentimes he had thoughts of a furlough, but that there were innumerable hindrances to it. The chief reason, he says, is that 'ever since the work began to prosper here, I have had no desire to leave it . . . I have so much work in hand'.[5] What a difference true blessing in God's work makes! It delivers from dissatisfaction and discontent, from hungering for material prosperity, from longings for natural pursuits and worldly pleasures. So it was in the case of John Davies. However, he could not have foreseen this experience when he first became acquainted with Thomas Haweis. The latter's first impressions of the new missionary candidate were very promising, and he conveyed them to Thomas Charles in a letter, dated February 8, 1800: 'Mr Davies arrived safe . . . He seems a truly precious man, and I hope will be a blessing to us. I wish you had two or three more, you could as comfortably recommend.'[6] Indeed, John Davies was to prove, in the words of one of the historians of the Society, Richard Lovett, 'one of the best missionaries it has ever had'.[7]

It was not without experiencing many inward fears and struggles that John Davies set sail for his field of service. In a letter to Thomas Charles, for instance, written from Portsmouth on September 8, 1800, he records the displeasure he had met with from his kith and kin on account of his missionary call: 'even though I met with bitter opposition from my family who reside in Llanfyllin, yet I have not the least doubt that the work is of God, even though I am myself one of the most unfitting and unworthy to have any part in it.'[8]

Apart from the missionaries *The Royal Admiral* carried some three hundred convicts who were placed under the spiritual supervision of the missionaries, and John Davies describes to Thomas Charles some of their early ministrations among them:

Respecting the convicts, I can with pleasure give a much more favourable report than I expected. Four or five of us visit them twice a day regularly, and in general they pay great attention to what is said to them. We distributed several religious tracts among them, with some Bibles and Testaments. They promised to read them, and we have reason to believe that many of them perform their promises, and if I speak my own opinion I have much more favourable thoughts of the convicts than of the ship's company. They are all of them officers and sailors; only the Capt. Surgeon, the ship's carpenter excepted, a set of the most wicked and ungodly characters. Oh! may the Lord make us as salt among them, may he direct, and guide us, and bless our feeble efforts. I see myself the most unworthy among my Brethren, and in continuous need of Divine assistance. We are placed in a situation where the eyes of all in the ship are upon us. Dear Sir, I request your prayers that our conduct may be such as becometh the Gospel of Christ.[9]

That letter was written in May 1800 as they sailed from Portsmouth, and the voyage for John Davies ended on July 10, 1801 when he saw the sphere of his future labours for the Lord, Tahiti, for the first time. Already four years had elapsed since the first L.M.S. missionaries had landed there, and their reports of progress would have given John Davies and the other newcomers very little encouragement. Ten days later he was chosen librarian for the Tahitian missionaries, a post which carried a great deal of responsibility, and entailed a great deal of hard work, combining as it did the work of general secretary, book-keeper, record-keeper, and archivist. He was to remain at his post for over fifty years until he died in 1855.

The difficulties which faced him were legion, and well-nigh insuperable. The language had to be learned and reduced to writing, the Tahitians taught to read and write, while at the same time he had to acclimatize himself to new surroundings. Due to the unreliable nature of their early contacts, who would just come and go as they pleased without discipline or regularity in their attendance at school or church, the prospect for some time for the missionaries was far from bright. After six years of tough, up-hill work, John Davies could report to Thomas Charles only limited success.

I could say much of the several means I have employed in an attempt to teach the Tahitian youths, but all to little purpose . . . the hindrances I met with were such that I had little hope of overcoming them. My entire labour in teaching the Tahitis to read for three years has, it seems, come to nought. And I have more or less given up all expectation of success in this direction

through any means I might use . . . My scholars number about thirty, some
of whom are beginning to read and write in Tahiti, and most are able to pronounce the words; but I fear their unreliable temperament will cause many
to give up before they have mastered reading to any profit. They require
more than a common measure of patience and wisdom, and yet in spite of
the many difficulties I reckon that, had we printed books in their own language, much might be achieved among the younger element . . . with regard
to the mission generally . . . some of the brethren continue to preach as they
have opportunity, but as far as we can see, with little success; yet, through
various means, knowledge is increasing in their midst . . . indisputably our
work has a discouraging aspect. If we look at the people among whom we
labour, their hostility to the Gospel, their indifference to every means used
for their good, their strong inclinations towards superstitions and sinful
practices in spite of all they have heard, understood, and acknowledged; or
if we look to ourselves, the work is surely hopeless; but when we are
enabled to look at the promises, and what is already accomplished in other
parts of the world, we are confident that He whose Word it is, in His own
time and way, will make it effectual here also . . .[10]

Meanwhile the work of translating the Bible into the Tahitian language was progressing under the joint energies of John Davies and
one of his colleagues, Mr Henry Nott. At the close of 1808 for instance they could report the completion of the historical books of
both Old and New Testaments.[11]

Towards the end of the same year the work suffered a serious set-
back with the outbreak of hostilities on the island, and many of the
missionaries had to evacuate to neighbouring islands. John Davies,
in a letter dated November 12 from Huahine, testified to the readiness with which the missionaries had been welcomed, and added: 'if
we are constrained, and if we have more personnel, we may start
missionary work in Ulitea, under the protection of [Chief] Tapoa.
We are praying that the Lord will over-rule in this unexpected and
grave turn of events to the further success of the missionary endeavour.'[12] Their prayers were answered in abundant measure during the
years 1813-1817 when God visited several of the islands in salvation
and righteousness. The resulting reformation in their midst was
evident in the changed lives of a good number of the people, the
emergence of a worshipping, witnessing church, the surging forward
of educational projects, the elevated moral tone of their primitive
society, and the clamouring need for more missionaries to cope with
the work.

The progress of these 'showers of blessing' was recorded by John Davies in his official diary of the mission's work and in the letters he sent regularly to his Welsh friends at home. Here is an extract from the diary relating to the early evidences of the blessing in their midst in 1813:

On Monday evening July 26th forty natives met the missionaries at the new chapel. The meeting was commenced with singing and prayer in Tahitian, and then those assembled were addressed by Mr N(ott) on the design of the meeting. Several appeared affected by what was said. They were then asked by me whether they were desirous of renouncing their false god, and cast away their evil practices, of receiving Jehova for their God, and Jesus Christ for their Saviour, and be instructed in the word of Jehova, etc., etc. To these questions, and to the number of thirty-one (they) requested their names to be written down as the professed worshippers of Jehova, who had resolved to cast away their evil practices and be instructed in the word of God. Others professed their desire to do the same, but deferred having their names put down for the present. No one was pressed to have his name put down, but all were urged to attend the means of instruction. This meeting rejoiced the hearts of the missionaries, it was a sight they hardly dared to expect.[13]

It was not only unexpected, it was also conducive to further spiritual exercise and discipline, for the same diary goes on to record that 'November 12 was observed by the missionaries as a day of humiliation and prayer; to acknowledge their sins and unfruitfulness, and to ask for pardon and special protection at this critical juncture . . . Also to acknowledge the Lord's mercy and goodness in prospering beyond their expectations their feeble attempts to make known the Gospel among the people.'[14]

Within a year the Tahitian missionaries urgently needed reinforcements of the right calibre, called of God and utterly dedicated to toil for their Master in the mammoth tasks which would face them. The missionaries' letter of appeal listed the qualities necessary for any missionary candidate: 'we can never press too much upon the Directors, that it is of no use to send an unqualified person here; it will cause great expence (sic), and issue in disappointment. Not only is true piety necessary, but also zeal, prudence, and perseverence, a heart truly devoted to the work, and abilities of acquiring the language, and if possible to assist in the translation of the Scriptures.'[15]

Numerically the work grew apace. At the end of 1814 'the numbers

of professors were increased (to) 150 and of the attendants on the
School to 242'; in January 1815 'were added 53 more names to the
worshippers of the true God among whom King Pomare requested
his name to be inserted. A large addition was made to the School
also this month of people from Tahiti', their 'constant hearers' by
that time being 'about 300, but sometimes many more so that the
house cannot contain them'. The total number throughout the missionary field in the islands 'of those who have renounced idolatry
... cannot be less than between 500 and 600 including most of the
principal chiefs'. In March the attendance at the School increased to
318; by July it was 643, while the number on the Church roll
increased in May by 56 and in September by a further 39. By the
beginning of 1816 'the missionaries had discontinued the practice of
writing down the names of the worshippers of the true (God), as it
could be no longer a distinctive mark, the profession of Christianity
having become national both in Tahiti and Eimeo.'[16]

Looking back over this period in 1817 John Davies summed up
the effects of these 'times of refreshing from the presence of the
Lord' in this way:

The awakening and reformation which began with us in 1813 and 14,
increased in 1815-16-17, so that at present the islands of Tahiti, Eimeo,
Teturoa, etc., have renounced idolatry altogether. The gods and altars are
entirely destroyed and the human sacrifices, infanticide, etc., have fully
ceased, and the worship of the true God and a Christian profession is general. There are 66 places of worship on Tahiti, 18 on Eimeo, where the people
gather for worship three times each Sabbath, as well as on Wednesday
evenings. The Lord's day is carefully observed throughout the Islands, and
family and private prayer is common among the people. Some 4,000 people
have learned to read and many can write. In a word, the transformation in
our midst is in every respect beyond all expectation. Truly 'the Lord has
done great things for us'.[17]

All this could not have been accomplished without the tireless
activity of the missionaries, and it clearly demonstrated the principle
that in periods of intense activity on the part of the Holy Spirit not
only are God's enemies brought into subjection to Christ's kingship,
but God's people are also strengthened and quickened for fuller
service in Christ's kingdom, witness Psalm 110:2-3 (R.S.V.), 'The
Lord sends forth from Zion your mighty sceptre. Rule in the midst
of your foes! Your people will offer themselves freely on the day

you lead your host upon the holy mountains.' During the gathering in of this tremendous spiritual harvest the missionaries were fully occupied with instructing, preaching, travelling, visiting, catechising, and a host of other necessary duties, and in February 1817 a printing press arrived for their use and to add, not only to their joys, but also to their labours. This press moved from one island to another until it was finally set up in Huahine, and in a letter of 12 September 1818 John Davies reported:

Mr [William] Ellis is the printer and Mr Nott and myself are the translators. Luke's Gospel is finished and some 3,000 copies are printed, but many more are needed. Mr Nott is translating the Acts of the Apostles, and I am busy with Mark's Gospel. I finished Matthew before leaving Eimeo, but it is not ready for the press because I have to prepare another edition of my Spelling Book for the use of the schools first; also a Tahitian Catechism and some hymns which I sought to write for use in our services. I even tried to make some of the Welsh hymns extol the praises of our Redeemer in the Tahitian language.[18]

Under the blessing of God the sustained efforts of the missionaries were bearing fruit and their needs were being met.

The missionaries were also privileged to witness the establishment of a regular church ministry and order, as in the case of Eimeo, an island where John Davies had spent much time and given a great deal of labour. The prosperous years for Christ's kingdom on Eimeo were 1819-1825, as the diary shows:

In June 1819 the missionaries agreed that a number of those that made a profession and had long enjoyed the means of instruction should be baptized, and consequently on the 27th of the month 22 adults viz 14 men and eight women, were selected and baptized together with 17 of their children. These adults were formed into a Christian church on the 2nd of July following and on the 4th being the sabbath day, the ordinance of the Lord's Supper was administered to them for the first time . . . After this the church at Papetoai continued without any other office bearers than Pastors, until the beginning of 1821 when it consisted of about 100 members, and several hundreds of the people had been baptized. Jany 10th 1821 six of the members were solemnly set apart to the office of Deacon, by fasting, prayer and imposition of hands. The labour of these Deacons contributed much to the increase and welfare of the church, and the furtherance of the Gospel, and prosperity of religion on the Island in general. In May 1822 an awakening which had previously commenced was much increased together with a spirit of inquiry, and thirst for the Word of God, which long continued, and the church prospered the three following years and was much increased . . . In 1825 most of the inhabitants of Eimeo had been baptized, and the greater part of the chiefs and judges had been received church members, among whom were the two principal chiefs . . . who had long held out in opposition to the Gospel, and they became as zealous promoters and supporters of the Christian religion, as they had been formerly of paganism . . . The power of the Gospel was strikingly displayed in the conversions of these aged, but lofty, proud and haughty chiefs, in bringing them to possess the spirit of little children, and to sit at the feet of their teachers to receive instruction.[19]

John Davies's more detailed account of missionary strategy in the founding of churches and settling their order was patterned largely on that obtaining in the Welsh Calvinistic Methodist movement during the latter part of the eighteenth century. It is found in his letter of 15 May 1821, referring to his work at Papara, the largest congregation of the islands, numbering 44 in full membership at that time, together with 284 baptized persons as adherents, and a further 280 candidates for baptism.

Those who show evidence of being under conviction are invited to come and converse with me, and if there are signs that they love God's word and people, I write their names in a book, and give them tickets so that they are accepted to the private fellowship meeting which is held every Thursday afternoon. Those who are baptized also attend, and our custom is very similar to that in the Welsh fellowship meetings. When they have been attending this for some appreciable time, and we have conversed much with them by way of a searching inquiry into their experience, etc., if they give satisfaction, I baptize them, and they are accepted into the other meeting which is held on Tuesday afternoons (the communicant members also attend) and when they have been here for a period on trial, if they give satisfaction, they are then received as communicant members. There is good order in our midst and a rigorous discipline. I do not accept any into the Church until I have the testimony and satisfaction of all the members. I administer the Lord's Supper on the first Sabbath of the month, and have a private fellowship meeting with all the members on the previous Friday.[20]

It is interesting to note that a further flood-tide of blessing was experienced in 1827 and as a result John Davies's communicants numbered 363, the baptized adherents 1,600, and the public congregation some 1,200.

Nevertheless, in the midst of such evident success, John Davies was very alarmed at certain incidents which took place in the years 1828 and 1829. There was a marked decline in fervour and zeal among the converts; there was news of the arrival of French Jesuit priests in the South Seas; and there was the delinquent effect of drink on the populace—through the visits of drunken sailors from various Western countries. All these factors weighed heavily on his mind and caused him much concern and grief.

By 1836 he had cause to expect a further deterioration in the religious climate with the settling on the island of the Jesuit priests. These made strenuous efforts to gain permission to found a mission station on Tahiti, but they were refused for some years, and eventually the two priests who had lived on the island were expelled. The French Consul—an ardent Catholic and able propagandist—insisted on restitution being made for this (what Lord Palmerston referred to as 'an uncalled-for act of violence', condemning the law against Roman Catholic teaching as an 'intolerant and indefensible Edict'), and in 1838 he received paid indemnity for their expulsion. 'By 1841, the attempt of the missionaries to exclude the Roman Catholics had been repudiated.' This led to the most miserable confusion, and when in 1847 Tahitian sovereignty was surrendered to France, the future of the Protestant mission was in jeopardy. A further blow was dealt to the work in 1852 by the passing of the law which gave the right of electing church deacons to all and sundry irrespective of their religious attachment. Subsequent negotiations finally secured the handing over of the Mission's work in these islands to the French Société des Missions Evangéliques and 'in 1863 the first two ministers of the Reformed Church of France arrived'.[21]

Although these events presented a gloomy aspect to the missionaries they were given encouragements as the storm clouds gathered. In 1837, for instance, John Davies could speak of another awakening in their midst, resulting in an appreciable addition to the church, many of them young people, and some of those who had backslidden were restored.[22] On the other hand, the coming of the Jesuits were not his only trial. During the course of his missionary life he had to bear much personal grief and sorrow, and on the death of his third wife on the island, he wrote of his feelings in this way:

The news was so unexpected that my feelings were inexpressible; for some time I could neither weep nor speak, but stood motionless as though encompassed with extreme misery! O the uncertainty and fragility of all our earthly comforts! The words of Eli came to mind, 'It is the Lord: let him do what

seemeth him good'. I could no longer think of returning to the house at
Papara. Such was the troubled state of my mind.[23]

Furthermore, for the last ten years of his life he was blind and in a
poignant note to his Welsh friends in 1844 he advised them 'that he
could no longer write with his own hand, and that it would be point-
less for any of his old friends to write any more in Welsh, since he
could not read, and no other person on the island could understand a
word of it'.[24]

Mention has already been made of his literary labours. These
included works of translation, such as parts of the Bible, and spiritual classics like Bunyan's *Pilgrim's Progress*, The Westminster
Assembly's Larger and Shorter Catechisms; the production of original material for the schools such as spelling books (the one printed in 1810 being the first in the Polynesian language), elementary
arithmetic, grammar, and in 1851 a Tahitian-English Dictionary. He
must have been adept at these languages for he also wrote the first
printed Alphabet and Spelling book in Fijian in 1825. In addition to
these were hymn-books, tracts, and catechisms. Of his thoroughness
in the work of Bible translation there could be no doubt: 'I have read
carefully from Genesis to the beginning of Job, comparing the translation (of his colleague, Mr Nott) with Dr Boothroyd's translation,
comparing it too with the English Authorized Version, and with the
excellent Welsh translation (which Mr Nott did not understand); also
with Mr Martin's French translation, with the Hebrew and Greek
Septuagint; also with Parkhurst and several other Hebrew Lexi-
cons.'[25]

In his laborious and careful manner the work progressed so that in
1828 he was able to rejoice that 'the whole of the New Testament
had been translated . . . I have lately been preparing the Book of
Psalms for the printers . . . at present, whenever I have some spare
time, I am translating *The Pilgrim's Progress*.'[26] Undaunted by ad-
verse external pressures, or personal grief, he redeemed the time
without sparing himself, and in 1836 commenced, at the instigation
of his fellow-labourers, a periodical which included articles of a pol-
emical as well as devotional nature. 'Amongst other things, in these
various issues, I printed articles on: The Church of Rome in her
beginnings and as she is at present; Proofs of the idolatry of the
Papists; Ave Maria with comments; the manner and commencement

of the chief heresies of the Church of Rome. And I have much more to add on false miracles and so on.'[27]

From this brief survey of John Davies's missionary career there is surely much to be learned by way of basic principles in missionary strategy. The exacting nature of the missionary life, the mammoth tasks to be undertaken, the difficulties to be overcome, all this and more beside demand an intense devotion and unflagging determination from body and soul. The importance of a teaching ministry, of careful, solid instruction, of strict discipline, of utter unswerving dependence on the Holy Spirit's power, these are vital in the founding and edifying of the churches. Unremitting toil, stemming from a clear call of God, should characterize the Christian missionary today more than ever before. The abiding awareness of Christ's commission should maintain in the heart not only a singleness of purpose but also a fervent commitment to the missionary task.

John Davies: a man of mere flesh and blood, content to live with only the basic necessities of life in a primitive society; a man who had known the luxuries and amenities of a more civilised country, content to live without ease and comfort; a man of intelligence and ability, content without the honours and acclaim of the world of learning. He was content even though God shut him up to a narrow sphere of service, a sphere where he was cast entirely upon his Master for every step of progress and evidence of success. At the same time he was consumed with this one passion: that of making Christ's Name known among the heathen. For him Christ's service, with all its divinely ordained limits and confinements, with all its discomforts and difficulties, with its crucifying of all humanly-conceived prospects and earth-bound ideas of success, was perfect freedom, in an enlarged place, and with the truest satisfaction. Such were the characteristics of this man of God, and the fruit of his labours brought much glory to the Saviour whom he served.

REFERENCES

1. 'Templus Experientiae Apertum'; neu Ddrws y Society Profiad, *Gweithiau Williams Pantycelyn*, N. Cynhafal Jones, vol.ii. 1891, pp.507-508.
2. Arthur Skevington Wood, *Thomas Haweis*, 1957, p.195, quoting John Morrison, *The Fathers and Founders of the London Missionary Society*, n.d. vol.ii. 170; D. E. Jenkins, *The Life of the Rev Thomas Charles, B.A. of Bala*, Denbigh, vol.ii.1908, 196 (abbreviated as TC).
3. National Library of Wales, Calvinistic Methodist Archives MS 16209, letter dated 15 May 1821, later printed at Bala as *Trefn Eglwysig Ynysoedd Mor y Dehau* (The Church Order of the South Sea Islands). Abbreviations: NLW and CMA.
4. TC ii.197
5. *Trefn Eglwysig*
6. NLW MS 4798E
7. TC ii.201
8. NLW MS 4798E
9. TC ii.199-200
10. *Trysorfa Ysbrydol*, 1800, pp.93-94, letter dated 11 June 1807 from Tahiti.
11. C. W. Newbury (Editor), *The History of the Tahitian Mission, 1799-1830*, (Hakluyt Society), Cambridge, 1961, p.127. (Abbreviated to Newbury).
12. *Trysorfa Ysbrydol*, 1800, 142
13. Newbury 164-5
14. Ibid. 168
15. Ibid. 170
16. Ibid. 181-197
17. *Newyddion Da*, 1892, p.44
18. NLW CMA MS 16207
19. Newbury 237-8
20. *Trefn Eglwysig*
21. Newbury 336-9
22. NLW CMA MS 16231
23. *Newyddion Da*, 1892, p.53
24. Ibid. 75
25. Ibid. 76
26. NLW CMA MS 16217
27. NLW CMA MS 16231

12
THE BEDDGELERT REVIVAL
No place too small: no heart too hard

In today's tourist brochures Beddgelert claims to be an excellent centre for exploring the Snowdonia National Park. It is not hard to see why. Situated some 13 miles south of Caernarfon, and a mere 5 miles from the summit of Snowdon, the village is compactly set in rural surroundings of exquisite beauty.

River and hills, forests and fields provide tranquility and invite exploration. Tourist facilities are plentiful, offering a whole range of countryside activities like hill-walking and climbing, together with the alluring prospect of visits to interesting craft shops and quaint woollen mills. A few years ago the hills to the south of Beddgelert provided the location for filming 'The Inn of the Sixth Happiness'.

Thousands converted

In 1817 Beddgelert was visited by large numbers of people for a very difference reason. The village was the scene of a remarkable spiritual awakening. It was one of the most powerful revivals seen in Wales, spreading throughout the North and many parts of the South. It was remarkable for the intensity of the convictions experienced in it, and the extent of its influence gave it a lasting significance. The churches were quickened, thousands were converted to Christ, and as a result, whole communities became spiritually active. For years to come a solid spirituality based on biblical principles was established in the churches.

At the time, the population would have consisted mainly of farm workers and craftsmen, such as carpenters, with slate-quarrying a new industry in the region. Poverty was the keynote of that period in Wales. 'The Great War' between Britain and France from 1793 to 1815 had impoverished the country. February 1797 had seen 'the last invasion of Britain', when the French had landed near Fishguard in South Wales, only to surrender within 48 hours. Even so, the event had spread terror throughout the countryside.

With the end of the war there came a period of depression, affecting the whole population. At the time of the revival the people had been through 'a year without a summer' with bad harvests. Food was scarce, unemployment was widespread, and prices were high. Inflation and unemployment do not inevitably turn men's thoughts to God, but together with a higher mortality rate, in 1817 they were used by God's Spirit to create a sense of spiritual need.

Until that time the people of Beddgelert had not been known for their spiritual liveliness. On the contrary, the Calvinistic Methodist cause in the village had quite stagnated. For more than twenty years the membership had remained at a steady forty. Hardness and indifference to spiritual realities were widespread, and no power attended the preaching of God's Word. The home-spun entertainment of the time, which the majority sought in the local public house, took the form of singing and reciting, but this would soon degenerate into an orgy of drinking, swearing and fighting. The young people were brazen in their worldliness, profanity and immorality. Neither the prayers of the saints nor the most earnest pleading from the pulpit had any effect on them.

The unknown preacher

Many church members would have remembered—some might even have heard—the great Welsh Calvinistic Methodist preachers, contemporaries of Whitefield and Wesley, like Daniel Rowland and William Williams. They would almost certainly have fresh memories of those who followed them. Thomas Charles of Bala (who died in 1814) and Thomas Jones of Denbigh (who was to die in 1820), were both able, strong leaders and preachers. The churches of Wales were still richly endowed with preachers of exceptional gifts and usefulness: John Elias (Calvinistic Methodist), Christmas Evans (Baptist), and William Williams of Wern (Congregationalist). Yet God, in His sovereign providence, used an insignificant and unknown preacher to manifest His power in revival at Beddgelert.

For the initial stirrings of revival at that time, however, it is necessary to travel some distance to the west, to Nant Chapel in the Lleyn Peninsula, and to go back in time to the summer of 1816. One of the elders, burdened with the church's spiritual deadness, brought the matter before the congregation. He requested that every member should set a time daily to pray for a visitation of God's Spirit in their midst. At the next meeting he would ask each one about their response.

Children's prayer meeting

In the event, all but one had taken his message to heart, feeling that the matter was from the Lord. There was also a quiet conviction that God would not long delay the answers to their prayers. Even the children and Sunday School scholars had met for prayer with the same burden.

Sunday School met in the evening, the afternoon meeting being a preaching service. One handicapped child could not make the journey home between meetings, and he began to spend time in a loft to be alone with God. Gradually he was joined by other children, each being allowed admission on the condition of good behaviour. The same spirit of supplication soon gripped the more mature believers, some praying far into the night for a spiritual awakening.

At the beginning of 1817 it was evident that the ministry of the Word was becoming more lively and powerful. The little girl who had been the first to join the handicapped boy at prayer was also the first to break out into praise, soon to be followed by four others. Within a fortnight some eighty or so, of all ages, were under strong spiritual impressions, and the entire neighbourhood was overwhelmed with a sense of God's presence.

The daily routine of work and business was curtailed; some neither slept nor ate for days, such was the conviction of sin which overpowered them. The powerful influences spread through the community like wildfire, people coming under conviction while in the fields, or at work, or in bed. The Spirit's working was spontaneous, general and irresistible. On one occasion a stable-hand came under conviction, so much so that he roared as with pain; it spread to others in the yard, and together they cried for mercy. The local parson urged the employer to dismiss the stable-hand, but this was refused with the comment, 'I would rather hear him praying than swearing at the horses, as he used to'.

Firstfruits

Reports of these incidents reached Beddgelert early in 1817. In the Sunday School one young teacher began weeping while reading the closing passage of John's Gospel. At the close of the school one of the elders warned the young people against a fair coming to the village, urging them to seek the blessings which 'come from above'. 'Light, warmth, and refreshing rain come from above; the blessings of salvation come from above; the outpouring of the Spirit is from above; though dark here, it is light above'. Everyone, young and old alike, were overcome by solemnity and weeping. The very young were so terrified that they cried out 'the day of judgment has come?'.

These things were only the firstfruits of the harvest, some mercy drops heralding a mighty downpour. The floods of blessing burst the banks one Sunday in August under the ministry of Richard Williams from Brynengan. The congregation regarded the occasion as social rather than spiritual, having little thirst for God or regard for the preacher. Meeting in a farm kitchen, his pulpit was a makeshift one, a stool on a table between the window and the fireplace. He had hardly started preaching on 'he that cometh to me I will in no wise cast out', when a change came over his voice and manner. Later he confessed that it was as if he was listening to someone else preaching, even the matter was new to him!

A fearful solemnity descended on the people, few sang the closing hymn, and all dispersed in silence and awe. Throughout the community the following day a similar solemnity prevailed. During that week the church meeting, which few customarily attended, was full. Bible reading was followed by singing a hymn. Suddenly the whole place was a seething mass of agitated people. Some were in prayer, others in praise; some were crying for mercy, others weeping for joy: it was both disorderly and universal.

News of the extraordinary events in the chapel spread rapidly, bringing curious spectators in haste to witness the strange happenings. These in turn were overwhelmed by the same influences, and people eventually dispersed only after the strongest restraints from the more experienced members of the fellowship. Before the revival at Beddgelert had subsided some 240 people had been added to the church.

Powerful preaching

As the revival spread throughout the Principality, its most prominent feature was the power of the preaching. What had been previously weak, ineffective, and barren was now authoritative and fruitful. The descriptive element in preaching was mightily used of God, as in a sermon on Hebrews 11:7, 'by faith Noah', describing the predicament of the unbelieving when the door was closed; in a sermon on Psalm 1:5; the ungodly unable to stand at the judgment. During the latter sermon, the preacher cried out, 'Lord Jesus, enough, the people are almost dying, they can't take any more'. 'No', came the reply, 'I have one more word, "Depart from Me, ye cursed, to everlasting fire"'. At this, several hundred cried out for mercy, and it was reported that about a thousand were converted under that sermon.

Through the Beddgelert revival, preaching regained its authority and influence in the land. Some of the leaders, like John Elias, aware of the danger of spurious conversions and superficial impressions, sought to establish converts in the faith by emphasising the primacy of God's Word: 'True religion does not consist in emotions. The passions of many are excited under sermons, without a change of heart! Others may be changed; their hearts broken, conscience tender, sin hated, self loathed, but perhaps without many tears. There is a great difference in the natural temperament of people, which accounts for the difference in their feelings under the Word preached. I confess that if people are easily moved under natural causes, but immoveable and unaffected under sermons, it is a very bad sign. But the thing we should aim at in hearing the Word is to see more of the greatness and majesty of God, the purity of the law, the evil of sin, our miserable state of nature, the preciousness and excellency of Christ, the privilege of giving ourselves to Him to be saved in His own way, and to serve Him all the days of our life; and the feelings may be affected by those circumstances as God may see proper.' These timely words were written in December 1819, in the midst of that season of refreshing that lasted until 1822. The publication of the Calvinist Methodist Confession of Faith in 1823 served to strengthen the teaching ministry of the churches, and in turn consolidated the fruit of the revival.

When God visited His people in 1817 it was in spite of their unpreparedness. True, there was a remnant thinking and praying in terms of revival. There was faithful preaching of God's Word. But God's power came in sovereign and spontaneous fashion, and matters passed from the hands of men. Above all, God vindicated His truth, revived His people, and changed the face of whole societies. What He did before He can do gloriously again!

13
HUMPHREY JONES
'The youngster who lit the fuse'

'The '59 Revival began at a funeral.' That pithy statement was made by Evan Isaac half a century ago. It is to be found in his Welsh book on Humphrey Jones and the 1859 Revival, and he is referring to his subject's first public engagement after returning to his birthplace at Tre'r-ddôl, some 10 miles north of Aberystwyth in Mid Wales. Humphrey Jones was 26 years of age at the time, and he had spent the previous three years preaching to the Welsh communities in North America. He prayed with such unction at the funeral as to create a keen sense of anticipation that he would do great things. Within two years the whole of Wales had heard of him, and the Welsh churches had received some 100,000 new members.

Revival was 'in the air', as it were, in Wales as well as in America. With the rapid growth of the religious press regular articles appeared on the subject. Thus in the first half of 1858 attention was given in the denominational periodicals to local revivals at Llanfairfechan, Llangybi and Swansea; and stories of similar movements were copied from American newspapers and journals. The matter was discussed at the Calvinistic Methodist Association in April and June, with the recommendation that churches should be involved by interest and prayer. The Baptists of Monmouthshire at their Conference in May decided to set aside the first Sunday of August as a day of prayer for revival, and their example was followed by the Independents in South Wales at their Assembly in June.

Such activities were neither new nor unusual: in 'the Land of Revivals' they were part of an acknowledged religious pattern. Revival was the divine intervention of God's Spirit, coming with constraint and often without expectation into the regular means of grace. This would be followed by a profuse measure of liveliness amongst church members, widespread conversions among the ungodly, a disturbing sense of God's presence throughout entire communities, and a moral reformation spilling over into contemporary society. Such phenomena were collectively referred to as a 'revival' or an 'awakening'. God's sovereignty in it would be emphasized by reference to the 'outpouring' of the Holy Spirit, something similar to what happened on the day of Pentecost.

In the atmosphere and religious mind of the fifth decade of the last century any unusual stirring in a church meeting would reawaken a longing for revival. And why not in a funeral? The funeral had been an unexpected engagement for Humphrey Jones, but what of the meetings which he presided over for the next five weeks? Had that been his purpose in returning to Tre'r-ddôl? On his journey through Liverpool that June he told one minister that 'he had come to set Wales ablaze'. He preached there on the Sunday morning instead of another minister, and told him 'that in returning to the old country his intention was to commence revival meetings in the Aberystwyth area'. Liverpool was not set alight by his sermon, nor was the city touched by revival influences until the summer of the following year.[1] Recounting his memories some forty years later, the Rev. H. P. Howell writes in a similar vein: 'I think it was in the summer of 1857 that he visited the Racine district, while steadily working his way to Wales with the intention, by God's Spirit, of stirring the whole of Wales out of its spiritual slumber.' If that was the case, Humphrey Jones kept his intentions very much to himself at the time. The first public notice of his mission at Tre'r-ddôl, which appeared in the *Herald Gymreig* for 7 August 1858, simply reported that 'this young Wesleyan minister has only recently come to visit his native locality, and has been holding revival meetings in the above place. His ministry is very powerful, and fifty people have joined the cause during the last month. He intends to spend a month in the several chapels of the circuit.'[2]

In the standard history of Welsh Wesleyan Methodism the record of the occasion is brief: 'In 1858 the Rev. Humphrey Jones came from America to his former home, and at the request of the fellowship at Tre'r-ddôl, a series of revival meetings were held, which initiated the '59 Revival'. A more expanded version of the events is found in a letter written by Jones in August 1858, a letter which betrays a measure of ignorance regarding the Welsh situation:

The sound of revival is quite unfamiliar in Wales these days. Religion is at a low ebb throughout the country. Church prayer and fellowship meetings are lifeless in tone and few in number. This locality and the surrounding area were no exception. But I happened to come home from America five weeks ago to visit my relatives, and as they heard of the great Revival in America, and saw in the newspapers my name linked with the Revival, the friends felt a strong urge that I should set the same programme in motion in this area. This I did and great was the effect . . . The influence of the stirrings here has spread far and near. Letters come from all parts asking me to hold similar meetings. I have already undertaken to visit a number of places before returning to America. This revival is more especially among the Wesleyans. I believe that a blessed time will soon dawn on Wales, and that revivals will be common throughout the country.

Events were conforming to the pattern he had hoped for, although he refrained from giving public expression to his convictions.[3]

The word 'programme' and the phrase 'to hold similar meetings' provide the key to an appreciation of Jones's thinking, especially with regard to his understanding of the nature of revival, and the means which were conducive to realizing it in any situation. They also suggest the new direction to which the churches' faith was being guided: where before God's intervention and timing would have been sought, now there was to be a reliance on man's methods and techniques. In order to analyse the significance of this in Jones's contribution to the Revival, and to the religious life of Wales for the remainder of the century, it is necessary to trace his experience and career while in America.

Humphrey Jones's parents, his two brothers and sister emigrated to America in 1847, leaving him, at fifteen years of age, in the care of his aunt who lived in the Half Way Inn, Tre'r-ddôl. Five years later the family had settled in Oshkosh, Wisconsin. Hugh Jones and his wife Elizabeth were among the first founders of the Welsh Wesleyan cause there in 1855.[4]

Meanwhile, Jones had come under strong religious impressions, although he had been a church member for three or four years: 'When I was fifteen I came under a strong, disturbing and terrifying conviction, which lasted for over seventeen months. I was sore broken as in the place of dragons (Ps.44:19). At that time I was constrained to preach, and in deference to others rather than from any personl inclination, I began to preach, when sixteen, even before I found release from conviction.' As to his educational attainments, it was said of him: 'Mr Jones had the best education available to him in the area where he was brought up. He spent a term in the school of Mr Edward Jones, Aberystwyth, who was considered at the time to be the best scholar in Cardiganshire.'

Notwithstanding his eductional competence, he was not accepted as a candidate for the ministry by the District meeting of 1854. The reason, according to Evan Isaac, lay in the fact 'that there was no need for more preachers at the time'. The District minutes, in an appeal to the Wesleyan conference, show that there were financial difficulties, if not a manpower shortage, in that year: 'All the circuits in this District except three are dependent, and very poor, and the other three, which have the name of being independent, are notable properly to make up the salaries of their own Preachers.' It is evident that the District was unwilling to undertake the support of more preachers as long as there was insufficient funding to meet the necessary expenses.[5]

Humphrey Jones did not see things in that light at all, and J. J. Morgan suggests that he crossed 'the Atlantic in a disappointed frame of mind'. He had, after all, seen substantial success in his preaching, and he could honestly say, 'I have reason to believe that the Lord in his grace blessed my ministry at this time to the salvation of hundreds of souls in the upper regions of Cardiganshire.' It was extremely galling, therefore, to have to accept the gloomy outlook for a ministerial future in Wales intimated to him by the District. Given his determination 'that he was resolved to preach and to enter the ministry in spite of all opposition', and his evident success in the work already, it would have required an extraordinary measure of patience and humility to submit to the ruling and wait quietly for better days. He was not to know at the time that the District would accept three candidates on probation within the year, one of them from the nearby Machynlleth circuit. For his part, he shunned the waiting and set his sights on a future in America.[6]

If the country was new to him, the people were not: he was coming to a Welsh community. Welsh people had settled in New York since the end of the eighteenth century, and in 1842 one exiled Welshman could recommend particularly one part of the country: 'As far as I can judge from hearsay, Wisconsin Territory is the place for Welshmen. It lies to the north of Illinois. They say that it is a very healthy country, with good water, pure air and a temperate climate. There are also mines of lead and copper there . . . In the matter of religion, there is here almost every sort of Churchmen, Wesleyans, Presbyterians, Methodists, Baptists, Socinians, Quakers, Universalists and Mormons.' Jones spent a short time in New York and, after his reception as a preacher on probation with the Episcopal Wesleyans in 1855, he laboured as a 'missioner' amongst the Welsh of Oshkosh, Wisconsin.[7]

He was instrumental in constituting the Wesleyan church there, consisting of fourteen members in 1856, and of which six were from the Jones family. To all appearances there was nothing unusual in Humphrey Jones's ministry of those days. He saw a measure of growth, but no revival. Here is a description of the conditions in which he ministered: 'At first Mr Jones preached in houses; but soon it became possible to use the Red Schoolhouse, and this was the place of worship until a church was erected in 1862. Building was begun in 1861 . . . At that time Mr Jones was a pleasant young man . . . who possessed a fine, strong voice, and whose spirit was ablaze with love of the truth and a desire to save sinners.' In 1856 his circumstances changed, once more at his own instigation: 'I broke my connection with the Conference, and so followed my own inclination to visit any denomination which gave me opportunity.' In taking this step the usual course of ordination was denied him. From that time he looked on himself as a 'revivalist', added 'Rowland' to his name, and was referred to by the American Welsh community as 'the Reverend Humphrey R. Jones'. Today, having a Billy Graham image as a familiar pattern, his standing would more correctly be that of 'evangelist'.[8]

Responding to the invitations he received, he moved freely from one mission to another through Wisconsin, Ohio, Pennsylvania, Illinois, and New York. In presenting his message he would aim directly at the individual conscience, pressing for a response as a matter of urgency, and at the end counselling any who showed interest. In his own words here is a summary of his labours for the period 1856-8:

I began labouring as a Revivalist in Cambria, Wisconsin. Twenty-one people stayed behind at the close of the first meeting in the series, that is, all of those present except one. As a result, some claimed that I had stood in the doorway preventing people from leaving. On the contrary, I expressly said that no-one should stay behind from excitement, that the door was open for them to leave. I remained in those parts for a month. Then I came to the

Oshkosh area, where I laboured for a fortnight . . . From there I went to the Waukesha settlement. This was the place where the great dawning and the most powerful revival in connection with my ministry in America really commenced. Thence I went to Milwaukee city; there I was in the same place each night, and three times a Sunday for a month, witnessing some of the most astonishing meetings in my whole life. Forty-five people joined the church. After that I spent a month at Racine, and a fortnight at nearby Pike Grove. Even though it was the hay harvest, people came together to pray at six in the morning, as well as at night. From there I went to Big Rock, Illinois . . . preaching to the English as well as the Welsh people. I was invited to the annual meetings held by the Wesleyans in Oneida County, New York. There I began a series of interdenominational revival meetings. About seven hundred souls were converted at Oneida during that period.

Contemporary with Humphrey Jones's campaigns, if not preceding them on occasions, was a widespread spiritual awakening which made religion a talking point throughout the country, and indeed a matter of great urgency. One periodical, *Y Cenhadwr Americanaidd*, spoke of the social crisis prevailing in America at that time, as advantageous to the success of the gospel:

Previously, almost everyone pursued the deceitful 'mammon', and worshipped their idols—riches and rank—instead of the true God . . . Worldliness was our general and public sin . . . Such an attitude called for God's reproving visitation. Relentlessly, the crisis came! Suddenly the commerce of this great country and that of the whole world was thrown into complete confusion. In one moment thousands lost all their wealth. Thousands upon thousands were thrown out of work . . . But God overruled these things so as to make thousands of souls consider their end, and apply their hearts to wisdom.

Whatever the motivation for the religious excitement, a pattern of recognizable activities emerged in Jones's ministry.[9]

In Oneida county the revival began when a young woman expressed concern for her spiritual state. Shortly afterwards Humphrey Jones preached at the Wesleyan Conference in that place. Reporting the event, *Y Cenhadwr Americanaidd* stated:

This brother had been holding revival meetings amongst the various denominations in Wisconsin . . . And he expressed his intention to stay in Oneida over the winter to hold similar meetings wherever he found permission and co-operation . . . The congregationalists started . . . to hold such meetings, and continued for 10 weeks . . . Then . . . the Wesleyan Chapel . . . for 5 or 6 weeks . . . Then brother Jones came to Capel Uchaf, Steuben, and Remsen, and four churches joined together . . . to hold meetings . . . They continued twice a day and three times on the Sabbath for 6 weeks . . . They started among the Welsh community about the beginning of October, and they ceased the middle of March. The entire neighbourhood did virtually nothing except go to the meetings for this whole time . . . It is only right to add that the congregations have been generous in their contributions . . . especially to the visiting brother, Mr H. R. Jones.[10]

Evidently for Jones it was a full-time ministry, and the reimbursement he received was his means of support.

An interesting description of his preaching is given in some recollections which appeared in *Y Drych* in 1895:

The message was simple, clear, unadorned, complete . . . Like Moody he had plenty of melting, interesting and telling anecdotes, which he recounted and applied with considerable effect . . . I never heard him boast of his success in convicting men, which is sometimes all too evident in American revivalists . . . When he first appeared, he was abreast of the contemporary understanding of gospel truths. He was a third of a century ahead of his Welsh generation in his grasp of the most effective means of awakening souls and convicting them of their duties. If he were to appear now, he would be abreast of the spirit of the age, and would perhaps give a kind of Moody leadership in Zion.[11]

The comparison with Moody, and the contrast to American revivalists, classifies Humphrey Jones in a convenient type, a type that was at the time quite an innovation—'a third of a century ahead of his Welsh generation in his grasp of the most effective means of awakening souls and convicting them of their duties'. What were those means? And what influences convinced Jones of their lawfulness and suitability to awaken the church and convert the world? In the same article notice is taken of the elements which were new in Jones's manner: 'Preaching at that time was mainly doctrinal and systematic . . . Mr Jones brought a new gospel to men's ears . . . His preaching sounded less like theological, orthodox compositions, and more like fervent, personal appeals for men to be reconciled at once to God.' The innovative means, the theological framework which supported them, and the itinerary campaigning suggest the influence of the American Charles G. Finney.

Finney was converted at a time of revival in 1821. Two years later he was licenced to preach as a missioner by the Presbyterians. In the years 1825-32 he laboured in west New York State, travelling and preaching tirelessly. At the time he saw much success, and the missions came to be known as 'the Western Revivals'. At these missions, Finney preached night and day to crowded congregations, often under inter-denominational auspices. Interestingly, one of Humphrey Jones's most fruitful spheres of ministry was Oneida County, as it had been for Finney thirty years before.

Finney's manner of preaching was fiery and tempestuous, deliberately so, depending on persuasion and reason to triumph over the audience. He would close with an appeal to those who had been influenced in any way to come forward to 'the anxious seat'. During this successful period the converts were numbered in thousands, but within three years Finney confessed, 'I learned, with pain, that the spirit of revival had greatly declined, . . . and that a spirit of jangling and controversy alarmingly prevailed.' Similar testimonies to the disturbingly low quality of the converts are given by some of Finney's friends, and critics estimated that only one in ten of them stood the test of time.[12]

Resulting from his experience as a 'revivalist', Finney gave lectures on 'revival'. They formed a kind of apologia to his theology and to his methods. They were published in 1835, some 12,000 copies being sold within a few months of their appearance. By 1839 a Welsh translation was off the press. The lectures give clear evidence of Finney's fundamental departure from the Calvinism of his denomination, affirming his belief that man's responsibility before God was dependent on his moral ability to choose what was right and good.

Finney's position can be summed up in this way. Revival is not a miracle on the part of God, but an activity on the part of man. In its essence Christianity is human rather than divine. Man has both choice and power in religious activity, to respond or otherwise to God's provision for him in the gospel. Therefore, a revivalist's work is to use every means to influence man's unprejudiced reason and unbiased will. This cannot be achieved, however, without God's help: the preacher still has a responsibility in the matter of diligent prayer and effective preaching. In addition, every means must be used to awaken the church to its responsibility towards the world, and to remove every conceivable hindrance on the path of blessing. New methods must be devised all the time, so as to overcome the natural tendency to despise what is familiar. One such innovation was 'the anxiety seat', an attempt to confront people with the need for decision while the sermon's influence was still fresh in their minds. If the means are used with thoroughness and sincerity, revival will inevitably follow. Indeed, such success is indispensable to any minister worthy of his calling. It is not faithfulness but success which vindicates his ministry. Having set out these propositions, Finney acknowledges that revival can be hindered if mechanical means are used to promote it! Many critics spoke of the serious declension in the churches which followed the departure of the 'revivalist'. They added that Finney had betrayed the scriptural and orthodox theology of the Puritan Fathers in America, as well as the proven teaching of Jonathan Edwards in the golden age of the Great Awakening.[13]

With that brief review of Finney's main teachings, it is possible to assess the extent to which they were adopted, intentionally or otherwise, by Humphrey Jones. His energetic labours have already been noted; according to one report, 'the meetings, held twice a day and three times on the Sabbath, lasted for six weeks'. Praying, preaching, pleading: that was the pattern of his ministerial life, and those were the memories people had of him in later years. 'He experienced what he preached; his sermon was an expression of his deep convictions and feelings. But his prayers were even more remarkable and more effective than his sermons. He had a solemn and striking personality, and on occasions his appeals were so electric that the congregations would be quite overcome.'[14] Here, then, were the resources he brought to the work: experience, conviction, feeling, prayer, personality, appeal. References to the Spirit's resources, and the need for them, are glaringly absent.

A survey of the texts of his sermons reveals two aspects to his ministry. One was a conscious attempt to awake believers within the churches ('Woe to them that are at ease in Zion'; 'Because thou art ... neither cold nor hot'; 'Awake thou that sleepest'); and the other was aimed at convincing the ungodly of their responsibility and danger ('What will ye do in the day of visitation?'; 'How long halt ye between two opinions?'; 'Behold, now is the accepted time'). But praying and preaching were not enough: another technique was required to bring men to the point of persuasion and decision there and then, without delay, and this is where 'the anxiety seat' and 'the penitent pew' were so useful. This was also where Humphrey Jones departed from the customary *seiat* (society or fellowship meeting), which was usually held during the week to give men time for a more leisurely consideration of gospel obligations.*

Writing in 1895, Dr H. O. Rowlands could reflect: 'the present was emphasized . . . "Tomorrow morning, O! sinner, you may be in hell!" Then a *seiat* followed the sermon, and sinners would be solemnly urged to remain behind to receive the offers of grace. There was an effective novelty in these means. In addition to this, the revivalist visited people's homes, and with solemn, personal entreaties and importunate prayers he implored and pleaded with men to yield to God's grace and call to them.'[15] There is in this feverish activity a classical, lively portrayal of the Finney type of 'revivalist'. This is not to condemn either Jones's godliness or his sermons. What it does is to show the origins of his new measures, and at the same time to suggest the dangers and weaknesses inherent in them. What if there was no response from church members, and what if there was no stirring among the ungodly? What would be the converts' ground for faith and hope when the elevated feeling and general excitement had been replaced by the burning trials of each day?

Humphrey Jones managed to evade these issues while in America for two reasons. One reason was that his evangelistic campaigns merged imperceptibly with the general revival movement which shook the whole of America, and indeed parts of Europe and many other countries throughout the world. The shock-waves of that great movement were felt by the business men of New York city as early as October 1857. The ripples spread irresistibly and spontaneously throughout the churches, and within a year the converts were numbering half a million.[16]

The other reason was Humphrey Jones's return to Wales. He landed in Liverpool in June 1858. In his heart burned the revival fire of America, and the hope, if not the intention, that he would be an instrument to light a similar blaze in Wales. Upon his arrival at Tre'r-ddôl he held a campaign in his home locality along the same lines as those he had adopted in America. Soon after the commencement

---

* The seiat—derived from the English word society—was the name given to the 'society' or 'experience' meetings of the converts of the Methodist Revival. In mid nineteenth-century Wales, however, by which time those early societies had long grown into churches, the term seiat was being used in a more general sense, usually to refer to a church fellowship meeting.

of those meetings he heard of a young student with the Calvinistic
Methodists who had been preaching at the next village of Taliesin.
He shared with him his vision in a letter:

When I heard of your style of preaching, that you aim at reaching the conscience, I rejoiced greatly . . . I believe that a great revival will soon come to
Wales. I would dearly love . . . to converse with you . . . so that I could tell
you . . . of the way to be a succesful preacher. Two things are necessary . . .
one is to be a man of much secret prayer . . . the other thing is to preach
reprovingly and severely, aiming at the conscience each time . . . preach
severe sermons to the church first. Strive to awake Zion. However much
you preach to the world, it will not achieve much unless you have first
stirred Zion from her sleep.[17]

Nothing came of the letter. To the vast majority of religious people
in Wales at the time Jones's ideas would have been strange if not
repulsive. They were at least contrary to the widely-held belief that
awakening the church and convincing the sinner were the province
of the Holy Spirit. Furthermore, the timing of such a heavenly visitation lay securely, but also secretly, in the providence of God.

Humphrey Jones remained at Tre'r-ddôl for five weeks, and there
were astonishing scenes. One talking-point was the crowd which
gathered around the chapel in the afternoons: 'Only with the greatest
difficulty was it possible to drive the carriage past the chapel, such
was the crowd. The chapel was crammed full, and the road in either
direction past it for about half a mile was packed with people, young
and old, some worshipping, some praying and others praising,
everyone behaving with self-control and in an orderly fashion.' At
dawn the scene was no different: 'People from the area congregated
at the chapel at five in the morning, even on the busiest days of harvest, and the sound of song and praise could be heard in the houses
and in the fields throughout the locality.'[18]

Humphrey Jones gives a triumphant account of the work: 'The
church was thoroughly revived, and prayer meetings were held each
night. At the close of the prayer meeting, we asked whether there
were any sinners present who wished to be mentioned in the prayers
of the church, and who wished to give themselves to the Saviour. If
so, then they should come to the front pew . . . Each night the procedure was the same. During the second week there was preaching
each night, and at the end some came forward each evening. To date
in this small locality 51 have been converted.' Similar things were

experienced during his next campaign, at Ystumtuen, and Jones could say, 'Even at the height of the revival blaze in America last winter we seldom saw such powerful influences. Already 76 have been converted here.'[19]

These remarkable manifestations followed him from Ystumtuen to Mynydd-bach at the beginning of September, and then on to Pont-rhyd-y-groes and Ysbyty Ystwyth in October. In this latter place the Calvinistic Methodist minister, Dafydd Morgan, experienced a new power in his life and ministry only after an acknowledged 'measure of prejudice'. Until that time he had been a very ordinary and unknown preacher, but later he was to take precedence over Humphrey Jones, such was the unction on his ministry. For three nights he faced a deep spiritual crisis in his soul, and then, in the middle of the following night the divine release and anointing came upon him. 'I awoke about four o'clock', he said later, 'remembering everything of a religious nature that I had ever learnt or heard. Everything that was told me I remembered.' Within a few weeks 'he had unutterable and glorious experiences' as he travelled over the hills between Llanilar and Devil's Bridge, spending 'hours' without knowing exactly where he was. The two worked together in the Ysbyty Ystwyth area until the middle of November, and by the end of the year over 200 conversions were recorded. For a while the two continued their association, visiting Pontrhydfendigaid, Tregaron, Blaenpennal, Swyddffynnon and Llanafan. Before the end of November they separated. Dafydd Morgan's son and biographer summarizes this period in this way: 'At the beginning of this time, people expected Humphrey Jones and Dafydd Morgan. Before the end, they were awaiting Dafydd Morgan and Humphrey Jones.' After separating, the latter went to the village of Llanfihangel-y-Creuddyn, and in the latter part of December he came to Aberystwyth. It was here that his mission came to a sad end.[20]

At this point it will be useful to summarize Dafydd Morgan's contribution to the Revival. The reason for his initial reservations with regard to the work can be readily ascertained. In common with others of the Calvinistic Methodists he feared what could be called 'a carnal revival', that is, an attempt on the part of men to imitate the effects of revival. Finney's influence had reached Wales as far back as 1839 when a Welsh translation of his lectures on the subject appeared. At the time it was instrumental in a measure of success in what was called 'the silent revival'. These new ideas, and they were widely regarded as such, found acceptance with some. The Calvinistic Methodist Association of April 1840, however, firmly resisted the measures, issuing a broadside against them by reaffirming the traditional stance on the matter: 'In order to have revival there is no need to change any article of doctrine; the Spirit will only anoint the old revealed truths. There is no need to try any measures other than those of divine appointment.' More explicit expressions were unnecessary, everyone understood the implied criticism of Finney's position.[21]

As to the lasting significance of Finney's 'Lectures' on Wales, John Thomas in his biography of the Rev. Thomas Rees of Swansea says of the Congregationalists: 'A definite transformation could be discerned in the character of our denominational ministry. In place of the old systematic treatment of the truth in a doctrinal manner, sermons took a more practical approach, to the heart and conscience, and to behaviour.' The convictions of the fathers, therefore, were different, not because of deficient reasoning, but from scriptural and theological considerations. As Dr Tudur Jones says of them: 'They insisted on defending the unmediated sovereignty of the Holy Spirit. He could influence men's minds directly, independently of means. For that very reason you could not command Him by using techniques. If revival came, it would be through the sovereign and gracious intervention of God.'[22]

Dafydd Morgan was nurtured in that Puritan strain, and he had read works of the leading Puritans such as Thomas Watson and John Owen. The revival he contemplated was the product of the Spirit's intervention, a divine visitation that would engulf everything in its path in blessed disorder. Predictably, therefore, after Humphrey Jones's departure from Ysbyty Ystwyth, he changed the character of the meetings, establishing something which he considered 'more edifying on some evenings to discuss the basic truths of the faith, with a view to establishing and maturing the converts'. In this, of course, he had an advantage over Jones, in that he was the settled minister of a congregation. At the same time it was an indication of a more disciplined and solid religious piety than that of Humphrey Jones.

Dafydd Morgan's revival activities lasted until the spring of 1860. The religious excitement gradually subsided, and Morgan settled once more into an ordinary level of preaching and influence. By that time the 1859 Revival was a fact of history, its effects covering the whole of Wales independently of the revivalist.

The most astonishing earnest of the Revival's general, spontaneous diffusion was experienced at Tregaron during the period of
the two revivalists' united efforts. There was nothing striking initially
at the meetings, but things changed when a heavenly anointing was
felt on the proceedings. 'The congregation was overcome with
something the like of which had not been experienced before . . .
there was precious little order on the meeting that night', according
to one witness; another testified, 'It was a meeting which altered the
complexion of the whole awakening: general rejoicing broke out . . .
By the following Sunday evening Llangeitho, Llwynpiod, Llanddewi-
brefi, and Pontrhydfendigaid [in the neighbouring area] were ablaze
. . . Soon . . . all the means of grace were under evident unction,
especially preaching.' Herein lay the difference. At Tre'r-ddôl,
notwithstanding the crowds and the excitement, everything was
localized and orderly; at Tregaron there was disorder and spontaneous rapture, the effects spreading to the nearby villages in a quite
unsolicitied and irresistible way. Revival had truly come.[23]

If Tregaron was a turning-point in the course of the Revival, there
are grounds for asserting that it was a crisis in Humphrey Jones's
experience. He had to face the possibility of failure in his mission.
At the first of the Tregaron meetings, 'he had a . . . very hard service; the heavenly breeze was absent, and although he spoke of . . .
profitable and timely things, somehow nothing gripped . . . He
appeared . . . as one trying to engineer a revival.' For him it was a
period of similar leanness at other places in the area—Llanafan,
Llanilar, Swyddffynnon. At Llanafan, 'since the meeting was so
hard he soon came down from the pulpit'; at Llanilar there was little
response, and he rebuked the congregation with the words 'I am
convinced that things are not as they should be with you'; and at
Swyddffynnon, 'having been in the pulpit for only a few minutes,
he came down and alleged that he could not preach in such a hard
atmosphere, and urged the brethren who had opened with prayer to
pray again.'[24] Preaching without success was, to him, a condemnation of the preacher. Something was wrong with the machinery, and
that had to be corrected before proceeding any further. Thus the sermon was displaced while the revival programme was reviewed. This
dilemma was at the root of Jones's sad decline.

In accordance with his long-standing intention, he came at last to labour among the Wesleyans of Aberystwyth, in hopes 'of a deeper and more excellent revival than any experienced in the outlying country areas'. By this time it was the middle of December 1858, but within a short time he was once more in difficulties: 'I don't know what will become of me in this town, they are so hard.' The disappointment and the uncertainty—'my afflictions' as he called them—overwhelmed him, and he became stubborn and unpredictable. J. J. Morgan describes the Aberystwyth period in this way: 'Mr Jones did not preach, nor would he allow anyone else to do so. There was only one sermon in the space of two months. Neither would he allow very much singing. Usually there was only a Scriptue reading, and praying. For a while the meetings were popular and influential. Scores expressed a desire to join the church, but Humphrey Jones would not receive them, claiming that the church at Queen Street (the Wesleyan church) was unfit to receive and nurture newly-born children . . . The meetings went into decline. The singing faded away, and eventually the saints could not even pray.'

The saints were not alone in their anguish, Jones himself was perplexed: 'Endeavouring to pray, but failing completely. Trying to exhort, but having to sit down.' Yet, he was hopeful of better times, as one of the congregation reported: 'He tells us that the dawn is about to break, that he has had a revelation from the Lord that something wonderful will happen.' As a result, Jones 'began to "prophesy"'. He announced . . . that on a certain day, at eleven in the morning, the Holy Spirit would descend visibly, and the Millenium would then be ushered in.'[25]

By this time Dafydd Morgan had also come to Aberystwyth—to Tabernacle—and the Calvinistic Methodists of that chapel, and of the whole town, were in a state of the highest spiritual fervour. A vivid contemporary description of the prevailing excitement and expectancy is given in a letter dated 1 March 1859:

Cardiganshire through the abounding grace of the Almighty God has had in these latter days what you may call a foretaste of the Millennium. The glorious old days of Howel Harris, Rowlands Llangeitho etc. are powerfully recall'd by the revival now going on in our neighbourhood. Think of people dancing and 'gorfoleddu' (joyfully praising) in the different chapels all about here . . . Call to mind the number that used to attend the prayer meetings in the old 'Tab' *Nos Lun 1af o'r mis* [at Tabernacle on the first Monday of the month]; what would you think if you saw the bottom of the chapel full on Monday nights in a prayer meeting, Tuesday, Wednesday and Friday nights the same, and the Society on Thursday night full up to the corners under the gallery [300-400 people]. On Tuesday nights prayer meetings are held at the same time in the Tabernacle, Trefechan, Tanycae, Penparciau, Skinner's Street, Morfa and Waun (related preaching stations), all well attended. Over 250 have in the last few weeks joined our Society.[26]

Such success corresponded to the commonly held belief that an effective and widespread propagation of the gospel was to usher in the thousand years which immediately preceded Christ's coming and the end of the world. Finney had insisted on linking this hope with the use of his means: 'If the whole Church, as a body, had gone to work ten years ago (when he was seeing remarkable things under his ministry in New York), and continued it as a few individuals . . . have done, there might not now have been an impenitent sinner in the land. The millennium would have fully come into the United States before this day . . . If the Church will do all her duty, the millenium may come in this country in three years.'

In the midst of the awakenings in America during the summer of 1858, a correspondent to one of the American Welsh periodicals could write: 'It appears that additions to the churches take place here, as in Wales, chiefly through occasional revivals of religion; indeed it is so in every age and in every country, under the gospel as under the former dispensation, and they multiply and are more powerful as they approach the great revival of the Millennium.'[27] Could these have been the authors that influenced Humphrey Jones at the beginning of 1859? Frequent references are found in his own letters to the present 'Dispensation' in which he and others found themselves, a dispensation which frustrated all spiritual activity and missionary endeavour. He wrote in July 1859:

This Dispensation is nothing other than the literal fulfilment of those words in Romans 9:28 ('For he will finish the work, and cut it short in righteousness: because a short work will the Lord make upon the earth'). Or in other words that 'spirit of judgment, and of burning' (Isa.4:4) which is to descend on the world as a *preparation* for the coming of the *Millennium* . . . I know that these words are to be completely fulfilled within the body of this year, that is, before July of next year.

His prophecy was not realized and Humphrey Jones disappeared from prominence in the revival altogether. He himself gave as the reason for his withdrawal, 'I became too weak'; others maintained that his health had failed, while some added the comment, 'a change of views as to the mode of promoting a revival'.[28]

His sun had set, and he spent some time at the Mental Hospital at Carmarthen. He was at a similar institution in America for a further period later in his life. It was on his return to America that someone recorded his impressions of Jones's 'first sermon at the Calvinistic Methodist chapel at Milwaukee . . . when he presented a rambling discussion on the heady theories of the Second Coming, and went to disorderly and unruly extremes'. After the Aberystwyth debacle his preaching was without unction, but his prayers were lively and appealing. He died at his brother's home in America in 1895 at the age of 62.[29]

What then were the results of the Revival, and what was Humphrey Jones's contribution to it?

A prior question, however, must be asked: What if there had been no Revival? Evidences of serious declension were everywhere, even though some hoped for better days, and the sporadic local revivals presaged a greater effusion. The 1859 Revival safeguarded a solid gospel witness for the second half of the century.

Reference has already been made to the number of converts during the Revival, a number which considerably strengthened the Nonconformist presence. This was later to prove a key factor in the move to disestablish the National Church in Wales. With regard to the quality of the converts, there is consistent evidence that few of them disowned their profession.[30] The churches were quickened, a new generation of preachers, missionaries and leaders emerged. The fruit of the Revival was consolidated by consistent preaching, both before and after 1859. In this context it is necessary to remember that although prayer meetings were the means of its commencement, with Humphrey Jones's efforts a kind of catalyst in the process, the Revival's fire descended on material which had been made ready by years of preaching. Attention was repeatedly drawn to the fact that many of the converts had come under conviction at the time of the Revival by means of a sermon which they had heard many years previously. Consequently, the Revival was widely regarded as the spiritual harvest of a long season of sowing and watering the seed. In reviewing the 1859 Revival, Robert Ellis of Ysgoldy quotes a saying of John Elias of Anglesey: 'We once heard Mr Elias say that in God's gracious dealings there was a similarity to the way men blast the rock in a quarry; to make the initial hole . . . and so on, the need is for determined, strong men; but any keen, lively youngster may be given the job of lighting the fuse . . . and it is this, of course, which effects the explosion. So it was in this revival. It was the result or the fruit of twenty years of preaching and of weary, sustained labour.'[31]

A new, strong social awareness accompanied the religious awakening. The desire for national educational establishments was intensified, and this was in turn regarded as a growing sense of national identity. However, it would be futile to expect the Revival to have any direct impact on politics. Both the Calvinistic and Wesleyan Methodists were opposed to organized intervention on the part of the churches. Social action was different, and many crusades against the social evils of the day, among children, the poor, and others, and the cause of temperance was given fresh impetus. The social conscience and moral standards of society were strongly influenced by the Revival. During the last half of the century the pattern of life and work for many was substantially changed. The God who had been real to so many in the 1859 Revival was the One who strengthened and guided them in the new Industrial Age.

What then of Humphrey Jones's contribution?

His sad withdrawal to Aberystwyth did not quench the revival fire. The divine influences continued to spread, deeply and effectively, spontaneously and generally, throughout Wales. Yet it must be conceded that Humphrey Jones's return to Tre'r-ddôl was its beginning. He could so easily and comfortably—if not so successfully and famously—have stayed amongst his family and the other Welsh exiles in America. Compelled, however, by love of God and love of Wales, he returned to the 'Old Country'. His personal godliness and evangelistic zeal are beyond question. He deserves to be honoured as one of the leading benefactors of his country and generation.

If the means he adopted exposed him to trouble and danger, he passionately believed them to be useful. If there was an imbalance in his interpretation of Scripture, he was not deficient in sincerity in his preaching of the gospel and in his earnest praying for the salvation of souls. If he was not one of those whom John Elias styled the determined, 'strong men', he was the 'keen, lively youngster' who was 'given the job of lighting the fuse'. Ultimately, it was that which caused the explosion that is known as the 1859 Revival.

FIRE IN THE THATCH

ABBREVIATIONS

EI: Evan Isaac, *Humphrey Jones a Diwygiad 1859* (Bala, 1930)
NLW: The National Library of Wales
JJM: J. J. Morgan, *The '59 Revival in Wales* (Mold, 1909)
DM: J. J. Morgan, *Hanes Dafydd Morgan Ysbyty a Diwygiad 59* ([Mold], 1906)

REFERENCES

1. JJM 3; DM 21,391-3; *Y Fwyell*, May 1894,61; *Yr Annibynwr*, June 1859, 144;
    J. Edwin Orr, *The Second Evangelical Awakening in Britain* (London, 1949),
    156
2. *Y Drych*, July 1895; DM 24
3. Hugh Jones, *Hanes Wesleyaeth Gymreig*, vol.iii (Bangor, 1912), 1251; *Yr Herald
    Gymreig*, 14 August 1858; DM 24,25
4. David Davies, *Hanes y Cymry 1847-1897 yn Swyddau Winnebago a Fond Du
    Lac, Wisconsin* (Oshkosh, Wisconsin, 1898), 75,168
5. EI 20,21; *Y Fwyell*, Sept 1894, 181; DM 19; NLW Wesleyan MS 358D
6. DM 19; NLW Wesleyan MS 358D, Minutes for 12-14 June 1855
7. *NLW Journal*, vol.ix (1955-6), 58-9; David Davies, op. cit ., 168,181; EI 24
8. David Davies, loc.cit.; DM 19-20
9. DM 20; *Y Cenhadwr Americanaidd*, May 1858, 167
10. *Y Cenhadwr Americanaidd*, May 1858, 1892-3
11. *Y Drych*, 18 July 1895
12. C. G. Finney, *Revivals of Religion* (London, 1913), vi,xiv, 27; see also William
    G. McLoughlin, *Revivals, Awakenings and Reform* (Chicago, 1978), 122-8;
    P. E. G. Cook, 'Finney on Revival', in *One Steadfast High Intent* [1965 Puritan
    Conference Papers] (London, 1966), 4-16; J. Edwin Orr, *The Light of the
    Nations* (Exeter, 1965), 58-9
13. See C. G. Finney, op. cit ., passim; Bennet Tyler and Andrew Bonar, *The Life and
    Labours of Asahel Nettleton* (London, 1975); John F. Thornbury, *God Sent
    Revival* (Welwyn, 1977); B. B. Warfield, *Perfectionism* (Philadelphia, 1958),
    125-214
14. EI 28-9
15. EI 35,52; *Y Fwyell*, Sept. 1894, 182; *Y Drych*, July 1895
16. J. Edwin Orr, *The Second Evangelical Awakening in Britain*, 35-7
17. DM 25-7
18. EI 37; Hugh Jones, op. cit ., vol.iii, 1251-2
19. DM 24-5,27-8
20. DM 33,42,43,98-9; JJM 16; EI 58-9
21. *Cymru*, vol.xxvii (1904), 282; see also Richard Parry, *Y Pentecost Cymreig*
    (Llanrwst, 1840), 3; *Y Drysorfa*, June 1840, 182
22. John Thomas, *Cofiant y Parch T. Rees, D D, Abertawy* (Dolgellau, 1888), 95-6;
    R. Tudur Jones, *Hanes Annibynwyr Cymru* (Swansea, 1966), 202; see also R. M.
    Jones, *Llên Cymru a Chrefydd* (Swansea, 1977), 485-6
23. *Y Fwyell*, July 1894, 110; *Y Geninen*, vol.xxiii (1905), 98; cf. DM 58-9; JJM 27-
    8,35-6; and NLW, Calvinistic Methodist Archives, General 871: 'Atgofion per-
    sonol Daniel Davies, Ton, o ddiwygiad 1859 yn Nhregaron'
24. DM 87,98,70

25. DM 146,147; JJM 16-17; EI 63-64
26. DM 149; NLW, CMA, General 12684
27. C. G. Finney, op. cit ., 345,346; *Y Cyfaill o'r Hen Wlad*, August 1858, 281; cf.Iain H. Murray, *The Puritan Hope* (London, 1971)
28. EI 67; DM 22; David Davies, op. cit ., 181; *Y Drych*, 4 and 18 July 1895; Thomas Phillips, *The Welsh Revival* (London, 1860), 138
29. *Y Drych,* 18 July 1895; EI 89,90
30. See e.g. *Yr Eurgrawn Wesleyaidd*, Dec. 1860, 429; *Cymru*, vol.xiii (1897), 13; Thomas Phillips, op. cit ., 135-6; Hugh Jones, op. cit ., vol.iii, 987
31. *Y Drysorfa,* 1859, 162-3,286,382; John Owen Jones, *Cofiant a Gweithiau y Parch Robert Ellis*, Ysgoldy, Arfon (Caernarfon, 1883), 264-5

14
DAFYDD MORGAN
'Commissioned by the King'

Several events made 1859 a memorable year. The appearance of Charles Darwin's *Origin of Species* made a profound impression on both science and religion, while social theories received a modifying influence in a book by John Stuart Mill called *On Liberty*. Charles Dickens's already substantial literary labours were supplemented by *A Tale of Two Cities*, and the country went to the polls for another General Election.

In one way or another each of these events affected historic Christianity. If Darwin's evolutionary theories hailed the liberation of man from the biological confines of special creation, and from the theological confines of divine revelation, Mill's thesis sought to liberate him socially from such external restraints as an inhibiting convention. The sharply contrasting pictures of tyranny and liberty drawn in *A Tale of Two Cities* raised the question as to how long it would be before the reign of reason and revolution in Paris replaced that of faith and revelation in London. During the General Election in Wales the curtailing of liberty by intimidation was already a reality: some tenants were evicted from their farms near Bala by W. W. E. Wynne for refusing him their electoral support. Their refusal was not altogether political; it was partly due to their deep misgivings about his Tractarian activities. Humanism, in its many forms, seemed set to rid man of the supposed shackles of divine revelation and sanction.

It was, however, another event which proved to have the greatest significance, namely, the religious Revival which swept through Ulster, Scotland, England and Wales. It determined the spiritual tone of the churches, the moral fibre of the nation, and the social improvement of the people for a whole generation. A powerful change was brought about by this spiritual awakening in the lives of some 100,000 people in the Principality. Such a transformation in so many people influenced attitudes, movements, social structures, and personal relationships far more fundamentally and extensively than any scientific theory, political manifesto, or social engineering could ever have achieved. In Wales the man at the centre of that spiritual awakening was Dafydd Morgan.

Social changes were certainly taking place in the area of north Cardiganshire where Morgan spent his entire life. Born in 1814 near the famous Devil's Bridge, his mill home was a place of industry and piety. In the Cardiganshire of his youth, standards of living were low and, apart from agriculture, most men found a living as carpenters, cobblers, tailors, masons, blacksmiths and woollen workers. By the 1840s there was a resurgence in the demand for lead, and the mines of the upper Rheidol and Ystwyth valleys proliferated and prospered. About 1824 the family moved to Pont-rhyd-y-groes, where Morgan's father built a mill within a stone's throw of a mine level. Morgan was living here in 1859 when mining and revival activities were at their most intense, combining the trade of carpentry with the calling of preacher in the Calvinistic Methodist Connexion.

The Calvinistic Methodist nurture to which he was heir and of which he was part was both distinctive and determinative. Its most distinguishing feature was an established pattern of assessing experimental religion exercised in the *seiat*. This stemmed from and reflected the Methodism of the eighteenth-century fathers of the movement, notably that of Howel Harris, Daniel Rowland and William Williams. Later leaders such as Thomas Charles, Thomas Jones and John Elias bequeathed a legacy of orthodoxy by an insistence on the disciplined understanding of biblical truth. To mention such names as Daniel Rowland and John Elias is to evoke other aspects of that rich heritage: the glorious tradition of powerful preaching with its exalted image of a gospel minister; and the periodic seasons of revival which kept fresh in the awareness of the people the dimension of sovereign and transforming visitations of the Holy Spirit. All these aspects of Calvinistic Methodist soul culture affected Morgan, and in turn they were determinative for the 1859 Revival in Wales.

Morgan's experience of God's grace began with his conversion under the ministry of Evan Evans at Cwmystwyth in 1836. At the time Evans was a schoolteacher at Nant-y-glo, was prominent in the Calvinistic Methodist Association preaching festivals, and had written a book on the Covenant of Works (*Y Cyfammod Gweithredoedd*, 1833).[1] Later in his life Morgan bore witness to the reality and authority of that experience. When preaching there himself during the Revival, he pointed to where he had sat on that occasion, saying that he would always remember that day and place 'when the new nature descended by the Holy Spirit's regeneration into his heart'. Even close to death one of his last sentences was 'The old covenant made at Cwmystwyth stands as firm as ever.'

Membership of the Calvinistic Methodist cause at Ysbyty Ystwyth followed, but this would have been neither automatic nor immediate. From the beginning of the Methodist movement there had been a concern for recognizing and nurturing a genuine work of grace in the heart. The emphasis had been on a warm, charitable encouragement of faith and fellowship in a thoroughly biblical framework: 'We meet to examine our faith and conduct, to glorify God thereby, to confirm our privileges in Christ, and to foster discipline, peace, purity and protection amongst ourselves'. If the societies had an exalted aim, they also had a tender approach, that 'special care be taken to refuse no-one, however weak, provided there are tokens of his acceptance by Christ'.

In assessing admission to the fellowship great care was to be taken to maintain the balance between the demands of charity on the one hand, and of purity on the other. Consequently, says Williams, the usual way is to put a person 'on trial', and for this he would need

to give his name to the stewards of the society some time beforehand; and for such stewards then to question him privately, and that on more than one occasion, also to ask his neighbours about him, and to ask some of his friends what difference they see in him, and to make a point of getting an account of him from the lips of the godly and the ungodly as far as possible; and when a month or two is spent on this enquiry into the reality of his state of grace—that is what is called a 'trial'. Then if the stewards find him fit to come before the entire body of the fellowship, let every one question him . . . asking for the testimony of all the members as to his being in a true state of grace, and let him be received if counted worthy—by the consent of the entire fellowship.

The 'Rules' which governed Morgan's admission into membership were those drawn up by Thomas Charles and Thomas Jones, first published in 1801, and subsequently issued in 1823 along with the newly-framed 'Confession of Faith'. Allowing for a modified terminology here and there, the procedure for admission was virtually unchanged:

Let none be admitted into membership hastily, but let every candidate for membership first inform one of the elders or members of his intention, before he appears personally at the church meeting; that they may have time to make enquiries concerning him and be fully satisfied respecting his life and conversation—not what he was, but what he is now; and when they are satisfied in their own minds, let him come himself before the church; then let him be examined, if he shows signs of repentance and conversion, and if his soul is awakened to seek salvation. If they are in doubt about him, let them take time to consider the matter . . .

A shift of emphasis, however, is discernible in seeking to evaluate the content of the candidate's faith. Before, 'questions' had been asked in order to examine the strength of the candidate's conviction, in the sense of spiritual enlightenment, personal need, submission to Christ and His people. From 1801, however, 'questions' were to be replaced by 'qualifications': 'None may be admitted into membership of whom we cannot entertain a reasonable hope that they possess these qualifications'. The shift suggested that entrance to the church involved a person's acceptability before men, as well as acceptance before God; a growth in grace as well as an experience of grace; a measure of sanctification as well as an evidence of justification. True, in the second-generation document, there was the probing for conviction as before, but the majority of the 'Rules' referred to sanctions about specific areas of conduct, from Sabbath observance to smuggling, from conscientiousness in work to a conscience about words. This was undoubtedly a tactical concession to the criticism and slander of opponents, and Thomas Charles had been involved in controversy at the turn of the century over the tenets and practices of the Methodists. At the same time, the extensive 'qualifications' tended to give the documents as a whole a legalistic flavour and exposed the church to the danger of adopting an over-scrupulous attitude. The whole matter was to have particular application for Dafydd Morgan during the Revival, affecting as it did the acceptance or otherwise of the converts. In this, facing as he did situations which paralleled those confronting Williams and the other early Methodists, he prudently reverted to their earlier practice of recognizing conviction, with a measure of caution.[2]

As a young convert, Dafydd Morgan was regular at family worship and at the means of grace. He took an enthusiastic interest in Sunday school and temperance activities, and was soon being urged to preach. This he refused until he was unable to resist any longer, and so he began the long and arduous task of preparation for recognition as a preacher with the denomination. Acceptance as a preacher was governed by the Monthly Meeting of Cardiganshire Calvinistic Methodist churches. It followed a pattern of probation usually lasting for several years, and culminating in ordination by the denomination's South Wales Association. The principle which governed the procedure was expressed in 1843 by the North Wales Association: 'Every branch of the Church among the Calvinistic Methodists should understand that their approval of a Candidate is not sufficient to appoint him a preacher since he is to be a preacher in other churches as well as their own; yet it is in the home church that enquiries about his character should be conducted first.' Careful scrutiny of the candidate was applied at every stage of the process, for maturity of spiritual experience, upright conduct, intellectual ability and ministerial gifts. Morgan was granted permission to preach by the Tregaron Monthly Meeting in January 1842. His first text was Revelation 6:17, 'For the great day of his wrath is come; and who shall be able to stand?'

Preaching in Wales had an illustrious history, and Morgan would have been aware of the galaxy of great preachers which his countrymen would have known. These included John Penry and Walter Cradock of the Puritan era, conforming to Bunyan's picture of a gospel minister: 'It had eyes lifted up to Heaven, the best of Books in his hand, the Law of Truth was written upon his lips, the World was behind his back; it stood as if it pleaded with men, and a Crown of Gold did hang over its head.' Within the more recent past, Morgan would have known of Daniel Rowland's exceptional reputation as being 'the greatest preacher in Europe'.[3]

Within that mould of piety and preaching lay the newly deceased and exemplary figure of John Elias of Anglesey. He had died in 1841, about the time of Dafydd Morgan's own call to the ministry. Such was the power and influence of his preaching that it was reckoned 'almost in every neighbourhood, village, and town, some persons may be met with who ascribe their conversion to impressions received under one of his sermons'. His famous sermon on the Fourth Commandment at Rhuddlan one Sunday was particularly remembered. A fair was in progress and Elias stood in the open air competing with all the clamour of music and trading. 'The fear of God fell upon the crowd, harps and fiddles were silenced . . . One man who had purchased a sickle let it fall to the ground, thinking in his heart that the arm which held it had withered, and was afraid to pick it up again lest the same thing should happen to the other. He lost his sickle, but on that day he found salvation. The Sabbath fair was never afterwards held, and many were brought, through that marvellous sermon, to seek the Lord.' Thus preaching in the Welsh tradition was more than a matter of gifts and abilities: God alone could anoint and clothe the preacher with authority to reach men's hearts and change their lives.[4]

Morgan was, from the start of his preaching career, cast in this typical mould: a little suspicious of education, eager for—and on occasions the subject of—the Spirit's power, itinerating endlessly, dissatisfied with anything less than dependence on God for enabling and success. In keeping with denominational practice, rather than as an index of his ministerial power, he itinerated widely—for example, his preaching engagements in 1849 and 1855 were in North Wales, in 1857 in South Wales.

As he prepared himself for preaching with the Calvinistic Methodists his own resources were minimal. His formal education was negligible, but his mind was stored with Scripture knowledge. He refused a college education, even though the opening of Trefecca in 1842 as a theological college might have been an enticement for him. Such refusal was not unusual. For his part, Morgan admitted to an older preacher of similarly unadorned qualification that he was content to be known as 'Dafydd Morgan from Ysbyty Ystwyth, who had not been and was not going to college, seeking to speak a Word occasionally, working at his craft during the week'.

When accepted at the Llangeitho Association in 1848, he was not deterred by the disapproval of Owen Thomas, who frowned on his lack of a college education. However, his reading included such Puritan authors as Thomas Watson and John Owen, and apart from this private study, his 'college' in many ways was the *seiat* of the Monthly Meeting. The subject matter would be set a month in advance, and the members would prepare avidly from the commentaries of Matthew Henry and Thomas Scott or the practical works of Thomas Goodwin and John Howe. Each would speak to the matter

in his own informed style. Even though few of the preachers part-
icipating would have been to college, their discussion was prolonged
and profitable. The elders present would note their remarks for repetition in their respective churches.[5]

On being ordained in 1857 Morgan would have had to satisfy the
Association of a mature spirituality and a firm orthodoxy, as defined
by the Calvinistic Methodist 'Confession of Faith' in terms of a
Trinitarian, Calvinistic and Evangelical position. One who worked
with him in the Revival, Evan Phillips, described him as one who
had a vivid imagination to portray spiritual things in natural dress.
'He understood the doctrines of the gospel, and was very familiar
with the themes of Scripture . . . In Dafydd Morgan's study there
were two important volumes: the divine *Testimony*, and *man*. We
never met anyone who understood man better than he did.'

Even before the Revival Dafydd Morgan's preaching on occasions produced conviction and edification, although he was generally esteemed more for his praying than for his preaching. In 1859
an elder from Ebbw Vale requested a visit from Morgan, who had
been there some years before the Revival. Morgan was reluctant to
yield, until the elder's argument became quite irresistible: 'Look
you, David my boy, we at Ebbw Vale were dealing with you when
you were carrying a basket on your arm and trading on a small scale,
and now that you have opened an emporium, don't think you can
turn the cold shoulder to your old customers.'[6]

Revival experiences were not entirely new to Dafydd Morgan. In
the early 1840s there were stirrings in various parts of Wales, and
Dafydd Morgan was involved in at least one of them. J. J. Morgan,
his son and biographer, records one particular meeting at which
Dafydd Morgan could not continue preaching on account of the out-
burst of praise. Morgan confessed to have prayed consistently,
'Lord, pour Thy Spirit mightily upon me', and for ten years before
the Revival 'a petition for the outpouring of the Holy Spirit was
never absent from his public prayers'. In a diary entry for 1855 he
reflects on this very subject:

It is a great thing to long for the Lord to revive his work. Whoever has this,
it will compel him to do all in his power to revive the Lord's work. Reading
church history we realize that the great work of God fluctuates up and
down, but whenever the Lord draws near to save there was among the godly
an expectancy for his coming. Together with prayer we should also strive

for the reviving of his work. This is how the godly have always done: they prayed and they worked.

Applying these thoughts to the contemporary situation in 1857 he wrote:

The gospel in power is God's instrument to quicken sinners. Are there signs that the gospel is quickening sinners today? We have so many advantages over our fathers, but we have lost the Spirit. We are quite satisfied to make use of the means of grace without the manifestations of the Spirit's influences. In the Bible, the saints would not go forth unless God went with them. Let us take every meeting to God, preacher and sermon. He is still the Living God, and the powers of God's Spirit are at our call.

Such was Dafydd Morgan before the 1859 Revival: a man whose spirituality was cast in a Calvinistic Methodist mould, preaching according to his ability and with the highest of ideals and examples before him, praying with the dimension of revival never far from his mind. All these influences were to have an important bearing on his contribution to that great awakening.

For a year or so before 1859 among the Welsh churches there had been an increasing awareness of their low spiritual state. Prayer meetings were lifeless and weak, and the preaching, though orthodox, was ineffective. Some churches were turning to literary pursuits and becoming bereft of their missionary vision, urgency and zeal. 'Before the 1859 Revival', said Principal T. C. Edwards of Bala, 'the churches were withering away in our country; a wave of spiritual apathy and practical infidelity had spread over Wales.' The world was becoming increasingly more blatant in its profanity and indifference. Young people were defecting from their earlier church affiliation, and the baser manifestations of a society adrift from its spiritual moorings were causing concern. When news of the American Revival reached Wales in 1858, the response was widespread and enthusiastic. Many churches and individuals were encouraged to pray for a similar work in Wales.

In June 1858 Humphrey Jones, a native of Cardiganshire, returned to Wales from that American scene. While in America the most important influence upon this Wesleyan preacher had been the revival teachings of Charles G. Finney.[7] Jones had travelled widely amongst the Welsh communities in America, convinced, as Finney taught, that revival inevitably followed the strenuous efforts and fervent prayers of God's people. His evangelistic activity had merged easily with the wider movement of God's Spirit in America. Armed with his theological convictions, his substantial personal success, and his first-hand experience of the American Revival, he saw his return as a desirable extension of that work.

His initial labours among the Wesleyan churches of north Cardiganshire in the summer of 1858 followed a pattern familiar to him. First he urged the churches to awake from their spiritual slumber, to repent, pray, and seek the conversion of the lost. Nor was he disappointed in the response: crowds flocked to his meetings and many were genuinely converted. On Thursday, 30 September, he arrived at Pont-rhyd-y-groes in response to the invitation of the Wesleyan church to hold three weeks of 'revival meetings' in their midst. Jones's sermon from the pulpit was directed at believers. This was followed by an exhortation from 'the big seat' (arranged in a semi-circle below the pulpit and in which the elders usually sat).

Having attended the early meetings Dafydd Morgan was at first hesitant and suspicious. He was now 44 years of age, and if his Calvinistic Methodism had taught him anything, it was that revivals are God-made rather than man-made. Of old the fathers, when faced with religious declension, had sought a genuine reviving work of God by recourse to prayer. Morgan was thus responding along the lines of an acknowledged tradition when he cautiously suggested to Humphrey Jones that the Wesleyan and Calvinistic Methodists should hold united prayer meetings.

Morgan was also labouring under a sense of reproof for ministerial neglect on his part, and a sense of misgiving at the innovative methods of Humphrey Jones. Such was the anguish and perplexity in his mind that he failed to keep his preaching engagement on the following Sunday morning. In the evening, however, he preached at Ysbyty Ystwyth on Matthew 25:10, 'They that were ready went in with him to the marriage: and the door was shut.' It was a passage he was to expound frequently during the Revival, but a sermon on it had been delivered on a previous occasion. Its theme was that of judgment, and urgency in preparing for eternity.[8] Nothing unusual took place, either at Ysbyty Ystwyth, or while preaching away the following day. After the Tuesday united prayer meeting he went to bed with his mind in spiritual turmoil, as it had been for some days. 'I awoke about four o'clock', he said later, 'remembering everything of a religious nature that I had ever learnt or heard.' That astonishing faculty of remembering details was to remain with him for some two years, and just as suddenly it departed from him. When he arose the next day he knew that God had endued him with unusual power, and he wrote in his diary against Wednesday, 6 October, 'The time the visitation started.'

Several similar visitations are recorded by Dafydd Morgan. A month later he was to be at the isolated preaching station of Soar-y-mynydd in the hills above Tregaron. His arrival was considerably delayed and his appearance was strange. 'He had left his home with the dawn,' says his biographer, 'but in crossing the mountain he had come to a desolate place that might be called Peniel, for there, secluded from mortal eye by barren knolls, a man wrestled with him. The dust of this mysterious encounter was on his clothes when he entered Soar. The service made a deep impression.'

On the last day of the year he had to travel from a preaching engagement over a lonely upland in the direction of his home.

He was on this mountain for hours; whether in the body or whether out of the body, he hardly knew. Beyond a doubt he went through experiences unspeakable and full of glory . . . On this strange night on the hill he grasped and clung to the furze-bushes, because he seemed to feel some mystical forces lifting him, as it were, body and soul from the earth. We cannot but think that One whose Name is Wonderful came out of the darkness to meet him . . . When he let go the Divine Sojourner, and awoke to his terrestrial surroundings, his puzzled beast was standing by him. Giving it the rein, he arrived home with a countenance so strange, and garments so spoiled, that his people hardly recognized him. When questioned, he replied, 'I have been wrestling for the blessing, and I have received it.'

At Devil's Bridge the following day there were scenes of extraordinary spiritual ecstasy under his ministry. An eye-witness records that his words 'were so like fire as to create terrible convictions. It was a fearful place, some sighing, others praying, still others praising.' Afterwards Dafydd Morgan remarked, 'The Lord would give us great things if He could trust us not to be thieves; if He could trust us not to steal the glory for ourselves.' Ever mindful of the sovereignty of God's Spirit in giving or withholding gifts or power, he spoke of these elevated experiences only with discretion and reserve. While they occasionally accompanied seasons of striving in prayer, the experiences themselves were spontaneous, unsought and

unexpected, neither stereotyped nor predictable, glorious in character and copiously profuse in measure. The sense of God's presence
at such times replaced awareness of time and space.

Morgan regarded these outpourings of the Spirit upon him as the
source of his spiritual blessings. Whatever freedom in prayer, power
in preaching, ability to discern converting grace at work in his meetings was given to him, came from this source. His phenomenal
memory in dealing with people, his confidence in the triumph of the
gospel from place to place, the enabling to meet the rigours of travelling and ministering for sustained periods of time—all these, too,
were given by God. For Morgan authentication of the awakening lay
here, and he accepted it gladly.

The work of revival was not the mere proliferation of personal
experiences, however sublime, but the declaration of God's mercy in
Jesus Christ. So Dafydd Morgan's methods of promoting the work
still revolved around the means of grace. Jointly with Humphrey
Jones until November, and then separately, Morgan's practice followed the traditional pattern of preaching, but there was a difference. It lay in the application of the message, and was sometimes
referred to as 'the double sermon'. Here is a description of Morgan's
typical approach:

As a rule his discourse would dwell upon truths specially applicable to
church members. Then, before giving out a hymn to be sung, he would ask
the whole congregation to remain for a short time after singing, as he had a
further message for them. He would then leave the pulpit and take his stand
in 'the big seat'. This message would be a fiery and urgent appeal to the
unconverted portion of the audience, when he would ply them with homely
arguments and telling illustrations to bring them to the 'valley of decision'.
All the converts who 'stayed behind' with the church members would be
invited to come forward to the front seat. Here the Revivalist would converse with them individually, inquiring with friendly interest about their
family connections and responsibilities, and after winning their confidence
he would proceed, like a skilful surgeon, to probe their spiritual wounds,
and administer the cordial or corrective which his diagnosis of the case
enjoined as necessary. Then he would kneel and commend the converts to
God, individually and by name, however numerous they might be, his pet-
itions moulded with minuteness and detail upon his conversations with
them.

How did Morgan come to change his mind regarding the work?

What influenced him to adopt this unusual method which was at least suspect and open to criticism? The answer lies in his understanding of revival, and in his conviction that having discerned the reality of revival conditions there must be openness for the leading of the Holy Spirit. At first hesitant, he was now convinced that the events of those days at Pont-rhyd-y-groes, including his own remarkable anointing, were not of human origin, but so many proofs of a manifestation of divine power. God had come down and visited His people. What had started on the human level of arranged 'revival meetings', God had seen fit to transform into a divinely spontaneous, irresistible and great awakening. Imperceptibly, but wonderfully and convincingly, things had passed from man's hands. Independent of human agency, men were turning to God, eternity was in the air, and God's presence in the whole neighbourhood was both glorious and fearful. Revival had come!

Given that Morgan was satisfied from the evidences he saw that an authentic spiritual harvest was upon them, he merely used what seemed the most appropriate means to reap that harvest. Further, he would have depended on the nurture and discipline already in existence in the churches, at least of his denomination, as providing a safeguard against possible excesses. He felt therefore that something more immediate and direct was called for to balance the more formal and rigid tendency of church discipline. On one occasion he gave as the reason for the 'double sermon' that there was a need 'to be closer and more personal. Remember that religion is a personal thing, dying is a personal thing, judgment, heaven and hell are personal things.'

An example of the kind of address which he used at the close of a meeting is given by J. J. Morgan:

My questions are for the unconverted, and I demand a straightforward answer to each question. This is the first: what is your opinion of Jesus Christ? What think ye of Christ? . . . Allow me to reply for you, and if I say a word too much, contradict me at once. 'He is the best we have ever heard of.' The next question is this: Do you follow Him? 'N-no, we don't.' You follow some one at any rate. Let us hear his name! . . . If he is worth following, he is worth owning. 'Then if we must say, his name is the devil.' . . . what sort of a being is the devil? . . . I will answer for you . . . 'He is the worst we have ever heard of.' Is that correct? Christ the best and Satan the worst, and you choose to follow the worst and not the best . . . The finest

Christians I have read about were folks who accepted Jesus Christ the first time He was offered them. One day Christ finds Matthew at the receipt of custom, and says, 'Come, follow Me.' He rises, and goes the first chance he ever had. 'Stay, Matthew, the auditors are coming round next week, and it is very probable that you will receive promotion at their hands.' 'Promotion!' cries Matthew; 'what is promotion to me? Jesus Christ for me!' 'Stay, Matthew; a fortnight's wages are due to you; don't forfeit your hard-won earnings; wait to draw your salary.' 'Salary!' cries Matthew; 'what is salary to me? Christ for me!' . . . All who have chosen Christ will remain behind, and you who follow the devil shall leave.

Of those who left some would return, unable to go home because of severe conviction of sin. Each of those remaining would usually be questioned regarding their spiritual state, prayed for by name, and given an opportunity to join the fellowship.[9] At such times Morgan could be severe or compassionate as the occasion demanded, but from each case he was able to display the progress of gospel grace, even from a poor illiterate painter:

'Well, John,' he exclaimed genially, 'you have stayed with us; there is something troubling your mind, I suppose?' 'Yes, there is something here', replied the old painter. 'Perhaps some word from the sermon, or the hymns, or the Scriptures has stuck to you. If so, let us hear what it is.' After a short silence John whispered huskily, but audibly, 'Sinner!' 'Do you hear, my people?' cried the minister; 'John has found the word "sinner", and the word "sinner" has found John. Come again, John bach;* tell us, has any other word from God's Book gripped you?' 'Yes', said he a little more boldly. 'What is it?' 'SALVATION!'. 'Do you hear, my people?' cried the elated evangelist. 'Here is a sinner who has seen the word "Salvation". Thanks be unto God! for a book that proclaims the word "Salvation" after thundering the word "Sinner". Well done, John! it was not flesh and blood that revealed these things to you. You are led step by step. Come again, John bach! has your soul grasped some further word?' The old fellow had by this gathered strength and confidence, and cried with electrifying effect, 'HALLELUJAH!'

The object of the exercise was always examination of personal experience and encouragement from God's Word, and its benefits were felt by all.

Many of the churches, especially among the Calvinistic Methodists, had misgivings about his methods, and criticized them as

* Bach, literally 'small', is also used in Welsh as a generic term of endearment.

man-centred and superficial. They were suspicious of human emotions and decisions divorced from a deep, solid work of conviction on the part of God's Spirit. They were also concerned about the increased risk of admitting into membership those whose conversion was counterfeit and unreal. Morgan, too, was aware of these dangers, but considered that the Spirit's presence and leading at the time was a sufficient safeguard. For him any particular occasion was part of a wider movement. While, in the midst of a divine visitation, the enemy's tare-sowing activity was not to be belittled or ignored, neither should it be allowed to restrict or reduce the privileges and joys of those who were the subjects of spiritual impressions.

In Calvinistic Methodist circles the practice of receiving new members into fellowship would normally take place at a weeknight *seiat* rather than at a Sabbath service.[10] At the January Monthly Meeting the issue was given an airing in a dialogue between Morgan and one of the leading ministers, John Jones of Blaenannerch:

'What means this lugging of people into church fellowship without giving them time to sit down and consider and count the cost before they begin to build?' 'What time ought a sinner to get to consider, Mr Jones?' 'More than you give them by all accounts.' 'You are criticising my method; what is your idea of a reasonable period for considering this great question?' . . . 'A month is not too much, at least.' David Morgan . . . replied, 'Well! well! God's Spirit says, "Today", the devil says "Tomorrow"; but the old evangelist of Blaenannerch says, "A month hence will do."'

Morgan's approach, however, was not altogether without its discipline. He always insisted on the self-denying aspects of a Christian profession, and gave prominence to family worship in the home, to temperance and personal godliness, and to a definite commitment to Christian fellowship.

At Ysbyty Ystwyth towards the end of 1858 he established meetings 'in which definite religious instruction was imparted, and the converts became catechumens'. Wherever he itinerated he 'urged the Societies to attack the drinking evil, and also the habit of courtship in improper hours'. When a minister expressed concern as to how he would shepherd the large numbers of converts in his area, Morgan replied, 'It will be easier for you to shepherd them in the fold than on the common.' Changing the metaphor, the minister expressed his sentiments to one of his elders, 'He (Morgan) only catches the fish, it is we that will have to salt them.' Another compared

the work of the Revival to that of a tailor at his first cutting the cloth
with a big scissors and joining it together by coarse stitching. The
fine stitching and more polished tailoring would come later.

After the Revival, Morgan often visited churches, much along the
lines of Paul's return to missionary centres as described in Acts
14:21-23 and 15:36. On one such return visit in his sermon on
Philippians 1:6,

He showed that it was not fair to judge a Christian before grace had finished
its work on him. It was not fair to judge a house in process of construction
while the scaffolding was in place and rubble disfigured its grounds. So the
Christian, it was not fair to judge him while the old man in him fought for
the ascendancy, with the world, the flesh and the devil beating him from
without; but on triumphing over the powers within and without he will not
need to fear, either being weighed in the balances, or the measuring rod of
the accuser of the brethren.[11]

During the Revival Morgan was clearly convinced that the beginnings of grace could be discerned, much as Paul had done in the
case of the lame man at Lystra (Acts 14:8-10), when he 'perceiving
that he had faith to be healed, said with a loud voice, Stand upright
on thy feet. And he leaped and walked.' Morgan also followed apostolic example in providing encouragement at the time to those who
made a profession: 'When the congregation was broken up, many of
the Jews and religious proselytes followed Paul and Barnabas: who,
speaking to them, persuaded them to continue in the grace of God'
(Acts 13:43). There is no record of Morgan's referring to these biblical passages, but he would have considered his practices to be
within this biblical framework, given the apostolic manifestations of
God's Spirit in 1859.

His message was also consistently biblical, and in keeping with
his denomination's 'Confession of Faith'. He was aware that the
1859 Revival represented the harvest of many years' sowing of the
Word of God by other faithful preachers, some 15 years, others as
long ago as 40 or 50 years previously.[12] Indeed, for the more scepti-
cal, one sign of the Revival's divine origin was the very fact that so
many of the older generation were being converted, even those who
had withstood the approaches of God's grace in previous awakenings. 'Awake, Zion, put on thy strength. Let the ungodly awake too
... Repent and turn, you travellers of the broad way. Wales's greatest preachers have been pleading with you to turn, but you persist in

walking in the counsel of the ungodly'—this in a sermon on Isaiah 51:1-2. Simple, homely illustrations and apt similitudes made his appeal more direct. When preaching on 'the just shall live by faith', he spoke of a man who had injured himself with an axe. Refusing medical help because he believed he could heal the wound himself, and that it was not such a bad wound after all, he finds to his cost that such stubborn pride makes it eventually necessary to amputate his leg.

Another pointer to the message delivered in the Revival is the type of hymn that was sung. The favourite hymns of the Revival were full of free grace, the atonement, and the glory of Christ. It was a singing revival as much as a preaching revival! Astonishing scenes accompanied the final hymn at one of Morgan's services at Tregaron:

Between the big seat and the pews there was a clear space, some yards across, in most chapels in Wales at that time. A godly old woman, named Nell, eighty years old, who had failed to attend the afternoon service owing to the very severe rheumatic pains in her limbs, and had only crept painfully to the evening meeting, advanced briskly across the open space and put her hand on Enoch Davies, a lame and decrepit deacon of seventy-two, who sat in the 'big seat'. This was high-backed, and a seat ran around it outside as well as inside. As if electrified by Nell's touch, Enoch stood on his feet, and with one vault cleared the high obstacle between him and her; and the two, soon joined by others, began to leap and dance, as if the days of youth had returned to them.

On one occasion the harmony of the singing was not to everyone's taste, but a convincing reason was given for that by the offender: 'You haven't got the right measure, Richard Jones' . . . 'Never mind the meter, Humphrey bach . . . I am not singing by measure tonight, but by weight.' Men were deeply stirred by the solid evangelical theology of those hymns, and Dafydd Morgan delighted in that as much as in their warmth and simplicity.

Morgan was also convinced of the need for a sense of expectancy and confidence toward God in preaching. Speaking of the Revival period he said, 'At that time I would go to the pulpit firmly believing that God would save sinners through me in that meeting, and he would invariably do so. Somehow I lost that faith, and with the faith I lost my power.' At one and the same time he was convinced both of his responsibility to warn the sinner, and of his own impotence in that great work: 'I can do nothing, but what is given me from above.'

Wherever he went during the Revival great crowds attended his ministry, quite simply because they had heard 'that God was with him'. On occasions he had to stand in the chapel window as there were more outside the building than inside. Perhaps the greatest crowd of all was at the Association at Bangor, 12-14 September 1859, when some 30,000 were present for a festival of preaching, praising and praying, singing and dancing. It reached a crescendo of rapturous exultation when John Jones, Blaenannerch, preaching on Isaiah 28:16, dwelt on the word 'ransom': 'This word fills a field . . . [it] fills the world . . . It fills eternity . . . Ransom, Ransom, RANSOM.' The impression created was to many unforgettable.

If the impressions remained, the Revival gradually waned. By the end of 1860 Morgan's revival ministry was over, as was that of others like Thomas Edwards, Evan Phillips and John Jones. The churches settled down to nurturing the new converts in the faith and in godliness. Morgan undertook the pastoral charge of Ysbyty Ystwyth and Swyddffynnon in 1868. Subsequent years showed a gradual decline in numbers at Ysbyty Ystwyth. Between 1878 and 1889, for example, the membership fell from 130 to 126; adherents from 450 to 400, and the Sunday school from 341 to 302.[13] The figures serve to show that Morgan's ministry after the revival was no different from that of his colleagues.

Morgan was often referred to in those years as 'the Old Apostle', a token of the respect in which he was held by God's people. His contemporaries in the ministry who had lived through the Revival had come to acknowledge the authenticity of the work and the validity of Morgan's part in it. Perhaps his preaching afterwards was more polished and structured, but the anointing of revival times was not upon him. This caused him much distress. J. J. Morgan records that

he told a brother minister that one of the most agonising experiences of his life was to find crowds still flocking after him, when the convicting and saving influences of his ministry had declined into comparative insignificence. A remarkable old blacksmith at Aberffrwd addressed some quaint remarks to him at this time. 'Well David bach,' said the veteran, 'you have lost your warrant, haven't you? I was an officer of the press-gang at one time, and my warrant allowed me to seize whom I would. My warrant lapsed in twenty-four hours, but I could renew it upon application. The Almighty gave you a commission, and really you had authority while it was in force—you could lay your hand on whom you would. Perhaps you could renew your commission. Go to the King, David bach, and get it renewed.

It was not to be. Dafydd Morgan did not spend the rest of his life in obscurity, but neither did he enjoy prominence and eminent success. The epitaph on his tombstone reads simply, 'In memory of the Reverend Dafydd Morgan, the Lord's chosen vessel in the 1859 Revival, minister with the Calvinistic Methodists for 26 years, who died October 27, 1883.' It was as if what was said of Paul and Barnabas on their return to Antioch after their first missionary journey was also applicable to Dafydd Morgan after his reviving ministry: 'the work was now completed' (Acts 14:26).

A quarter of a century on from the first breaking forth of the Revival, and also the year of Morgan's death, the North Cardiganshire Monthly Meeting was engaged in discussion about the need for a religious revival. The same meeting considered the desirability of securing a copy of the 'Confession of Faith' for each church member and of arranging suitable occasions for its study and application.[14] Morgan was still enjoying reasonable health and would undoubtedly have been present as it was held at Ysbyty Ystwyth. Maintaining for a whole generation the standard of doctrinal purity and the dimension of spiritual awakening had been one of the achievements of the Revival. There were others, reckoned in terms of social improvement, of educational advances, of cultural developments, of missionary expansion.

Whatever revolutionary forces were at work in the world during the latter half of the nineteenth century, whether scientific or social, the 1859 Revival fundamentally influenced the British response to them. A striking illustration of this is afforded by a recent social commentator:

In 1855 the slate-quarrymen of Trelazé, discontented with their economic conditions, decided to take action: they marched on Angers and proclaimed an insurrectionary Commune, presumably with the memory of the Commune of 1792 in their minds. Nine years later the coal-miners of Ebbw Vale were equally agitated. The lodges from the valley villages marched on to the mountains, headed by bands. Speeches were made, tea provided by the Ebbw Vale lodge at 6d. a head and the meeting ended with the singing of the Doxology. Both Welsh miners and Breton quarry-men were engaged on rather similar economic agitations. Clearly they differed, because the histories of their respective countries had differed. The stock of past exper-

ience, upon which they drew when learning how to organize, what to organize for, where to pick their cadre of leaders, and the ideology of those leaders embodied, in part at least, specific French and British elements: broadly
speaking we may say, in the former case, the revolutionary, in the latter the
radical-nonconformist traditions.[15]

The different reaction could not be due to temperamental factors:
both localities were Celtic, but the fact that Wales had been swept
by the major spiritual awakening of 1859 may be of no little significance.

Societies do not just drift into decline or posterity, they are driven
in one direction or the other by the power of those convictions
which are at work in men's hearts. There is no ideological, or moral,
or spiritual vacuum. There is only the power of unbelief or of faith,
of spiritual death or of spiritual life. It is only when every sphere of
human experience and activity is seen as stemming from the conviction of the heart, when man's culture and his economics, as well as
his religion, are recognized as flowing from an inner disposition,
and as governed by faith or unbelief, that social and national movements are seen in their total reality.

In 1859 Dafydd Morgan was God's instrument to turn many from
unbelief to faith, from death to life. Changed lives determined the
response to influences at work throughout society. For this reason
Morgan's contribution to the Wales of the latter half of the century
can hardly be overestimated. He would have been the first to
attribute that contribution to God's gracious intervention and powerful activity. On that clear understanding also the lessons of his life
and ministry remain of timeless relevance.

REFERENCES

Matters of fact relating to Dafydd Morgan are drawn from J. J. Morgan, *The '59
Revival in Wales* (Mold, 1909), and J. J. Morgan, *Hanes Dafydd Morgan Ysbyty a
Diwygiad '59* ([Mold], 1906). Henceforth shortened to JJM and DM respectively.

1. For Evan Evans (1804-86) see the *Dictionary of Welsh Biography*; John Robin-
     son, *Can 'Mlynedd o Gymdeithasfaoedd* (Caernarfon, 1900), 67,70,72
2. See chapter 7; *The History, Constitution, Rules of Discipline, and Confession of
     Faith, of the Calvinistic Methodists* (Caernarfon, 1900), 23 ff.
3. John Bunyan, *The Pilgrim's Progress* (Edinburgh, 1977), 25; [A. C. H.
     Seymour], *The Life and Times of Selina Countess of Huntingdon*, vol.ii
     (London, 1839), 118

4. William Williams, *Welsh Calvinistic Methodism*, second edition (London, 1884), 221,218-19

5. J. J. Roberts, *Cofiant y Parchedig Owen Thomas* (Caernarfon, [1912]), 170-1; *Y Drysorfa*, May 1911, 216-23—'Cyfarfod Misol Sir Aberteifi yn 1853 gan Mr D. Davies, Ton'

6. *Y Goleuad*, 23 Oct 1914

7. See pages 193-6;199

8. NLW, CMA, General 12813

9. John Owen Jones, op. cit., 265; *Y Drysorfa*, April 1859, 110

10. *Y Geninen*, vol.xxiii (1905), 97

11. *Y Goleuad*, 6 Nov 1914

12. John Owen Jones, op. cit., 264; *Y Cyfaill o'r Hen Wlad*, August 1859; DM 119,178,411; JJM 68,137-8,140-1

13. *Yr Arweinydd*, July 1879, 156; June 1881, 140

14. NLW, CMA, 'Cofnodion Cyfarfod Misol Gogledd Aberteifi', 1a (14-15 June 1883)

15. E. J. Hobsbawm, *Labouring Men: Studies in the History of Labour*, (London, 1964), 371-2, quoted in Bernard Semmel, *The Methodist Revolution* (London, 1974), 200, n.9

15
WHY NO REVIVAL?

Consider, first of all, these accounts of revival:

In the latter part of December 1734 the Spirit of God began extraordinarily to set in, and wonderfully to work among us; and there were very suddenly, one after another, five or six persons, who were to all appearance savingly converted, and some of them wrought upon in a very remarkable manner ... A great and earnest concern about the great things of religion and the eternal world became universal in all parts of the town ... all talk except about spiritual and eternal things was soon thrown by ... It was then a dreadful thing among us to lie out of Christ, in danger every day of dropping into hell; and what persons' minds were intent upon was to escape for their lives, and to fly from wrath to come. All would eagerly lay hold of opportunities for their souls, and were wont very often to meet together in private houses for religious purposes, and such meetings were greatly thronged ... And the work of conversion was carried on in a most astonishing manner ... souls did as it were come by flocks to Jesus Christ. From day to day for many months together might be seen evident instances of sinners brought out of darkness into marvellous light ... In the spring of 1735 the town seemed full of the presence of God, it never was so full of love, nor of joy, and yet so full of distress, as it was then.

Jonathan Edwards

While you preach the Word of Life, I do my utmost to restrain myself, lest I cause others to stumble ... and I often cannot stop my tongue from crying out, "God is good!" ... the earliest opportunity I get, while Christ's love burns within me, and I give vent to my spiritual emotions, it is inevitable that I shout the Lord's praises; I bless and magnify God, I leap and shout for joy in so great salvation. At such time my memory is more alert, and innumerable Scriptures flood my mind, all of this one strain—praising God for His free grace. My senses are sharpened; I understand the things of God in clearer light; my reason and emotions are so disciplined, that I am careful not to say or do anything which would cause my brethren to stumble, or the ungodly to blaspheme ...

William Williams, 1762

Some 30,000 were present in the field that day, many from six in the morning until midnight. As each public meeting ended, prayer began in several groups around the field. Most of those who prayed were ordinary people without any polished language, but there was about their praying a strange anointing. Sometimes there would be general praying all around the field, interspersed with loud shouts of praise. It seemed almost as if hundreds were drunk with wine. They held hands, weaved in and out of the crowd, prayed, praised, danced, jumped, sang, shouted . . . And so they continued until the next preaching service.

Bangor Calvinistic Methodist Association, September 1859

Here is a scene witnessed during the first days of revival: a crowded church, the service is over; the congregation, reluctant to disperse, stand outside the church in a silence that is tense. Suddenly a cry is heard within: a young man, burdened for the souls of his fellow men, is pouring out his soul in intercession. He prays until he falls into a trance and lies prostrate on the floor of the church. But heaven has heard, and the congregation, moved by a power that they could not resist, came back into the church, and a wave of conviction of sin swept over the gathering, moving strong men to cry to God for mercy. This service continued until the small hours of the morning, but so great was the distress and so deep the hunger which gripped men and women, that they refused to go home, and already were assembling in another part of the parish . . . a number made their way to the church, moved by a power they had not experienced before; others were deeply convicted of their sin and crying for mercy in their own homes, before ever coming near the church.

The Lewis Awakening, Scotland, 1949

These accounts of revival are taken almost at random from historical sources. They provide a painful reminder of the low state of religion in our own day. At the time, there were those who found fault with various aspects of these movements of God's Spirit, and all of them experienced decline. Why?

We must begin by considering the nature of true revival. Briefly, we can say that revival is God coming down in life-stirring power among His people. It takes place when the Church is spiritually low and ineffective. At such times, preaching lacks authority and is at a discount. Christians are cold, worldly, and unheeding in their concern; their prayers are lifeless and infrequent. Above all else, a sense of God's presence and power is missing. Meanwhile, the world's unbelief and ungodliness are rampant and aggressive.

In contrast, as a result of revival, spiritual truths become real, eternity seems near, and gospel preaching is powerful. There is a general hunger and thirst for God, and an overwhelming sense of

His presence. Often there is an acutely painful awareness of sin. All in all, it seems as if the apostolic times of the New Testament are restored to the Church. Incidents bordering on the miraculous were witnessed: in the Welsh Revival of 1904, a teapot which had held only beer reverted to its intended purpose on the conversion of the man of the house; in Korea in 1907, tiles for shrines were no longer needed, and were sold to roof a new church building. No less astonishing are facts like these: vast numbers are added to the Church; the Scriptures are treasured; the moral awareness of society is transformed and elevated.

Such manifestations of revival activity may not all be found at once, or together, or in the same degree, in every revival. There is about revivals a blessed variety, and in each a uniqueness, which confounds stereotype and duplication. There may also be some confusion, spurious experiences, and doctrinal controversies, some or all of which may cause great concern. But all in all, the spiritual impact upon church and society can only be attributed to the sovereign and powerful activity of the Holy Spirit.

So much for a time of revival, but what then? Consolidation, edification, decline, barrenness, deadness, desolation? Is this cycle inevitable and unavoidable? And what if the churches of our land are moribund, is revival impossible? Why no revival? Why is the question important? We must not allow anything to deprive us of the biblical dimension of revival. What God has done in the past He can do again. It is still the Day of grace, and not yet the Day of judgment. The Holy Spirit's work is still to exalt Christ and draw sinners to Him in repentance and faith. Nor should we think anything is too hard or impossible for God. We must therefore examine the Scriptures to find reasons for declension and hope for revival. In this task it may help us to consider a case-history of the experience of the church at Ephesus.

The church at Ephesus was born in revival, an account of which is found in Acts 19. Certain features of that work deserve notice. It was Bible-based inasmuch as Paul's activity at Ephesus revolved around 'the word of the Lord' (v.10). For three months he argued persuasively 'about the kingdom of God' (v.8), and the success of his two-year mission is described in verse 20 by the phrase, 'the word of the Lord spread widely and grew in power.' Later, Paul described his task as 'testifying to the gospel of God's grace'

(20:24), a task that demanded nothing less from people than 'that they must turn to God in repentance and have faith in our Lord Jesus' (20:21). For this, there must be the recognition 'that man-made gods are no gods at all' (19:26), and that God's people, the church, are 'bought with his own blood' (20:28). The foundation on which the work at Ephesus was built was nothing if not doctrinally comprehensive ('the whole will of God' 20:27), and ministerially demanding ('with great humility and with tears, although I was severely tested' 20:19, 'taught you publicly and from house to house' 20:20; 'warning each of you night and day with tears' 20:31). This was no fleeting, superficial, quick-fire, city-wide crusade, but a costly, solid gospel ministry in the face of satanic superstition and religious bigotry. God granted a plentiful harvest in conversions, miracles, the burning of books of sorcery, exposure of counterfeit experiences, and preservation from harm at the hands of a riotous reaction. Supremely, 'the name of the Lord Jesus was held in high honour' (19:17). Such was the revival at Ephesus, and the beginning of a gospel church in that place.

Paul's letter to the Ephesian believers provides a window to view the church's life in those early years. They enjoyed a profusion of blessings. Their teaching was laid on solid foundations, 'the apostles and prophets, with Christ Jesus himself as the chief cornerstone' (Eph. 2:20). As well as Paul, Timothy, and later, the apostle John, ministered to them. Prayers offered on their behalf used superlative terms and much fervency: 'the riches of his glorious inheritance', 'his incomparably great power', 'far above all', 'he may strengthen you with power through his Spirit'; 'to know this love that surpasses knowledge', 'filled to the measure of all the fullness of God', 'able to do immeasurably more than all we ask or imagine'; 'I have not stopped giving thanks for you', 'I keep asking . . . ' (Eph. 1:15-23; 3:14-21). They had the most profound experiences: forgiveness, new life, unity, growth, holy living, spiritual conflict, and mutual submission. How could the Ephesian church know anything except spiritual prosperity?

It is with no small surprise, therefore, that we read of the Spirit's indictment of this church in the book of Revelation (2:1-7). The ardency, purity, and simplicity of her first love have declined. Hard work, doctrinal integrity, and perseverance in the face of suffering remain, but where now the lively graces and vigorous devotion of

their first espousals (Jer.2:2)? In but a few years, the church at
Ephesus was no more, the lampstand was removed from its place!
Must it always be like that? Why do revivals wane? And how do
revivals begin?

Revivals wane because, while they are divine in cause, they are
human in effect. Men and women are the stuff of revival, frail, frag-
ile, faulty human beings. They are limited in physical, mental, and
emotional endurance. They are fallible in their understanding and
perception. The heart is deceitful and desperately wicked. The devil
sows tares while God's servants are doing gospel-work. There are
counterfeit conversions, false professions, superficial responses.
There is a saturation point for gospel preaching to a congregation in
the day of opportunity: some submit to the gospel yoke, others
become hardened in unbelief and the opportunity is lost. True
believers are partakers of the divine nature, but daily dependent on
divine sustenance. They do not have a reservoir of grace and goodness. Each day graces need to be quickened, sins have to be mort-
ified, faith must be in constant exercise. Apart from daily communion
with God the soul languishes and spiritual declension becomes a
personal reality.

If the objects of revival are human, the origin of revival is divine.
In the matter of revival, God's sovereignty is all-embracing. He
chooses the instruments (no-one would have heard of Dafydd
Morgan apart from God's anointing in 1859); the places (God's
visitation in revival made Llangeitho a household word for the best
part of a century); the manner of a revival's commencement, its
extent, and progress. Revivals cannot be 'held' by men; they have to
be 'sent' by God. Why was there revival in Ephesus and not in
Athens, when the same messenger preached the same message to
people with the same needs? Why was there no response to Noah,
that 'preacher of righteousness' for 120 years, when the people of
Nineveh repented within 40 days under the ministry of the runaway
prophet, Jonah? The answer lies among 'the secret things' that
'belong to the Lord our God' (Deut. 29:29).

By the same token, however, we are to understand that God has
ordained means as well as ends. We are not to sit back and say to
ourselves, 'since God is sovereign in the matter of revival, there is
nothing for us to do, we may as well forget all about it.' The verse
quoted continues: 'but the things revealed belong to us and to our

children for ever, that we may follow all the words of this law.' So we are to work for revival in our own souls, and in the souls of others. Pray for personal quickening in the soul, attend lively preaching of God's Word, remember Christ's willingness to save, and be concerned about the awful state and destiny of the ungodly.

As we have seen, sound, sustained gospel preaching is the chief means that God uses when He sends an extraordinary outpouring of the Holy Spirit in revival. In seeking revival, therefore, we seek God's face to provide godly ministers, powerful preaching, and persevering expectancy for God's intervention. The Bala revival of 1791–2 is an example of this. Thomas Charles had preached and laboured faithfully in the town for some years, not without seeing some fruit. However, things changed unexpectedly one Sunday, as he tells us:

This glorious work began on a Sunday afternoon, in the Chapel, where I preached twice on that day, and cannot say, that there was any thing particular in the ministry of that day, more than what I had often experienced among our dear people here. But, towards the close of the evening service, the Spirit of God seemed to work in a very powerful manner on the minds of great numbers present, who never appeared before to seek the Lord's face; but now there was a general crying, 'What must I do to be saved', and 'God be merciful to me a sinner'. And, about nine or ten o'clock at night, there was nothing to be heard from one end of the town to the other, but the cries and groans of people in distress of soul. And the very same night, a spirit of deep conviction, and serious concern, fell upon whole congregations, in this neighbourhood, when calling upon the name of the Lord. In the course of the following week, we had nothing but prayer-meetings, and general concern about eternal things swallowed up all other concerns.

As to the nature of the work, Thomas Charles assures us that it was growing and thriving 'in the souls of those where it is begun':

It is most pleasing and comfortable to observe, how those whom, at first, we perceived enveloped in great darkness, only full of fear and dreadful apprehensions of futurity, now enlightened in the truths, and established in the doctrines of the Gospel. When evangelical truths become the *food* of souls, and they desire them as the new-born babes do the breast, they must necessarily thrive and grow. Human, speculative knowledge, even of divine truths, freeze and starve the soul; whilst divine, experimental knowledge, warms, enlivens, and invigorates those who are blessed with it from above.

They then become not truths to *talk* of only, but to *feed* and live upon; and when we *live* on this *living* bread, we cannot but be *lively* and *strong* ourselves.

And two years later his assessment of the converts of that revival was encouraging:

most of those of whom we had any degree of satisfaction as to a work of deep *conviction* on their minds, and not only *terror* for the moment, have stood their ground amazingly well; we have lost very few of them . . . There is a work going on still among us, though not so powerful . . . I must add also, though with sorrow, that a great many who have felt most powerful supernatural workings upon their minds have entirely lost them, and are quite fallen off; they will yet come to hear, but *hearing* is all . . .

Thus, mature leaders such as Thomas Charles recognized both the centrality of preaching and the inevitability of declension with regard to revival. John Newton's comment about this revival was pithy, and appropriate: 'There are many more blossoms on the tree in spring, than apples in autumn; yet we are glad to see blossoms, because we know that if there be no blossoms, there can be no fruit.'

First, then, in the light of these things, what should be our response? We must ever keep before us the dimension of revival. We do this by reading about revivals, in Scripture and in history. Look up the accounts of God's marvellous deeds under Josiah and Hezekiah, on the Day of Pentecost, at Antioch as well as Ephesus. Read about the Reformers and the Puritans; about men like Richard Baxter, Jonathan Edwards and Daniel Rowland; study the seasons of refreshing that God sent in 1859, 1904, and 1949; acquaint yourself with the Kentucky Revival of 1800, the Boston (New England) Revival of 1842, the Korean Revival of 1907; give time to explore books on the theme of 'Revival' by such men as Jonathan Edwards and W. B. Sprague. Consider also hymns like 'Jesus shall reign where'er the sun'; 'O'er the gloomy hills of darkness'; and 'Hail to the Lord's Anointed'.

Secondly, we must familiarise ourselves with God's promises relating to revival. Some of them are found in the Old Testament: 2 Chronicles 7:14 and Isaiah 35 are two notable examples. William Carey's 'text', too, came from Isaiah (54:2-3): 'Enlarge the place of your tent, stretch your tent curtains wide, do not hold back; lengthen your cords, strengthen your stakes. For you will spread out to the right and to the left; your descendants will dispossess nations and settle in their desolate cities.' It was on the basis of such a promise that he could 'expect great things from God, and attempt great things for God'. Another promise from Isaiah enabled two sisters on the island of Lewis (Scotland) to pray for revival for several months. One was blind and the other arthritic, but they believed God would honour the Word that He had sealed on their hearts (Isa. 44:3): 'For I will pour water on the thirsty land, and streams on the dry ground; I will pour out my Spirit on your offspring, and my blessings on your descendants.' In the New Testament we have a text which gives us both expectancy and hope for revival: Romans 11:12,15, 'But if their transgression [that of the Jews] . . . means riches for the Gentiles, how much greater riches will their fullness bring! . . . For if their rejection is the reconciliation of the world, what will their acceptance be but life from the dead?' The day of grace will not be over until the Jewish nation experiences the power of the gospel. This has yet to happen, and when it does what world-wide success will attend the everlasting gospel!

Thirdly, we are encouraged to pray for revival. Some of the Psalms lead the way for us: Psalms 79, 80, 85; followed by the closing chapters of Isaiah 64-66. Paul's prayers challenge us, too, as we have seen. Passages like 1 Thessalonians 1 and 1 Peter 1 fuel our prayers, and buttress our faith. And it may be for us as it was for others in a low spiritual condition, that God will yet visit His people:

At last, forced by cowardice, unbelief, and the onslaughts of Satan, we resolved to give up our special meeting, and now we were about to offer a final prayer, fully intending never again to meet thus in fellowship. But it is when man reaches his lowest depths of unbelief that God imparts faith, and when man has failed, that God reveals Himself. So here with us, in such straits, on the brink of despair, with the door shut on every hope of success, God Himself entered into our midst, and the light of day from on high dawned upon us. One of the brethren, yes, the most timid of us all, the one who was strongest in his belief that God would never visit us, while in prayer, was stirred in his spirit and laid hold powerfully on heaven as one who would never let go. His tongue spoke unusual words, his voice was raised, his spirit was aflame. He pleaded, he cried to God, he struggled, he wrestled in earnest like Jacob, in the agony of his soul. The fire took hold of others, all were awakened, the coldest to the most heedless took hold and were warmed; the spirit of struggling and wrestling fell on all, we all went with him into the battle; with him we laid hold upon God, His attributes, His

Word, and His promises, resolving that we would never let go our hold until all our desire should be satisfied. (William Williams, 1762)

The revival which began in that unpromising way spread powerfully and irresistibly throughout the land. It healed divisions, restored to Zion the beauty of holiness, spread far and wide the glorious majesty of the Saviour, transformed communities, and secured for Wales a Christian presence that was to last well into the next century. May not we, in the depths of a cold and hostile spiritual winter, yet pray for, and hope for, such a 'blessed summer's day'? 'Oh, that you would rend the heavens and come down, that the mountains would tremble before you' (Isa. 64:1).

Books on revival and related subject from the Evangelical Press of Wales

Voices from the Welsh Revival by Brynmor P. Jones

An anthology of testimonies, reports and eyewitness accounts, gathered from relatively inaccessible sources, which provides first-hand information on the powerful revival which swept Wales in 1904–05. 304pp.

Revival Comes to Wales by *Eifion Evans*

A moving and thrilling account of the mighty working of God the Holy Spirit in Wales at the time of the 1859 Revival, a year in which an estimated 110,000 were converted. 132pp.

The Welsh Revival of 1904 by *Eifion Evans*

A thorough and readable study of the 1904 Revival. Foreword by D. M. Lloyd-Jones. Now in its third edition (with index). 224pp.

Howell Harris and the Dawn of Revival
by Richard Bennett; introduction by *D. M. Lloyd-Jones*

A study of the early spiritual life of Howell Harris and the beginnings of the Great Awakening of the eighteenth century in Wales. 212pp.

The Christian Heritage of Welsh Education
by *R. M. Jones* & *Gwyn Davies*

A bird's-eye view of Christian education in Wales down the centuries which demonstrates its close inter-relationship with revival. 120pp.

'Excuse Me, Mr Davies—Hallelujah!'
by *Geraint D. Fielder*: foreword by *Lady Catherwood*

The absorbing story of evangelical student witness in Wales in the twentieth century, a story which includes periods of quite remarkable spiritual blessing. 264pp.

Three companion volumes from the Evangelical Press of Wales

Christian Hymn-writers by *Elsie Houghton*. 288pp.

Fifty chapters on great hymn-writers through the ages. This popular book, now in its fourth reprint, includes over 60 illustrations and a valuable index.

'This book is a gem . . . It will inform the mind and warm the heart'—*Evangelical Times*.

Christian Preachers by *Nigel Clifford*. 320pp.

Published in 1994 this book provides an introduction to the lives and achievements of 31 of some of the outstanding men of the Christian Church, from Chrysostom and Augustine to Tozer and Martyn Lloyd-Jones.

'An interesting and illuminating study'—*The Methodist Recorder*.

Christian Missionaries by *Owen Milton*. 264pp.

Our most recent title includes biographies of 33 missionaries, mostly from the English-speaking world, from John Eliot, 'the Apostle to the Indians' in the seventeenth century, to Clarence Jones, the founder of the world Radio Missionary Fellowship. Also included are well-known figures like Carey, Hudson Taylor and John Paton, the Welshmen Griffith John and Thomas Coke, and five women missionaries.

Books by Dr D. Martyn Lloyd-Jones from the Evangelical Press of Wales

Out of the Depths
An exposition of Psalm 51 which shows repentance to be the divine remedy for human failure and guilt.

Why Does God Allow War?
Biblical teaching on how Christians should face evil and suffering.

Truth Unchanged, Unchanging
A powerful and penetrating examination of life's fundamental questions and God's answers.

Water in the Desert
This evangelistic sermon points to the only source of true happiness and fulfilment.

Martyn Lloyd-Jones: The Man and His Books
by Frederick & Elizabeth Catherwood
A fascinating personal account of 'the Doctor' by his daughter and son-in-law.

Books from EPW for the earnest seeker and the new Christian

by *Peter Jeffery*

I will Never Become a Christian

carefully and convincingly dismantles the reasons and excuses given by the convinced unbeliever and includes some remarkable testimonies of believers who once said, 'I will never become a Christian!'

Seeking God

a clear explanation of the gospel, written for the earnest seeker after faith.

All Things New

a help for those beginning the Christian life.

Walk Worthy

a sequel to *All Things New*, setting out clear guidelines on issues with which the new Christian will have to grapple during the early years after conversion.

Firm Foundations (with *Owen Milton*)

a two-month Bible-reading course introducing readings to 62 key chapters of the Bible and to some of the most important teachings of the Word of God.

Stand Firm

a young Christian's guide to the armour of God.

Christian Handbook

a well-illustrated and straightforward guide to the Bible, Church history and Christian doctrine.